INSPIRING PARTICIPATORY DEMOCRACY

I, uh, was one of the authors of the Port Huron Statement—uh, the original Port Huron Statement … not the compromised second draft.

—Jeffrey "The Dude Lebowski," The Big Lebowski, 1998

Students for a Democratic Society? That's a hell of a focus group.

—Don Draper, Mad Men, 2008

INSPIRING PARTICIPATORY DEMOCRACY

STUDENT MOVEMENTS FROM PORT HURON TO TODAY

BY
TOM HAYDEN,
EDITOR

With reflections by Port Huron veterans

Becky Adams, Paul Booth, Robb Burlage, Mickey Flacks,
Richard Flacks, Sharon Jeffrey Lehrer, Alan Haber, Barbara Haber,
Casey Hayden, Charles McDew, James Monsonis,
Maria Varela, and Michael Vester

Additional commentary by Robert Cohen, Diana Turk,
Stacie Brensilver Berman, and Linda Gordon

Research assistance by Wesley Saver

Paradigm Publishers
Boulder • London

Copyright © 2013 Paradigm Publishers

Published in the United States by Paradigm Publishers, 5589 Arapahoe Avenue, Boulder, CO 80303 USA.

Paradigm Publishers is the trade name of Birkenkamp & Company, LLC, Dean Birkenkamp, President and Publisher.

Cover photo: SDS National Council meeting, Bloomington, Indiana, 1963. (Photo credit: C. Clark Kissinger)

Back row, from left: Don McKelvey, Jon Seldin, Steve Max, Vernon Grizzard, Carl Wittman, Steve Johnson, Lee Webb, Richard Flacks, Robb Burlage, Rennie Davis
Middle row, from left: Nada Chandler, Dan Millstone, Paul Booth, Todd Gitlin, Richard Flacks, Mickey Flacks
Front row, from left: Tom Hayden, Nancy Hollander, Mary McGroarty, Sarah Murphy

Library of Congress Cataloging-in-Publication Data

Inspiring participatory democracy : student movements from Port Huron to today / by Tom Hayden, editor ; with reflections by Port Huron veterans Becky Adams ... [et al.].
    p. cm.
  Includes bibliographical references.
  ISBN 978-1-61205-261-8 (hc : alk. paper) — ISBN 978-1-61205-262-5 (pbk : alk. paper) — ISBN 978-1-61205-277-9 (q) — ISBN 978-1-61205-278-6 (e)
  1. College students—Political activity—United States. 2. Student movements—United States. 3. New Left—United States. 4. Democracy—United States. 5. United States—Politics and government. I. Hayden, Tom.
  LB3610.I526 2012
  378.1'981—dc23

                                                                    2012024052

Printed and bound in the United States of America on acid-free paper that meets the standards of the American National Standard for Permanence of Paper for Printed Library Materials.

Designed and Typeset by Straight Creek Bookmakers.

17 16 15 14 13   1 2 3 4 5

CONTENTS

PART I

PREFACE AND INTRODUCTION

THE PORT HURON STATEMENT AT 50

By Robert Cohen

Last fall, *The New York Post* spent months denouncing Occupy Wall Street (OWS) protesters as 1960s retreads, dirty hippies, and violent radicals. Similarly, on November 8, 2011, *Wall Street Journal* columnist William McGurn mocked the Occupy Wall Street Movement as "a lark. For Woodstock wannabes, [for whom] it's a romantic trip back to the Vietnam War protests.... Occupy Wall Street has taken a high-profile part of Manhattan and turned it into an anarchist campground ... of the homeless and a haven for drug dealing."[1]

This evocation of the radical '60s, drugs, and anarchy is by now an old trope of the American Right. As Bernard von Bothmer documents in his book *Framing the Sixties: The Use and Abuse of a Decade from Ronald Reagan to George W. Bush* (2010), for generations right-wing politicians, dating back to Ronald Reagan, have used negative images of the 1960s (an emotionally charged caricature of that decade) that amount to demonization to discredit—or at least try to discredit—even moderately liberal forces for political change. This was what that noise John McCain and Sarah Palin were making was all about during the last presidential race when they used this 1960s–guilt by association discourse to try to slander Barack Obama. Remember? Palin repeatedly trumpeted Obama's connection to the left-wing "terrorist" Bill Ayers—she said Obama was "palling around with terrorists,"[2] as if the Democratic presidential nominee was an honorary member of the Weather Underground, when in fact Obama was an 8-year-old child at the time when Weather formed. As a historian of the 1960s who has been reading these politicians and their campaigns '60s-bashing screeds for decades, I find them as significant for what they leave out as for what they use as targets of this demonization. For example, they never mention Berkeley Free Speech Movement leader Mario Savio (the subject of a biography I published in 2009), and they also are averse to mentioning or focusing upon the Port Huron Statement (PHS). In fact, von Bothmer interviewed scores of conservative Republican politicos for his book *Framing the Sixties* and not one of them mentioned the PHS or Savio. And I think there are pretty much identical reasons why neither Savio nor the PHS has been a major target of this '60s-bashing. Neither the PHS nor Savio's speeches are susceptible to being caricatured to fit the Republican cartoon version of the 1960s as a violent, irrational, frighteningly subversive, drug-filled, immoral nightmare. Yes, it is true that a couple of extreme right-wingers—David Horowitz and Robert Bork—have tried to treat the PHS as a commie plot, but this attempt to mistake the New Left for the Old Left never gained any traction with Republicans involved in the real world of electoral politics, probably because that argument is so over the top (the PHS, after all, criticized *both* sides in the Cold War, and advocated participatory democracy) that it never had the slightest chance of resonating with voters, especially since the Cold War has been over for decades.

The PHS represents a part of the 1960s that the American Right would prefer we forget: the early 1960s, when Students for a Democratic Society (SDS) activists at Port Huron, Student Nonviolent Coordinating Committee (SNCC) civil-rights organizers in Mississippi, and Free Speech Movement protesters at Berkeley were organizing *nonviolently* to make America a more democratic, egalitarian, and free society. The only activist students who were violent in the early 1960s were not organizers on the Left, but racists on the Right who, at the University of Georgia in 1961 and the University of Mississippi in 1962, fomented segregationist riots to oppose the admissions of the first black students on their Deep South campuses. As for the student Left in the Port Huron era, these activists were doing historic work envisioning a new America, and struggling to push the nation beyond its Cold War limitations, away from the arms race, counter-revolutionary military coups and wars, the anti-democratic legacies of Jim Crow and Joseph McCarthy, and the paralysis of political indifference and apathy. The early New Left aspired to a reinvigorated form of political community that the Port Huron Statement termed *participatory democracy*. So yes, most politicians of the Right stay away from the PHS statement because they cannot rebut its deeply felt and idealistic democratic faith and cannot handle the questions it raises as to why a wealthy nation is marred by poverty, why an America that prides itself on its peaceful nature is so addicted to the use of force abroad, why its two-party system offers so little choice and disengages millions of its citizens, why its universities do so little to use their resources and expertise to battle social inequality, why its black community remains so separate and unequal.

Read into historical context, the PHS (authored by Tom Hayden and 60 or so SDS activists at Port Huron, Michigan, in 1962) connects with traditions of dissent that go back to way before the 1960s. Its challenge to the two-party system's compromises with racism and segregation calls to mind William Lloyd Garrison's *Liberator* and Frederick Douglass's *North Star* editorials breaking with the antebellum American two-party system's consensus over permitting slavery to exist in the South. The PHS statement's dissent from Cold War America's infatuation with military solutions and the arms race calls to mind Henry David Thoreau's classic essay *On Civil Disobedience,* where he explains and justifies his refusal to pay taxes for an unjust war, which results in his going to jail for nonviolent resistance. Additionally, Thoreau and the PHS shared a commitment to participatory democracy, displayed when—in referring to civil disobedience—Thoreau urged Americans to vote "not merely with a strip of paper *but with your whole life.*" And as surely as the women's movement's 1848 Declaration of Sentiments constituted its declaration of independence from a male monopoly on power and voting, the PHS was the 1960s student movement's declaration of independence from Cold War America's politics of inequality, its "warfare state" mentality, and its skewed budget priorities.

Historian Howard Zinn dubbed as "new abolitionists" SNCC's civil-rights organizers, who spearheaded the black-led student movement of the 1960s. These new abolitionists risked their lives in the struggle to free the South from racism, segregation, and black disfranchisement.[3] And there are a number of levels on which the PHS's authors can also be seen as new abolitionists. First, because some of the leading figures in SDS and the New Left, most notably Tom Hayden, developed their hyper-democratic politics in part under the influence of SNCC. Hayden had worked with SNCC in its daring freedom-organizing in Mississippi and came to Port Huron shortly after risking his life as a Freedom Rider in SNCC's courageous campaign against Jim Crow in Albany, Georgia. Since activists in that movement were putting their bodies and their very lives on the line, all were active participants in its decisions, and the freedom movement modeled—actually lived and breathed—the ethos of participatory democracy.

The PHS was political, but its concerns were deeply moral as well. This too resembles the abolitionists, for as the historian Richard Hofstadter noted, "the abolitionist movement was based upon a moral ... not an economic discontent.... Almost all abolitionists were middle class people who had no material stake in the slave system," but were founding a movement to abolish slavery out of moral concerns.[4] Similarly, the mostly middle-class students who wrote the

PHS were fired not by their own economic grievances—and in fact the opening lines of the PHS speak of their having been "bred in at least modest comfort" and "housed now in universities." They were seeking, as Bob Moses put it, to "bring morality to politics," unlike their compromising elders who too often seemed to bring "politics to their morality."[5] In fact, the PHS started off not with a laundry list of political demands, but with a morally focused section on "values." As Tom Hayden explained in his 2005 retrospective on Port Huron, "We chose to put 'values' forward as the first priority in challenging the conditions of apathy and forging a new politics. Embracing values meant making choices as morally autonomous human beings against a world that advertised in every possible way that there were no choices, that the present was just a warm up for the future."[6]

I have highlighted the connections between PHS and this long tradition of dissent to show that we can learn much about the PHS if we think about its historical roots and avoid lumping it with sensationalized images of the late 1960s. But while connected to that earlier tradition of dissent we ought not lose sight of what was distinctive about the PHS, about the time of its writing in the early 1960s, for this was a time very different from the polarized world of late-1960s America, when so much of the political discourse had been poisoned by violence—the bloodshed of Vietnam and the tragedies of one assassination after another, from Medgar Evers to JFK, Martin Luther King, and RFK. The early '60s was a time of promise when liberals and radicals were not yet enemies (before Atlantic City—where Lyndon Johnson's Democratic establishment refused to support the Mississippi Freedom Democratic Party's challenge to the Magnolia State's Jim Crow delegation—and Vietnam had soured many radicals on liberalism's opportunism); it was a period when both were involved in extraordinarily deep explorations of the limitations of American political, social, and intellectual life. Reminding us of the distinctiveness of what Tom Hayden has referred to as this "Port Huron moment" of the early 1960s, intellectual historian David A. Hollinger concluded in our recent email exchange that

> The Port Huron Statement, whatever else it may be as a historical document, is a compelling example of the political and intellectual creativity of the very special historical moment of the early 1960s. That historical moment is too often conflated in popular memory with events of the later 1960s and early 1970s, which sometimes produced works of a quite different character. Mixing a forthright commitment to "reason" with a candid and explicit celebration of the human capacity for "love," the Port Huron Statement was a deliberate, non-sloganeering, carefully formulated presentation of a vision of democracy very similar to that developed much earlier

by John Dewey. The Port Huron Statement shares a distinctive historical moment with Rachel Carson's *Silent Spring,* Jane Jacobs's *Death and Life of Great American Cities,* Michael Harrington's *The Other America,* and Betty Friedan's *The Feminine Mystique,* plus a number of less politically salient works that continue to provide basic vocabularies with which we discuss central aspects of our culture, including Thomas S. Kuhn's *The Structure of Scientific Revolutions,* Joseph Heller's *Catch-22,* and Clark Kerr's *The Uses of the University.*[7]

What was it that made the early 1960s, the Port Huron moment, such a time of intellectual creativity and searching social criticism? Perhaps it was the relief of finally being done with the dark night of McCarthyism. Or the sense of possibility of democratic renewal fostered both by a young and energetic president—JFK—and by the sit-in movement, born in Greensboro, North Carolina, and quickly spreading, first across the South and then from coast to coast. The Port Huron Statement's sense of generational mission seems to have been, then, more than baby-boomer egotism, but reflected the fact that by 1962 youth were already beginning to lead the way towards democratic change from the Deep South to the White House. And yet this was a youth movement that lacked generational chauvinism; it was not merely willing but eager to build on the insights of dissident elders, symbolized by the attendance at Port Huron of Michigan Philosophy professor Arnold Kaufman, whose participatory-democracy idealism—along with that of John Dewey's—helped set the tone of the PHS, as did the critical sensibility of the late Columbia sociologist C. Wright Mills, with his memorable indictment of the American power elites for monopolizing political and economic decision-making.

Despite its strong element of social criticism, there was almost a sweetness to some of the rhetoric and tone of the PHS, a faith in reason, and an optimism about the possibilities of converting dysfunctional or status quo–oriented institutions, like the two-party system and the universities, into instruments of progressive social change. As Hollinger put it, the PHS offered "deliberate language' in its effort" to outline a program based on both theoretical reflection and an empirical view of the historical circumstances of the moment.[8] The document's identification of "reason, freedom, and love" as key ideals and "the cultivation of the mind" as central to university education made it a call to action that wedded an upbeat and moderate tone to a radically democratic sensibility.

This was emblematic of, as Mario Savio put it, the New Left's early and most appealing phase, when it was speaking in plain language, a rhetoric of "communication," eager to reach out to others and build a mass nonviolent movement. A world away from the angry and dogmatic rhetoric of the late '60s that Savio termed the rhetoric of "confrontation," a rhetoric born of the Vietnam tragedy, and the urgent need to stop the war and the killing by any means necessary.[9]

Part of what made the Port Huron Statement such an exciting document for students on the Left was that it departed from not just the sloganeering but the hierarchical approach to political organizing that had made the Old Left seem so archaic and irrelevant. For red-diaper babies—those who came from families of Communist Party members—such as historian Michael Nash, encountering the PHS as a high-school student was "like a breath of fresh air" because its stress on participatory democracy made for a communal approach to decision-making and organizing that differed fundamentally from the cadre-style elitism of their parents' generation. It was an open and indigenous American radicalism free of all that baggage from the Communist past. The PHS's authors saw themselves as writing a "living document," grounded in experience and empirical evidence, not dogma; a document that could be modified based on further experience. This was a pragmatic approach to organizing, and a world removed from the "party line" pronouncements of the Old Left.

Journalist Jack Newfield, in his pioneering history of the New Left, referred to these new student radicals as a "prophetic minority."[10] And when you think of how much of the PHS anticipated the imminent student rebellion, the word "prophetic" does not seem an exaggeration. Just two years after the Port Huron Conference, Berkeley's student protesters were—without necessarily having studied the PHS—living its highest ideals. They led a mass movement for free speech in fall 1964, which lived and breathed the PHS spirit of participatory democracy, using consensus decision-making to defeat a hierarchical and repressive campus administration and generating much thought and organizing to try to realize the PH dream of a university that, instead of being a service station for the military-industrial complex, assisted in a process of democratic renewal by having the campus serve as a base for a freedom movement challenging not only Jim Crow in the South but racial discrimination and poverty in the ostensibly liberal North. And the campuses would, as the PHS's authors hoped, become a base for the mass peace movement opposing the U.S. warfare state in the Vietnam era.

And as to legacies, the PHS ethos of participatory democracy is today shaking the walls of power even in the most unlikely of places, Wall Street. The Occupy Wall Street movement, with its General Assembly, its consensus decision-making, its wariness about the status quo/two-party system, its refusal—much to the consternation of the mass media—to focus on a few narrow demands but instead to offer a larger (if not yet fully articulated) PHS-style hyper-democratic *vision*, suggests that the path the PHS generation blazed in demanding accountability and change of the American power elite is one that has immense appeal to a new generation in a new century.

Professor Robert Cohen teaches social studies and history at NYU and is the author of Freedom's Orator: Mario Savio and the Radical Legacy of the 1960s.

Notes

1. William McGurn, "Bloomberg's Broken Windows—The Mayor's Message: When the Crazies Come You Are on Your Own," *The Wall Street Journal,* Nov. 8, 2011.

2. Kate Phillips, "Palin: Obama Is 'Palling Around with Terrorists'," *The Caucus: The Politics and Government Blog of the New York Times,* Oct. 4, 2008.

3. Howard Zinn, *SNCC: The New Abolitionists* (Boston: South End Press, 2002).

4. Richard Hofstadter, *The American Political Tradition and the Men Who Made It* (New York: Knopf, 1996), 141–142.

5. Tom Hayden, *The Port Huron Statement: The Visionary Call of the 1960s Revolution* (New York: Thunder Mouth's Press, 2005), 20.

6. Ibid, 5.

7. David A. Hollinger email to the author, Nov. 17, 2011, copy in author's possession.

8. Ibid.

9. Robert Cohen, *Freedom's Orator: Mario Savio and the Radical Legacy of the 1960s* (New York: Oxford University Press, 2009), 259–260.

10. Jack Newfield, *A Prophetic Minority* (New York: New American Library, 1966).

THE DREAM OF PORT HURON

By Tom Hayden

This is the 50th-anniversary year of the Port Huron Statement, the found-ing document of Students for a Democratic Society (SDS), issued as a "living document" in 1962. The SDS call for a participatory democracy echoes today in student-led democracy movements around the world, even appearing as the first principle of the Occupy Wall Street September 17th, 2011, declaration.

As a relic of the idealistic early years of the '60s, the Port Huron Statement is worth treasuring for its idealism, its rhetoric, and the spark it ignited in many an imagination. But in addition to nostalgia, the document's advocacy of par-ticipatory democracy still resonates as a rallying cry that could unite progressives in America

The Port Huron call for a life and politics built on moral values as opposed to a morality based on expedient politics; its condemnation of the Cold War, which is echoed in today's questioning of the War on Terrorism; its grounding in social movements against racism and poverty; its first-ever identification of students as agents of social change; and the proposed extension of participatory democracy to the economic sphere still constitute much of today's progressive sensibility. The Statement was prophetic in condemning the One Percent who then owned 80 percent of corporate stock and state and local bonds. The Port Huron Statement noted that despite waves of earlier reform, the slice of wealth of the One Percent had remained constant since the 1920s.

The first principle of the September 17, 2011, declaration of Occupy Wall Street demanded a "direct and transparent participatory democracy." In recent years, the concept of a "participatory democracy" arose in the Bolivarian circles, which led to the Venezuelan government of Hugo Chávez. Its strains of popular participation drove the electoral successes of Latin American nations emerging from dictatorships in the 1990s. It suddenly appeared among the slogans of young people in Tunisia, Egypt, and Middle Eastern countries in the Arab Spring of 2011. Spontaneous democratic demonstrations erupted in Russia in 2012, organized on Facebook by young people who considered themselves only "plankton" for the regime's power appetite.

The technological revolution of the Internet and social media is propelling a global revival of participatory democracy on levels we never expected. For example, Wikipedia, which was introduced only in 2001, is supported by a volunteer force that has inscribed four million entries and participatory publishing in the here and now, with its editorial disputes resolved by editors who are elected to adjudicate those disputes. (The error rate is the same as for the previous versions of handed-down encyclopedias.) Facebook, emerging only in 2004, is credited with a key role in youth movements from Cairo to the volunteer campaign for Barack Obama's 2008 presidential election. For the next generations, perhaps the most important issue for participatory democracy will be the ownership and control of the means of producing information.

These issues were prefigured in the briefest of complaints about computerized problem-solving in the Port Huron Statement, and the Berkeley outcry two years later about students being processed like IBM punch cards. The Port Huron Statement criticized the profit motive behind the introduction of automation, while noting that the new technology, if democratically controlled, could eliminate much drudgery at work, open more leisure time, and make education "a continuing process for all people."[1]

According to Kirkpatrick Sale's *SDS*, published in 1970 and still the most comprehensive organizational history, the Port Huron Statement "may have been the most widely distributed document of the American left in the sixties," with 60,000 copies printed and sold for 25 cents each between 1962 and 1966.

Sale made two observations about the Statement: First, the Port Huron Statement contained "a power and excitement rare to any document, rarer still in the documents of this time, with a dignity in its language, persuasiveness in its arguments, catholicity in its scope, and quiet skill in its presentation … a summary of beliefs for much of the student generation as a whole, then and for several years to come."

Second, "it was set firmly in mainstream politics, seeking the reform of mainstream institutions rather than their abolition, and it had no comprehension of the dynamics of capitalism, of imperialism, of class conflict, certainly no conception of revolution. But none of that mattered."[2]

Sale's conclusions may suggest the lasting power of the document as well as its later rejection as "reformist" by SDS leaders. In discarding the authentic language and radical populism of Port Huron, a later generation of activists turned in only five years to what the SDS president Carl Oglesby called "ancestor-worship" instead of the experimentalism of something new.

Who We Were, What We Said

Even today I find it hard to explain the "power and excitement," the "dignity," and the "persuasiveness" of this document, which sprawls over 124 pages in book form. Though I was already a student editor, and a budding pamphleteer, just 22 years old, I remember myself as a kind of vessel for channeling a larger spirit that was simply in the air—blowin' in the wind—and coursing through the lives of my friends.

The original draft began as follows:

> Every generation inherits from the past a set of problems—personal and social—and a dominant set of insights and perspectives by which the problems are to be understood and, hopefully, managed. The critical feature of this generation's inheritance is that the problems are so serious as to actually threaten civilization, while the conventional perspectives are of dubious worth. Horrors are regarded as commonplace; we take universal strife in stride; we treat newness with a normalcy that suggests a deliberate flight from reality.

Then followed sections about students, politics, the economy, international affairs, and so on. The Port Huron conferees, however, insisted that it begin with an emphasis on "we," to be followed immediately by a section on values. And so it opened by describing ourselves as a new generation "raised in modest comfort, looking uncomfortably at the world we inherit." Not exactly the Communist Manifesto. Why did it resonate with so many activists in 1960?

In fact there were present a few sons and daughters of former Communist Party members, but their previous family dogmas and loyalties lay shattered by the crushing of the democratic Hungarian revolution in 1956 and the revelations about the Stalinist gulag by Nikita Khrushchev. There were also children of New Deal Democratic Socialists, now experiencing liberal middle-class lives. There were plenty of mainstream idealistic student leaders, graduate sociology students, a few pacifists, and a number of the spiritually inspired.

Though not in attendance at Port Huron, there were others at the time who were philosophical searchers who practiced participatory democracy. Bob Moses, perhaps the single greatest influence on the early Student Nonviolent Coordinating Committee (SNCC) and SDS, could be described as a Socratic existentialist. The Berkeley Free Speech Movement's Mario Savio described himself as a non-Marxist radical shaped by secular Liberation Theology who was "an avid supporter of participatory democracy."[3] We all were influenced by Ella Baker, an elder advisor to SNCC with a great amount of experience of NAACP organizing in the South. Ms. Baker, as everyone referred to her, was critical of the top-down methods of black preachers and organizations, including her friend Dr. King. She argued that SNCC remain autonomous, not a youth branch of the older organizations. She spoke of and personified participatory democracy.

SNCC played a direct role in the shaping of my values, as it did with many SDS founders in the 1960–64 period. SNCC's early organizing method was based on listening to local people, and taking action on behalf of their demands. This was a style of organizing in which speaking and listening in clear vernacular English was key. Books were treasured, but where you stood, with whom, and against what risks, was even more important, because if the people you were organizing couldn't understand your theories, you had to adjust. This led to a language and a form of thinking cleansed of ideological infections, with an emphasis on trying to say what people already were thinking but hadn't put into words.

The right to vote was no intellectual matter as it was for many on the left who felt it was based on illusions about where real power lay. The SNCC organizers again and again heard rural black people emphasize how much they wanted the right to vote. Typically they would say, "I fought in World War II, I fought in Korea, and all I want before I die is the right to vote."

Many decades before, the 22-year-old Emma Goldman learned from a similar experience, after an early lecture when she scornfully dismissed the eight-hour day as a stupid and token demand. The language and thinking of her intellectual mentor, Johann Most, had "paralyzed her efforts to speak naturally." When a worker in her audience replied that he couldn't wait for the overthrow of capitalism, that he needed two hours less work "to feel human, to read a book, or take a walk in daylight," the experience gave Emma Goldman the consciousness of a great organizer.[4]

The first notes towards Port Huron were written while I was briefly in an Albany, Georgia, jail cell after a Freedom Ride in December 1961. When I met the high-school and college students engaged in direct action, they changed my life. I had never met young people willing to take a risk, perhaps an ultimate risk, for a cause they believed in. Quite simply, I wanted to live like them. These feelings might explain the utopian urgency of the final sentence of the PHS:

> If we appear to seek the unattainable, as it has been said, then let it be known that we do so to avoid the unimaginable.[5]

The "Values" section, which was pushed to the forefront of the Statement, reflected our eclectic, existential, sometimes apocalyptic, take on life: "We have no sure formulas, no closed theories." We would accept no hand-me-down ideologies: "A first task of any social movement is to convince people that the search for orienting theories and the creation of human values is complex but worthwhile." We agreed with the French novelist-existentialist and former Resistance fighter Albert Camus that a previous generation of revolutionaries had sometimes rationalized horrific slaughters in the name of future utopias like "land reform." Still, we wanted to argue, carefully, for a restoration of the utopian spirit amidst the deadening compromises all around us. We wrote that "we are imbued with urgency, yet the message of our society is that there is no viable alternative to the present," the same phrase later employed by Margaret Thatcher. Our diagnosis of the prevailing apathy was that deep anxieties had fostered "a developed indifference" about public life, but also a yearning to believe in something better: "It is to this latter yearning, at once the spark and engine of change, that we direct our present appeal."

We even thrashed out basic views of human nature day after day, not the usual subject of political platforms. We asserted a belief that "men [are] infinitely precious and possessed of unfulfilled capacities for reason, freedom, and love." Use of the term "men" was unquestioned at the time; Betty Friedan's *The Feminine Mystique* was one year away. This formulation followed long discussions in which we repudiated doctrines of pessimism about the fallen human condition, as well as the liberal-humanist belief in human "perfectibility." It may have been influenced also by the Vatican II reforms then sweeping the Catholic Church.[6] The formulation about "unrealized potential" was the premise for believing that human beings were capable of participating in the decisions affecting their lives, a sharp difference from the dominant view that an irrational mass society could be managed only by experts, or the too-hopeful Enlightenment view of Tom Paine that our world could be created anew.

We even embraced individualism, though of a certain kind, defined as finding a "meaning in life that is personally authentic" instead of one imposed by manipulation or advertising: "the object is not to have one's way so much as it is to have a way of one's own." From there we asserted that human relationships should be based on "fraternity and honesty," on a recognition of interdependence, as against the "loneliness, estrangement and isolation" that characterized so much of the '50s American culture. In our sweeping conclusion, "we would replace power rooted in possession, privilege or circumstance by power and uniqueness rooted in love, reflectiveness, reason and creativity."

What Participatory Democracy Meant

Much was omitted because, in 1962, awakenings just around the corner were not anticipated. Many of us read Doris Lessing and Simone de Beauvoir, but the first women's participatory consciousness-raising groups were two years in the future, and would be provoked by our own chauvinism. Vietnam was on the far horizon, though the Statement opposed U.S. support for the "free world's" dictators, including Ngo Dinh Diem. Rachel Carson's *Silent Spring* was published just two months after Port Huron, and all the Statement observed about the environment was that "uncontrolled exploitation governs the sapping of the earth's physical resources."[7] There was no counterculture, no drug culture, and there were no hippies. There was folk music, not rock and roll—all that was to come.

The Statement would need huge updating, but its passionate democratic core was of permanent value.

What did we mean by participatory democracy? Obviously the concept arose from our common desire to participate in making our own destiny, and in response to the severe limitations of an undemocratic system, which we saw as representing an oligarchy. At its most basic, participatory meant the right to vote, as Henry David Thoreau wrote, not with "a mere strip of paper but your whole influence."[8] It meant simplicity in registration and voting, unfettered by the dominance of wealth, property requirements, literacy tests, and poll taxes. It meant exercising the right to popular initiatives, referendums, and recall, as achieved by Progressives in the early 20th century. And it meant widening participation to include the economic sphere (workplace democracy and consumer watchdogs), neighborhood assemblies, the process of learning by doing, and family life itself, where women and children were subordinates. It meant a greater role for citizens in the ultimate questions of war and peace, then considered the secret and inbred realm of experts.

Participatory democracy was a psychologically liberating antidote to the paralysis of the apathetic Lonely Crowd depicted in 1950 by David Riesman. The kind of democracy we were proposing was more than a blueprint for structural rearrangements. It was a form of empowering the individual as autonomous but interdependent, and the community as a civic society. Without this empowerment on both levels, the Port Huron Statement warned, we were living in "a democracy without publics," taking the concept from C. Wright Mills.[9]

The Statement's economic program was an extension of the New Deal and a call for deeper participatory democratic reform. Proposals for a government-led poverty program and "medical care as a lifetime human right" anticipated the Medicare legislation that came in 1965, and the Port Huron Statement's concept of a government-led antipoverty program foreshadowed the official Office of Economic Opportunity project envisioned by Kennedy, adopted by Johnson, and led by Sargent Shriver.

But the Statement also called for economic democracy as distinct from the New Deal's more bureaucratic approach: while the major resources and means of production should be "open to democratic participation and subject to democratic regulation" there also was a danger of "bureaucratic coagulation" and too much emphasis in the New Frontier on "problems that are easiest for computers to solve." There should be experiments in decentralization, we said, devolving the power of "monster cities" to local communities seeded with more developmental incentives. Returning to the Statement's moral focus, since a human being's whole economic experience has "crucial influence on habits, perceptions and individual ethics," we insisted that economics include incentives beyond money or survival, ones that are "educative, not stultifying; creative, not mechanical; self-directed, not manipulated; encouraging independence, a respect for others, a sense of dignity, and a willingness to accept social responsibility."

Breaking the Political Stalemate by Party Realignment

According to historian Michael Kazin and many others, the role of the American Left has been to make lasting cultural and normative contributions while never actually coming to power. We were dreamers too, but dreamers who had a plan for achieving political influence and power.[10]

Again, SNCC's influence in the beginning was extremely important. According to Charles McDew, the first SNCC organizers committed themselves by a blood oath to spend five years in the center of white terror, the communities with large black populations suffocating under Dixiecrat rule. A score of people were killed, and thousands were injured, evicted, or convicted or incarcerated, but the plan began to threaten power.

Also according to McDew, SNCC came to Port Huron intentionally to recruit SDS activists, and northern white students in general, to join the Southern struggle in the belief that the federal government and media might respond more rapidly if white skin were in the game. They pointed out that when early

SDS leader Paul Potter and I were beaten during an October 12, 1961, trip to McComb, Mississippi, a photo of the violence appeared in the national and international press. But there was no coverage or photo when Herbert Lee, a black farmer working for voting rights, was murdered in the same town by a Mississippi state representative only 17 days earlier.[11]

SDS advocated breaking the stranglehold of the Southern segregationist Dixiecrat power bloc over the national Democratic Party, a "political realignment" to end the "organized stalemate" in Washington and open the possibility of a more progressive party.[12]

At a Chapel Hill workshop that preceded Port Huron, the SNCC leadership argued that "moral realignment" through direct action had to precede any political realignment, but a political strategy inevitably arose from their work. Dixiecrats represented 10 of 17 Senate committees and 13 of 21 House committees, "consolidating the irresponsible power of military and business interests." It was impossible for young civil-rights workers not to notice that politicians and plantation owners constituted a "natural interlocking" that blocked black people at the registrars' doors all over the South.[13]

The Kennedy administration was placed in a political crossfire between two forces on a collision course: the demands of the Freedom Riders, SNCC in Mississippi and the larger civil-rights movement, versus the political dinosaurs of the Dixiecrat South on which the party depended for its national majority. The New Frontier's gradualism and tokenism, which we fiercely criticized, reflected the compromised political order as a whole. John and Robert Kennedy sometimes complained about the impatience of the Freedom Riders and the radical "sons of bitches" of SNCC,[14] but eventually they were motivated to funnel large sums of private foundation money into voter drives where black majorities were suppressed, a plan intended to undermine the entrenched seniority power of the Dixiecrats. As early as 1961, top Justice Department officials like Burke Marshall (deputy attorney general) and Harris Wofford (special assistant to Kennedy for civil rights) were participating in meetings with executives from the Taconic and Field foundations and the Stern Family Fund to channel thousands of dollars to black-voter registration in the South.[15] The funds were channeled through the Atlanta-based Voter Education Fund, headed by Wiley Branton, which received a "prompt" tax exemption at Bobby Kennedy's direct request.[16] Arguments within SNCC over direct action versus voter registration were dissipated when it became obvious that southern blacks would be fired, beaten, and killed for attempting to vote. By risking their lives daily in both sit-ins and voter drives, SNCC and rural black people would soon crumble the foundation of Dixiecrat power.

In just five years, the Voting Rights Act passed, establishing federal oversight over Deep South voting patterns. The Port Huron Statement was perhaps the first document to articulate the strategy, as suggested to SDS by SNCC leaders like Charles McDew, Timothy Jenkins, and Bob Zellner, all three of whom attended Port Huron. Realignment was embraced by Martin Luther King, Jr. and was the political agenda of the vast March on Washington for Jobs and Justice in August 1963. Soon Northern students were streaming south for the Mississippi Summer Project in 1964, whose aim was to literally unseat the white Mississippi Democratic delegation and replace it with a democratically chosen slate called the Mississippi Freedom Democratic Party.

The energy of some SNCC and SDS organizers also overflowed into the rising farmworkers' organizing efforts in the Southwest around the same time. The Port Huron Statement condemned the disenfranchisement of migrant workers while also citing them as a potential base for rebirth of a "broader and more forceful unionism."[17] When I visited Berkeley in 1960, among the first experiences I had was a trip to migrant-labor fields in the Central Valley. By 1964, César Chávez "turned to the nation's most experienced protestors, the youthful members of SNCC and SDS, who had recently emerged from the cauldron of civil rights activism in the Deep South, as well as the Berkeley Free Speech Movement," writes labor historian Philip Dray.[18] Chávez recruited from Stanford and Berkeley, while SNCC organizers like Marshall Ganz moved from the Black Belt to the "factories in the fields," and Maria Varela eventually went to the tiny towns of northern New Mexico. In 1964, the federal government's hated *bracero* program was forced to its end. Political realignment was advanced that same year when the U.S. Supreme Court decreed that voter representation would be based on population rather than the land holdings of the growers. By 1966, the United Farm Workers was bringing new energy to the organized labor movement; in that same year, Congress moved to include minimum-wage protections for farmworkers who had been excluded for the previous 28 years under the Fair Labor Standards Act. The formation of the United Farmworkers Association in 1964 was followed by the Delano grape strike in 1966, the emergence of the United Farm Workers (UFW) and a four-year global consumer boycott of grapes. The boycott was a channel of participatory democracy by many thousands of activists inspired by the early '60s.

One linkage between these events was the leadership of Walter Reuther, his brother Victor, and a United Auto Workers (UAW) top officer, Mildred Jeffrey, who was the mother of Sharon, a key SDS founder at Port Huron. Reuther helped fund and support the early SDS, the UFW, and the Southern voter-registration campaigns and marches. The overall strategy of realignment, as I will point out, was derailed by Vietnam and Democratic Party internal politics, but it was indeed a rational objective.

The strategy was this: a vision of participatory democracy directly connected to a new social movement, one capable of forging a new governing majority in the

United States, with young people as shock troops building a bridge to political power composed of liberal Democrats, peace groups, organized labor, and the civil rights movement. For the first time, students were thinking of themselves as an agency of social change. The buoyancy of this strategy, perhaps carried on the innocence of the young, represented a momentous break from the culture of the Left in those times, which was dispirited by McCarthyism, bogged down in poisonous factional disputes, and weighted with the ideological language and baggage of a Marxism that remained foreign to most Americans.

A Legacy of Isms and Schisms

Not that Marxism was irrelevant to the Port Huron gathering. Most of the participants were shaped and informed in part by Marxist traditions. But the convention was never intended as a revival ceremony for Marxism. The document at one point mentioned a need to bring together "liberals and socialists, the former for their relevance and the latter for their sense of thoroughgoing reforms in the system."[19] But even those at Port Huron who were children of the Old Left had concluded that moral values and democracy were more important than any ideological construct of Marxism, Trotskyism, Maoism, or Anarchism—at least for the moment. We seemed agreed that we were something new—a movement—perhaps an embryonic blessed community. When those from an earlier tradition pointed out, sometimes vehemently, that we were not only not new, but descendants of the Left, the New Left became our hybrid brand. No one complained when C. Wright Mills, our intellectual hero, suggested the label.

The great value of the participatory-democracy concept lay in its participatory nature. There could be no fixed dogma, no left-wing catechism handed down to disciples, if the ideas were an open-ended contribution to a living dialogue as the Port Huron Statement proclaimed. Many of us struggled with how to keep doubt and hope alive at the very same time, without depending on the crutch of a dogmatic overview. This was a spiritual and moral question, not simply an intellectual or political one. Any person trying to decide whether to take a risk feels a certain need to replace doubt with faith. But faith, whether in a cause, an ideology, a leader, or a party, has a tendency to become dogma when doubt is erased.

The founding generation of SDS and SNCC, including thinker-activists like Moses and Savio, learned in the course of experience to take great risks without becoming dogmatic thinkers.[20] When their words became The Word, when they themselves became idols, they retired from their leading roles without a resolution of the question. Later the void was filled by doctrines, which, in seeming to explain everything, in leaving no room for doubt, could not possibly be open-ended or provisional in spirit like the sensibility of Port Huron.

The Derailing

The Port Huron vision of winning seemed entirely possible to those who debated the strategy and set forth earnestly to carry it out. But even the "best and brightest" among the young radicals were thwarted by a constant inability to predict the future until it was too late.

First, there was the assassination of John Kennedy, which devastated any rational basis for strategy. The assassination of a president simply wasn't factored into any models we took seriously about reform or revolution. Whether or not the Kennedy killing was accomplished by a larger conspiracy, as many still believe, a mood of paranoid conjecturing took root in which it seemed that any notions of peaceful democratic transfers of power were wishful. For most of us, Kennedy (and later, his brother Robert, Martin Luther King, Jr., and even the murdered Malcolm X) had been a central figure in the transformation we hoped to see realized. The power of the independent movement came first, but it was also necessary to pressure and persuade the president to follow, to recognize and legitimize and legalize the victory and pursue a transition to a more participatory and egalitarian democracy. Groups like SDS and SNCC, we thought, would be the impatient radical vanguards of a new majority, and would continue to play such roles in a new and reformed world.

The historic parallel to John Kennedy's assassination was the Confederate murder of Abraham Lincoln on Good Friday, 1865, and the subsequent demise of Reconstruction, the brief effort when thousands of Freedmen and Northern volunteers set forth to empower black voters, redistribute land ("our 40 acres and a mule") and reform public education through politics and organizing under the protections of federal power. Ours was to be the Second Reconstruction.

Many today argue that Kennedy's assassination made no difference in the history of the disasters that followed. Similar claims were made after the killing of Lincoln, who often is portrayed as a hesitating gradualist forced by pressure into abolition and war, and whose Reconstruction policies, therefore, would also be token in nature. Who knows? But can it really be said that the close election of 1860, when a political realignment forced by the abolition movement gave birth to the Republican Party and gave Lincoln 39.8 percent of the vote, was irrelevant?[21] As the conflict ended, didn't Frederick Douglass come to look kindly on Lincoln's role? What we know as fact is that Confederate conspirators killed Lincoln, Northern troops subsequently were withdrawn from the South; Reconstruction was rolled back and Jim Crow was brutally installed for a century.[22]

I do not believe the historical record supports the account of my revered friend Noam Chomsky, who thinks that Kennedy, if re-elected in 1964, would have escalated the Vietnam War in the way that Lyndon Johnson did. The truth is hard to excavate from the hidden files and smiles of apologists, of course. Yes, John Kennedy was the exuberant creator of the Green Berets, and the president who authorized the Bay of Pigs invasion of Cuba. But he also supported—and actually installed—a neutralist government in Laos, including Communists, when the Joint Chiefs wanted to unleash their air power. Kennedy supported 17,000 U.S. military advisers in South Vietnam as well, to back a dictatorship, which the Port Huron Statement denounced. But there is no evidence that Kennedy would have bombed North Vietnam at the Tonkin Gulf in August 1964, and none that he would have sent 100,000 ground troops into combat in 1965. Robert Kennedy later told Daniel Ellsberg, who was then at RAND, "We would have fuzzed it up. We would have gotten a government that asked us out or that would have negotiated with the other side. We would have handled it like Laos."[23] Again, according to Ellsberg, the official paperwork justifying an expanded war was finalized in the week of Johnson's 1964 election, when he promised to never send American boys to fight a ground war in Asia.

Bobby Kennedy took up his brother's mantle and identified himself more than any previous candidate with the poor, the racial minorities, and the alienated youth of America. His 1968 anti-Vietnam position actually was vaguer than Obama's 2008 pledge to end the Iraq War; his nomination fight with Eugene McCarthy, a foreshadowing of the nasty Obama–Hillary Clinton contest 30 years later, left RFK's image tarnished from white-liberal attacks. But on the night he died, the UFW's Dolores Huerta and the UAW's Paul Shrade were at his side, powerful evidence that the Port Huron strategy still flickered with hope. I participated in the honor guard at his coffin in St. Patrick's, adding an antiwar presence to the grieving circle.

Vietnam Destroys the Great Society

The Port Huron vision of a democratic movement demanding domestic priorities to replace those of the Cold War was destroyed by Vietnam. The document correctly predicted that if nuclear war with the Soviets could be prevented, there still would be an ongoing "international civil war" between proxies of the United States and the Soviet Union. Cuba was one such focal point, and we opposed Kennedy's "unexpected" CIA-sponsored invasion of April 1961. Vietnam was another unexpected folly. The Vietnam War diverted public attention and drained public resources away from the budding War on Poverty. I was one of many hundreds who moved into inner-city communities to engage in community organizing against poverty, building community organizations that took over local boards in Newark, New Jersey.[24] But Vietnam wrecked all that, plunging our young movement into five years of draft and war resistance, and provoking an escalated militancy against the war-makers. It was no accident that the Vietnam escalation also was accompanied by hundreds of uprisings in black communities, with the cost in lives still uncounted and billions of dollars wasted. Any possibility, however remote or delusional, of our being the left wing of Johnson's Great Society was rendered impossible and was rejected in disgust.

The consequences for political realignment were far different than our predictions. As a result of the civil-rights movement, there came a generation of white-liberal national politicians like Jimmy Carter, Bill Clinton, and Al Gore; a huge complement of black elected officials from the South, from local sheriffs to congressmen like John Lewis (of SNCC) and Jim Clyburn (vice chairman under Charles McDew of the Orangeburg State student movement in 1960). The climate of officially sponsored terrorism ebbed in the South, and leaders like the Rev. Jesse Jackson would run impressive presidential campaigns where none were possible in the previous 100 years. Barack Obama, born in 1961, the year the Freedom Rides began, very much owes his election to the voting-rights reforms that brought about this realignment. As Attorney General Eric Holder said at SNCC's 50th reunion in 2010, "there is a straight line from the lunch counters and Freedom Rides to the office where I sit today."

The Other Realignment

On the other hand, as Richard Flacks, a principle coauthor of the Port Huron Statement, has noted, there was another realignment, which we underestimated: the morphing of white Southern Democratic voters through the 1964 Goldwater Republican campaign and Nixon's 1968 "southern strategy" designed to attract white Southern voters away from the blacks, draft resisters, hippies, and homosexuals who were alleged to have seized the Democratic Party.[25] The SDS realignment project, in summary, peaked in the Democratic Party's rejection of the seating of the Mississippi Freedom Democrats at the 1964 convention, and resulted in two backlash victories by Republicans (Nixon, Reagan), the deaths of three national leaders (the Kennedys and King), and the election of three living Democratic centrists (Carter, Clinton, and Obama). The political civil war between so-called Red and Blue continues without end, with the red lines eerily drawn around the old Confederacy and the Wild West.

My argument so far is that the Port Huron vision and proposed progressive alliance would have succeeded in bringing a new governing majority to power in 1964 with a likelihood of avoiding Vietnam were it not for the murder of John Kennedy and Johnson's subsequent escalation. The argument may be criticized as purely hypothetical, but it tries to capture the immensity of our dream and how close it seemed to our grasp. It is also a measure of the bottoms of despair we fell to in the years to come, a despair that lingers today among those who experienced both the beautiful struggle and the bitter fruit.

Is There a System Preventing Change?

There was yet a third obstacle to Port Huron's dream, in addition to the assassinations and the Vietnam War. For want of another term, it was the System itself, or the powerful paradigms we defied but could not defeat. By "System" I mean the intersecting (though not coordinated) hierarchies of banks, corporations, the military, media, and religion, which were dominant then and are now (with a far greater sample of women and people of color at the upper levels today). This was the "power elite" described by C. Wright Mills, a Texas-born rebel sociologist at Columbia University, who died of heart failure just before Port Huron in 1962. His was a broader conception of power than that of an economic ruling class, one of an establishment far more flexible, even liberal, that had presided over the growth of the middle classes in the 1950s. Mills's open 1960 "Letter to the New Left" is properly credited with sparking campus and intellectual excitement, and first announcing the label. He most aroused us when he named our generation as the new agency of global change:

> Who is it that is thinking and acting in radical ways? All over the world—in the bloc, outside the bloc and in between—the answer's the same: it is the young intelligentsia.[26]

As the Statement emphasized, however, the New Left called for more than a revolt of the "young intelligentsia" of Mills's letter. That term, after all, could describe the Beat Generation of poets and artists. The exemplary figure in the early SDS period was the organizer; the "young intelligentsia" needed to listen and connect with forces beyond the campus because university students could not, as the PHS put it, "complete a movement of ordinary people making demands for a better life." This is the point Mills missed. Ironically, while he idealized the Cuban Revolution and visited with Fidel Castro, Mills never traveled to interview SNCC people or attend an SDS gathering.

By the "paradigm" we defied, I mean an understanding of power as cultural hegemony or dominance, a thought system where there seems to be no alternative. Previous hegemonies—such as monarchism, aristocracy, white or male supremacy—were discredited by social movements or revolutions. The oppressive paradigm of power, which the Port Huron Statement attempted to discredit, was the power elite's one of a Cold War between two blocs engaged in nuclear brinksmanship. We were the first generation in history to grow up with the Bomb, to learn to hide under desks or in bomb shelters, to witness mushroom clouds and disfigured Japanese survivors. During the Cuban Missile Crisis, three months after Port Huron, journalist I.F. Stone told us that the superpower deadlines had passed and the nuclear warheads would shortly be launched. We were exposed to the mad logic, humorized in the *Dr. Strangelove* film, of "mutual assured destruction" and the cynical realpolitik of Free World and Soviet blocs controlling alliances of servile authoritarians. And we knew the grim math: the trillions spent on weapons were dollars that could have been invested in economic development, health care, and education. President Dwight Eisenhower had a name for the institutional form of this System—the military-industrial complex—and we noted that he dared name it only as he was leaving office. This paradigm at first froze us in fear. The legacy of McCarthyism, if continued in the '60s, would mean that all our work, from sit-ins to the Freedom Rides to the Port Huron Statement, would be marginalized as taking the wrong side in the Cold War.

The Statement therefore included a 20-page attack on this Cold War mentality, half devoted to a proposal for phased nuclear disarmament, half to a welcoming attitude towards anti-colonial revolutions. Since it did not occur to us—nor to virtually anyone else—that the Soviet Union would collapse in the decades ahead, our proposal was to de-escalate the bipolar nuclear confrontation. We differed with most of the left-liberalism of the time by suggesting that our own government was partly to blame for the Cold War, and by denying that the Soviet Union sought to take over the world by force. There was a growing peace movement symbolized by the 100,000 who marched in Britain against atomic weapons in April 1960, and the formation of Women Strike for Peace on November 1, 1961, which many in our ranks eagerly joined. Despite, or perhaps because of, the near nuclear miss over Cuba, President Kennedy became an important critic of the Cold War shortly after Port Huron and before his assassination. The Port Huron Statement borrowed the phrase "peace race" from a Kennedy speech to the UN on September 25, 1961. Kennedy went further in his June 10, 1963, speech, when he called for the end of the Cold War, just two months before the

March on Washington. It appeared that the SDS demand for new priorities was being recognized when Kennedy initiated and signed a partial nuclear test ban treaty with the Soviets on October 7, 1963.

We had surprising connections for transmitting our criticisms and proposals to the White House. Immediately after Port Huron, for example, Al Haber and I drove to Washington, D.C., where we met with presidential advisor Arthur Schlesinger and Sen. Joseph Clark, a leading critic of the arms race. Perhaps we felt, mistakenly, that our liberal elders could be persuaded back to their earlier idealism. Some of our connections included the UAW's Mildred Jeffrey; Haber's own father, William Haber, at the University of Michigan Law School; and Norman Cousins, the crusading editor of *The Saturday Review*. For whatever reason, access to the White House seemed greater in those days than at later times. Not that it would matter all that much.

SDS, the CIA, and the Power Elite

As the killing of JFK and escalation of Vietnam buried the original hopes of SDS, a new politics of radical resistance was taking root, and with it, new ideological searching. The second generation of SDS, and the movement generally, were learning hard lessons from experience, which were not available to us in 1960–62. Black people who played by the rules would see those rules changed when power was threatened. Presidents were assassinated in a climate of hate if they moved in a progressive direction. Politicians would lie about taking us to war. Vietnam seemed to prove that militarism and imperialism were central features of American society whether liberals or conservatives were in power. And finally, there was a power elite that ruled beyond elected officials. To take one example among many, official disclosures in 1984 revealed that John McCone, Kennedy's CIA director, head of the Atomic Energy Commission, and Bechtel corporation executive, conspired with the FBI in a "psychological warfare campaign" against the Free Speech Movement and to elect Ronald Reagan governor of California.[27] Rampant conspiracy theories seemed to negate the prospects of popular movements and peaceful transitions through elections. Such speculation could destabilize the best of us. Even if the paranoia went too far, as it usually did, there still were real grounds for believing there were manipulators behind the curtain.

In 1961, I found a yellow pad during a National Student Association convention with a chart identifying SDS in a box on the left, Young Americans for Freedom on the right, and an entity named the "control group" in the center-top. Six years later it was revealed by *Ramparts* magazine (February 1967 issue) that the secretive control group included CIA agents whose work was to promote a pro–Cold War student movement globally. The CIA also ran covert operations through the AFL-CIO's international-affairs department under Jay Lovestone. AFL-CIO president George Meany's special assistant, and later director of the AFL-CIO's foreign operations, was Tom Kahn, the very person at the League for Industrial Democracy who in 1961 tried to fire Al Haber and myself and locked us out of the SDS headquarters in New York, because he believed the Port Huron Statement was anti–Cold War and soft on the Soviets. I have no concrete evidence that Kahn, who also was a leading civil-rights activist and died of AIDS in 1986, was himself a CIA agent, but he would have had intimate knowledge of the Agency's longstanding ties with Lovestone.[28]

The CIA's role in the AFL-CIO and foreign policy came to light as the byproduct of hearings into tax-exempt foundations by Rep. Wright Patman (D-Texas) on September 1, 1964, immediately after the Tonkin Gulf bombing, the rejection of the Mississippi Freedom Democratic Party, and the Atlantic City Convention. "Patman Attacks 'Secret' CIA Link," declared the *New York Times* headline that day. Our worst suspicions were confirmed. AFL-CIO staff was also involved in the U.S. invasion of the Dominican Republic in 1965, and in controlling Saigon's labor federation protecting the flow of U.S. military supplies into South Vietnam's ports during the war.[29]

The importance of this sojourn into left-wing history is that SDS and SNCC (and Martin Luther King, among others) were unaware of the company we were keeping. The unmovable obstacle to the coalition we hoped to build with organized labor was the secret pro–Cold War element within liberalism, directly and indirectly tied to the CIA, which was fiercely opposed to our break from Cold War thinking. On the one hand, there were the UAW's Reuther brothers, who helped fund and provide conference quarters at Port Huron, supported the March on Washington and the early UFW organizing effort, and were frustrated by Meany's arch-conservative views. On the other hand, there was the right-wing AFL-CIO foreign-affairs department with its covert operations carrying on the anti-Communist crusade. There was no way, in other words, that the New Left could have combined with organized labor in 1964–65 around the Port Huron foreign-policy vision because the AFL-CIO at the time was shackled to the CIA without our knowledge. The Reuthers were the great hope, but they were loath to break from Johnson over Atlantic City and Vietnam. Finally, when the UAW broke from Meany's AFL-CIO and demanded a cease-fire in Vietnam, SDS and SNCC were too radicalized and factionalized for it to matter anymore. Death, our old nemesis, also intervened again. On May 9, 1970, one week after Kent State, and after Walter Reuther demanded an immediate withdrawal from Vietnam, he and five others were killed in a charter-jet crash in northern Michigan.

Marxism Replaces Participatory Democracy in SDS

While the Port Huron Statement was criticized by the elders for being too far left, an opposite attack came from the mid-'60s generation that followed Port Huron. Beginning in 1966, the Port Huron Statement was rejected by the new SDS leaders as "too reformist." It was certainly true that the Port Huron Statement did envision reforms, substantive rather than token, rapid though not overnight, and revolution was seen more as an undefined aspiration or long-term hope than as a defined objective. The strategy of radical reform depended on independent social movements in combination with awakened progressives within political institutions rather than any revolutionary conquest of state and corporate power. This strategy was criticized as based on delusional liberal hopes. In place of the Port Huron vision came a "turn in SDS toward revolutionary Marxism and a further break with the group's social-democratic past as codified in the 'Port Huron Statement,'" writes Carl Davidson, an SDS leader from the mid '60s who remains a stalwart of the Left today.[30] Bob Gottlieb, Gerry Tenney, and David Gilbert, all from the New School, authored what they dubbed the Port Authority Statement, which made an important contribution in theorizing the rise of a "new working class" of "knowledge workers."[31] The notion had appeared only in embryonic form in the Port Huron Statement, which noted that the perversion of the universities by the nuclear-weapons lobby, big agribusiness, and corporations also demonstrated the "reliance of men of power on ... the storehouses of knowledge [making] the universities tied to society in new ways, revealing new potentialities, new levers of change." The next year Berkeley president Clark Kerr gave his fateful analysis of the university as serving the industrial needs of a new knowledge-based economy. The Free Speech Movement took up opposition to this "knowledge factory" by wearing badges that declared "do not fold, bend, mutilate or spindle," the message of the technocratic IBM punch cards then used in the admissions process.

FSM activists like Jackie Goldberg recall carrying their Port Huron Statements to study groups, and their new understanding of the "multiversity" was an organic extension of the Port Huron Statement vision, based on their an evolving experience. Why then was it so necessary for SDS leaders to reject Port Huron as "reformist"? The main reasons were external—the escalation of the war and draft by the liberal Democrats—but there was an internal dynamic as well. The new SDS leaders, in search of an ideology, turned steadily to Marxism, then to Marxism-Leninism and Maoism. Since the Port Huron Statement wasn't based on Marxist analysis, it had to be rejected as defective.

This was a stunning turn for a "new" Left, because it implied a broad rejection of all the new social movements of the '60s as basically "reformist" too, since none of them were led by Marxists; none were openly or dogmatically reliant on Marx, Lenin, Mao, or Trotsky; and none favored vanguard parties. None were demanding Socialism, though many within the movements were Socialists themselves or at least informed by Socialism as a powerful legacy. The implication was that no genuine explanatory framework existed for a radical American social movement outside of Marxism, a thesis that ignored or downplayed the deep historical currents of populism, pacifism, religious reform, Anarchism, or slave rebellions in American history. Most of the thinkers who inspired the early SDS—C. Wright Mills, John Dewey, Albert Camus, Doris Lessing, James Baldwin—were shelved in search of a higher knowledge that only Marxism seemed to offer.

The Port Authority Statement relied on European Marxists like Antonio Gramsci, Serge Mallet, and Andre Gorz, though the 1967 document opened with quotations from Marx and Lenin. The new definition of the proletariat took account of the rapid growth of the highly educated, technical sectors of the workforce since Marx's time. Then it sought to develop a student "class consciousness" as the highest of priorities, for otherwise the new left would become "one more epiphenomena of protest movements that can be absorbed by the economic growth of American society." It was an interesting challenge, but it opened the floodgates to many sectarian attempts to fit—some might say straitjacket—the new movements into Marxist theory. Tellingly, the Port Authority Statement, according to Davidson, was swallowed in a "factional struggle [that] prevented the bulk of it from ever being published" until 2010.[32]

Soon the open, participatory structure of the early SDS was being penetrated and disrupted by the Progressive Labor Party, a tightly disciplined, highly secretive organization dedicated to recruiting SDS members in support a Communist revolution on the inspiration of China and Albania. They proved impossible to dislodge from the organization, and pushed all internal discussions in a poisonous sectarian direction.

Beginning in 1968, the Weatherman (later the Weather Underground) faction surfaced as new "Communist revolutionaries" modeled after Vietnam, Cuba, and the Black Panthers at home. Instead of the Port Huron concept of a majority progressive coalition, they favored forming clandestine cells behind enemy lines, and regarded the white American majority as hopelessly racist and privileged. Their ideological heroes included Lin Piao, a hero of the Chinese revolution who was later condemned by Mao for "revisionism" and "Confucian thinking"; and Che Guevara and the young French intellectual Régis Debray with their "foco" theory that small bands of armed guerrillas could themselves set off popular revolutions, and their vision of a "tri-continental" alternative to the "revisionist" Soviet Union. For an American hero, they turned to John

Brown, who led a largely white handful to an armed and suicidal uprising against slavery. That uprising, to the Weathermen (and many African-Americans) was vindicated by the vast swelling of support for John Brown during and after his martyrdom. Perhaps it would take a vanguard of martyrs to incite an American revolution, or so the thinking went.

These were compelling notions to SDS radicals desperate to stop the Vietnam War and disillusioned with liberalism's default. But by 1969, the factional wrangling resulted in the end of SDS, less than eight years after its founding.

The Movements Rise Again, with SDS Underground

I am not describing these post–Port Huron Marxist tendencies as mad delusions, as many have. That brief generation tried to make sense of the terrible and traumatizing history around them. History was rich with failed uprisings—John Brown, Denmark Vesey, Joe Hill, Haymarket—where the sacrifices indeed paved the way for later reforms. Even as they quarreled over Marx, the SDS factions continued to have some impact: on the antiwar, antidraft resistance; on solidarity movements; and especially in raising the costs of the Vietnam War to a U.S. government worried about its stability and reputation. The Black Panther shootouts with police, the bombings and property destruction, and the little-reported violence by GIs against their military commanders all eroded America's image and security, though the costs to the movements were greater.

Nor were the late-'60s revolutionaries as isolated as conventional histories claim. In the case of the tiny Weather Underground and its many emulators, there were over 100 bombings and arson attacks on college and high-school campuses in 1969, costing $8.9 million in damage in the first eight months, according to the insurance industry.[33] Bombs, which were first used by the white left in 1968, were set off at least 255 times in the next 18 months, mainly against ROTC buildings, induction centers, and corporate headquarters.[34]

Nor was their deep radical paranoia unjustified. In late 1967, Johnson screamed at his top security advisers, "I'm not going to let the communists take this government and they're doing it right now!"[35] Fifteen hundred army intelligence officers, dressed as civilians, conducted domestic surveillance on 100,000 Americans.[36] Two thousand full-time FBI agents, the massive use of informants, counter-intelligence programs, and Hoover's orders to "neutralize" protest leaders are well documented.[37] Scores of young people were killed or wounded, well beyond the widely remembered shootings at Kent State and Black Panther offices. One near-victim of an assassination attempt in 1969 was Richard Flacks, a principal coauthor of the Port Huron Statement.[38] Targeted politically by Hoover and the Chicago police "red squad," Flacks was later attacked in his office with a claw hammer wielded by an individual who was never apprehended. A top Justice Department official, Richard Kleindeinst, advocated detention camps for SDS members and "draft-dodgers."[39] SDS was banned on many campuses. Outside police or troops occupied at least 127 campuses, and 1,000 students were expelled in the spring of 1968 (which, as Sale notes, made them instantly draftable).[40] Softer counterinsurgency techniques included screening out the "protest-prone" by many campus admissions officials, and employing psychological counseling to "treat" alienated students.[41] Making the paranoia all the more justified was the palpable sense of being abandoned by many of our parents; a Gallup survey indicated that 82 percent of Americans wanted student demonstrators expelled.[42] If that was true, what was the point of depending on mainstream public opinion?

But the heightened militancy became disconnected from a comprehensible narrative that the wider public might have understood. In abandoning the Port Huron vision and strategy as times worsened, SDS was offering a fringe analysis at best, and no longer was able to offer leadership and organizing resources to the vast swelling of campus protest that occurred after the doors of the SDS office were closed by an SDS leader who literally said, "We offed the pig" (referring to the reformist SDS). I agree with Carl Oglesby, an SDS president who died in 2011, in his 1969 complaint that our "attempt to reduce the New Left's inchoate vision to the Old Left's perfected remembrance has produced a layer of bewilderment and demoralization which no cop with his club and no senator with his committee could ever have induced."[43]

The greatest outpouring of youth, student, GI, liberal, feminist, and environmentalist sentiment in the '60s—or perhaps any previous era—occurred after SDS had closed its doors:

- In November 1969 came the largest peace march in American history, a moratorium largely organized by liberal students and Democrats who were radicalized by the Vietnam and Nixon.
- In April 1970, 20 million young people turned out for Earth Day, organized by an ad hoc group led by Sen. Gaylord Nelson and a Harvard student named Denis Hayes.
- In May 1970, after Nixon invaded Cambodia, the campuses rose up like never before. Sale estimates that 4.3 million Americans took part that May at half the colleges in the country, 536 of which closed down due to strikes or were shut down for the semester.[44]
- Instead of a repeat of McCarthyism, jury after jury exonerated antiwar defendants in proceedings like the Chicago Eight and the Catonsville

Nine trials; charges against Bobby Seale were dropped in Chicago and New Haven; a New York jury acquitted the Panther 21.

- Presidential commissions backed much of the early movement's reformist agenda. The Kerner Commission (1968), appointed by Johnson, lamented America becoming two societies—one black and one white—and called for immediate creation of two million government jobs. The Scranton Commission (1970), appointed by Nixon, warned of the greatest crisis since the Civil War, and endorsed "the new cultural revolution in lifestyles" and the students "who seek a community of companions and scholars but find an impersonal multiversity" instead. The Scranton report emphasized, "Nothing is more important than an end to the war in Indochina."[45]
- Returning Vietnam veterans were leading the antiwar movement by marching on the government and battling their officers.
- Less than two years later, the Democratic Party was taken over by the likes of Jesse Jackson, Gloria Steinem, and the Mississippi Freedom Democrats. The old insiders like Daley and Meany were suddenly outsiders. All this was much too rapid and radical for most voters, as the 1972 election results showed, but the Port Huron prophecy of realignment had proven to be more feasible than anyone imagined.

The '60s stumbled to an end after that American Spring of 1972, in large part due to the major reforms we achieved: the end of Vietnam and the draft; passage of the War Powers Act, the 1965 voter laws, the Freedom of Information Act, Nixon's environmental laws, and the amnesty for war resisters; the popular removal of two presidents from office; the 18-year-old vote; the union recognition of public employees and farmworkers; disability rights; the decline of censorship; the emergence of gays and lesbians from shadow existence—perhaps never had so many changes occurred in so short a time in American history, all driven by the vibrancy of participatory democracy.

Those who warned us of the System's unbendable durability, like Howard Zinn, a mentor I dearly loved, seemed at times to undervalue these achievements while celebrating the very movements that made them possible. For Zinn, the reforms were at best reluctant concessions "aimed at quieting the popular uprisings, not making fundamental changes."[46] The System would continue unchanged. As if to prove this thesis, the global Cold War quickly morphed into the rise of neoliberal globalization, the militarized war on narco-terrorism and, by 2001, the Global War on Terrorism. The old threat of international communist conspiracies was replaced by the alleged new threats from the narco-terrorists; global jihadists; and the insurgents in Iraq, Afghanistan, Pakistan, and the Mexican borderlands and beyond. The secrecy of the State expanded even in times of peace. And in response, new movements arose across the planet, against war, sweatshops, hunger, and environmental destruction. The elite of the World Economic Forum, flying into Davos, Switzerland, on corporate jets, was challenged by the World Social Forum, whose thousands of *campesinos,* indigenous people, workers, students, and artists made their way to Porto Alegre, Brazil, mainly by bus. The city of Porto Alegre showcased a model of "participatory budgeting" in which local citizens are directly involved in decisions to allocate public funds to neighborhood needs.

Starting in the 1980s, pro-democracy movements flourished across Latin and Central America in the wake of guerrilla campaigns, Liberation Theology communities, strikes, and road blockings by the indigenous. Where at least 20 guerrilla risings after the Cuba Revolution were blocked by U.S.-backed dictators and death squads, social movements and popular parties later came to power democratically. After Latin America's democratic transitions came the uprisings across the Arab world. Driven by direct action, forming coalitions to forge majorities and contest for power, these movements across Tunisia, Egypt, Yemen, Syria, Libya, Palestine, and even in such opposite places as Saudi Arabia and Israel, were described as participatory democracy by Phyllis Bennis on *Democracy Now!* Where the uprisings were repelled or derailed, the only forward path still seemed to be toward participatory democracy.

In 2011 came the still-ongoing Wisconsin revolt against the Tea Party governor Scott Walker, a model of participatory democracy in action, arising unexpectedly out of official insult and material grievance, flowing into months of building occupations in freezing storms, backed by organized labor and Democratic senators who took the extra-parliamentary step of leaving the state, collecting 900,000 valid recall signatures over a two-month period, rolling on movement energy into every open or even bureaucratic channel available. Unfortunately, this mass movement was defeated in 2012, partly by Big Money, partly by the Wisconsin process that requires the selection of a new governor, not simply an up-or-down vote on a particular law. By comparison, voters in Ohio voted by initiative to repeal a law like that of Wisconsin.*

---

*It is historically noteworthy that the national organizing director of the American Federation of State, County and Municipal Employees (AFSCME) during the Wisconsin revolt was none other than Paul Booth. He was a Swarthmore student at Port Huron who played a key role in SDS during the early to middle '60s. Booth was the architect of a "build, not burn" strategy, seeking an alternative to the military draft, which was condemned by SDS leaders as too reformist. From there, he became a leader in public-employee union organizing.

Participatory Democracy and Occupy Wall Street

Finally came Occupy Wall Street, two years after a historic volunteer movement led by young people and African-Americans, reminiscent of 1961, helped elect Barack Obama. Was it only coincidence that SDS and SNCC had risen during the three years of Kennedy's campaign and presidency? Or that Occupy Wall Street took up the very issues of economic inequality that died in Vietnam while Dr. King valiantly tried to forge a Poor People's Campaign? I don't know whether history begins anew or just repeats its sputtering cycles again and again. What is clear enough is that the Occupy movement began without pundit predictions, without funding, without organization, with only determined people in tents, countless Davids taking on the smug Goliath in spontaneous planetary resistance. While Occupy could not and would not agree on making detailed demands, it did agree on direct and transparent participatory democracy as its first principle.

There is endless speculation these days about the future of Occupy Wall Street. Since I was pleasantly surprised by its birth, I am not one to predict its growth. I prefer to wait and see, although the evictions from encampments in 2012 caused a weakening and lack of focus. Across the Western world, the smoldering conflict is becoming one between unelected, wealthy, and foreign private investors and the participatory democracies of civic societies and their faltering elected governments. Perhaps nowhere was this plainer than in Greece, the ancient birthplace of participatory democracy (for nonslaves, at least). The prime minister there was George Papandreou, son of a former prime minister, Andreas Papandreou, who once taught at Berkeley and was overthrown in a 1967 military coup. According to a longtime Papandreou advisor, Spyros Draenos, the "theme of participatory democracy resonated deeply with Andreas Papandreou, who was already in 1961 an advocate of decentralized economic programming for Greece."[47] When then-prime minister George Papandreou proposed a voter referendum on October 10, 2011, asking voters to decide on austerity measures imposed by foreign investors, he so offended institutional forces that he was forced to resign immediately.

There are differences between the Port Huron Statement and the Occupy Wall Street manifesto, though they should not be overstated. One of the major differences has to do with Anarchism, or "direct democracy," which plays a major role in the thinking, structure, and practice of many Occupy activists. The early SDS certainly identified with the Wobblies, the Anarchists who organized the 1912 Bread and Roses strike in Lawrence, Massachusetts; the Haymarket Square martyrs; and the historic wildcat strikes across the Western mining country. We sang of Joe Hill, knew all about "Big Bill" Haywood, Emma Goldman, and Mother Jones, lamented the executions of Sacco and Vanzetti. We believed that social movements could and should insist on the democratic reform of state and corporation, not expect their overthrow or collapse. We carefully managed to avoid adopting any of the previous ideologies of the Left, including Anarchism, in our search for something new. Ours was a democratic populist heritage in which we naively believed that many factions could bloom but none could choke our growth.

Once again today, there are questions about reform. Strict Anarchist theory suggests that any reforms only legitimize and strengthen structures that should be toppled or dissolved. But the early SDS saw no alternative to winning substantive reforms from the state and corporate sectors, fully aware of the dangers of being co-opted into the system, the managed cooling of street heat in the process, and the predictable countermovements that would rise to weaken those reforms over time. Even a philosophical Anarchist (or "Libertarian Socialist") like Noam Chomsky has written in favor of radical reform:

> There is a state sector that does awful things, but it also happens to do some good things. As a result of centuries of extensive popular struggle, there is a minimal welfare system that provides support for poor mothers and children. That's under attack in an effort to minimize the state. Well, anarchists can't seem to understand that they are to support that.... Minimizing the state means strengthening the private sectors. It narrows the domain within which public influence can be expressed. I know that a lot of people find that hard to deal with, and personally I'm under constant attack from the left for not being principled.[48]

Chomsky has said something else that is very important to understanding the early SDS-SNCC-UFW organizing approach:

> Try asking somebody to explain to you the latest essay by Derrida or somebody in terms you can understand. They can't do it. At least they can't do it to me. I don't understand.[49]

Coming full circle to the earliest influences on Port Huron, without intending to do so, Chomsky cites John Dewey, the parent of participatory democracy, as among the great humanist philosophers worth reading:

> He was straight out of mainstream America ... [believing] "the ultimate aim of production to be free human beings associated with one another on terms of equality" in education, the workplace, and every other sphere of life.[50]

I don't mean to say that all Occupiers today oppose reform. But there is a broad suspicion of seeking reforms, which require alliances with "top-down" organizations, especially with progressive elected officials. Many Occupiers stress the avoidance of "diluting themselves to meet the needs of already-institution-alized groups who aren't going anywhere."[51] The same dilemmas arose in the '60s in the relationships between SNCC and the national civil-rights leadership, and between SDS and liberal Democrats we blamed for starting Vietnam. In retrospect, however, it's impossible to reach a majority, or the 99 Percent, while rejecting coalition politics. Nevertheless, some theorists seem to believe so. For example, Micah White, a quite brilliant theorist at *Adbusters,* writes that "an insurrectionary challenge to the capitalist state" will be mounted by "culture-jammers" who create "fluid, immersive, evocative meta-gaming experiences that are playfully thrilling and [that] as a natural result of their gameplay" a social revolution will arise as "pure manifestation of an anonymous will of a dispersed, networked collective."[52] The *Adbusters'* collective draws its inspiration from French philosopher Guy Debord and the Situationists of 1968 France. They do not dwell on how the French trade unions turned against them and the security forces of De Gaulle crushed their barricades. It is as if the pure insurrectionary act is more important to memorialize as performance art than any consequence.

They are on to something new, however; a new engine of decentralized democratic power available to *Adbusters,* Occupy, Facebook, and WikiLeaks, which was never available at Port Huron. When I first saw a computer in 1964 it was the size of a room, and the professor who predicted microprocessors seemed nuts. Twenty years after the Gestetner machines and long-distance phone lines of SDS and SNCC came the Internet. We are full circle from the FSM's outrage at IBM punch cards to the exploding vista of instant information and interaction that has played a critical role since in the Zapatista uprising and the Seattle occupation, down to the present moment of instant interactive participatory democracy all over the world, including such weird and unexpected phenomena as Russia's self-described "young and connected office plankton," operating from the Social Network Agency, meeting in the Red October Chocolate Factory, and communicating with 50,000 Facebook friends.[53]

There is a utopian belief that downloading and freeing information, especially secret information, will bring about a decentralized revolution on its own, anony-mously, one might say. The download replaces the overthrow in the imaginary of some in this new movement. The invention of open-source technology may be the single greatest pathway to participatory democracy in our lifetimes, not only in coordinating social movements but also in making possible democratic decision-making without passing through representatives or gatekeepers. But like it or not, reform also is needed within the existing institutions, if only to protect the open source or the whistleblowers. The vast constituency of Occupy surely knows that a participatory future cannot be protected without engaging in some sort of politics in the present.

A useful model was implicit in the Port Huron Statement, one transmitted from our parents' generation, the last until now to weather Wall Street scandal, foreclosures, bankruptcies, and unemployment (without any safety net). Our parents wanted a New Deal and Franklin Roosevelt to meet their basic needs, just as black people in Mississippi wanted the vote and Kennedy, and workers wanted the eight-hour day in Emma Goldman's time. After waiting two years for Wall Street to self-correct or FDR to act, the people of the 1930s began demanding what became the Wagner Act, Social Security, the Works Progress Administration, the Civilian Conservation Corps, and the Federal Writers' Project. These reforms came about, as Zinn would rightly warn, as pragmatic institutional responses or concessions meant largely to restore order, but the process known as the New Deal itself was driven by a chaotic, eclectic, sectarian, combative, fanatic, and passionate energy force including Anarchists, Communists, musicians, muralists, liberals, progressives, prairie populists, industrial union organizers, and—yes—reformers from Al Smith to Upton Sinclair to Eleanor Roosevelt. They were pushed from below by waves of insurrectionary strikes in Seattle; factory occupations in Flint; and writings and art of government-subsidized poets and intellectuals who went forth to interview the poor, the migrants and the unemployed, and who brought forth "This Land Is Your Land" and *The Grapes of Wrath*. It was a splendid bedlam of participatory democracy, which led neither to Socialism nor Fascism, but to Keynesian economics and a definition of the state as an instrument, which sometimes can be bent to the popular will and public interest. After 20 years of celebration, we decided in 1960 that those New Deal reforms were stagnating and insufficient, and that it was time to begin again.

We are not yet in the '30s at present, if only because of the safety-net reforms that were achieved in that earlier dangerous time. Globally, however, the unfettered appetites of capitalism have created an intolerable human condition. It is time for a participatory New Deal to bring the banks and corporations under the regulations and reforms they have escaped through runaway globalization. The year 2012 marks the first presidential campaign in our lifetime when the gluttony of Wall Street, the failures of capitalism, the evils of big money in politics, and a debate over fundamental reform will be front and center in an election debate. No doubt the crisis that gave rise to Occupy will not be fixed by an election, but that is beside the point. Elections produce mandates. It's a time to organize a progressive majority, and the vision and strategy of Port Huron is worth considering as a guide.

Tom Hayden is director of the Peace and Justice Resource Center in Culver City, California. He has taught recently at UCLA, Scripps College, Pitzer College, Occidental College, and the Harvard Institute of Politics, among other institutions, and is the author or editor of 20 books and hundreds of articles for publications ranging from The New York Times *to* The Los Angeles Times *and from* The Nation *to* The Chronicle of Higher Education.

Notes

1. Hayden, Tom. *The Port Huron Statement: The Visionary Call of the 1960s Revolution,* Avalon, 2005, p. 81.
2. Sale, Kirkpatrick. *SDS,* Random House, 1970, p. 50.
3. Cohen, Robert. *Freedom's Orator: Mario Savio and the Radical Legacy of the Sixties,* Oxford, 2009, p. 110.
4. Gornick, Vivian. *Emma Goldman, Revolution As a Way of Life,* Yale, 2011, p. 28.
5. I have no recollection of where this exhortation originated.
6. On May 15, 1961, one year before Port Huron, Pope John XXIII issued the encyclical "Mater and Magistra," which promoted social justice and asserted that economic activity be conducted "not merely for private gain but also in the interests of the common good." The encyclical also called for "the participation of workers in the economy as a whole." "Pacem in Terris," the April 11, 1963, encyclical, which followed Port Huron by nine months, encouraged dramatic steps away from the Cold War and nuclear-arms race.
7. Port Huron Statement, p. 46.
8. Thoreau, Henry David. "Civil Disobedience," *Walden and Other Writings,* Modern Library, 1992, p. 679.
9. C. Wright Mills, *The Power Elite,* Oxford, 1956, pp. 298–324.
10. Kazin, Michael. *American Dreamers, How the Left Changed a Nation,* Knopf, 2011.
11. The Herbert Lee killing occurred on September 25, 1961, in broad daylight. A local witness, Louis Allen, was killed three years later, in 1964.
12. There are similarities in today's alliances between Tea Party Republicans and Blue Dog Democrats. It would take defiant direct action combined with methodical organizing to undermine the stalemate and compromise that preserved the status quo, as it may again today in breaking the grip of the Republican and Democratic conservatives over the boundaries of the politically possible.
13. Port Huron Statement, p. 67.

14. The "sons of bitches" statement is from a presidential transcript of September 19, 1963. During the Freedom Rides crisis, Robert Kennedy once said, "the problem with you people [is that] you want too much too fast." Cited in Jonathan Rosenberg and Zachary Karabell, *Kennedy, Johnson, and the Quest for Justice: The Civil Rights Tapes,* Norton, 2003, pp. 31, 172.

15. Zinn, Howard. *SNCC, The New Abolitionists,* Beacon, 1964, p.58. Wofford confirms this account in his *Of Kennedy and Kings,* Farrar, Straus and Giroux, 1980, pp. 158, 159.

16. Wofford, p. 159.

17. Port Huron Statement, pp. 68, 85.

18. Dray, Philip. *There Is Power in a Union,* Anchor, 2010, p. 560.

19. Port Huron Statement, p. 167.

20. "I am dreaming, and I want to do good. For the good you do is never lost. Not even in dreams" were the handwritten words of Mario Savio, carried inside his jacket during the Free Speech Movement. Cohen, *Freedom's Orator: Mario Savio and the Radical Legacy of the Sixties,* Oxford, 2009, preface.

21. The results were Lincoln 39.8 percent, Stephen Douglas 29.5 percent, John Breckenridge 18.1 percent, and John Bell 12.6 percent.

22. When I listen to the same denunciations of Barack Obama's gradualism and centrism, and the virulent hatred of him on the far-right, incidentally, my mind flashes to both the criticisms and ultimate fates of Lincoln and Kennedy. I experience post-traumatic stress syndrome still lingering from the wars of the '60s, and know I am not alone.

23. Ellsberg, *Secrets: A Memoir of Vietnam and the Pentagon Papers,* 2002, p. 195.

24. As a student editor, I was an original proponent of the Peace Corps. As a community organizer in Newark, I was once invited to join the Peace Corps in Latin America. I declined, since Vietnam had eclipsed any potential of the program. Years later, former presidential assistant Richard Goodwin sent a personal note saying that I had "inspired" the Great Society without knowing so.

25. The phrase "southern strategy" is attributed to Kevin Phillips, then a political strategist or Richard Nixon, who came to regret the idea in later years.

26. Mills, C. Wright. "Letter to the New Young Left." http://www.marxists.org/subject/humanism/mills-c-wright/letter-new-left.htm

27. "The Campus Files," *San Francisco Chronicle,* via SFGate.com, http://www.sfgate.com/news/special/pages/2002/campusfiles/

28. http://rightweb.irc-online.org/articles/display/League_for_ Industrial_ Democracy

29. Dray, Philip. *There Is Power in a Union,* Anchor, 2010, p. 572.

30. Davidson, Carl. *Revolutionary Youth and the New Working Class,* Changemaker Publications, Pittsburgh, 2011, p. 52.

31. Sale, Kirkpatrick. *SDS,* Random House, 1970, p. 338. Their statement was written in an apartment near the New York Port Authority.

32. Davidson, Carl. *Revolutionary Youth and the New Working Class,* 2011, p. 52.

33. Sale, Kirkpatrick. *SDS,* Random House, 1970, p. 513.

34. Sale, ibid., p. 632.

35. Weiner, Tim. *Enemies: A History of the FBI,* Random House, 2011, p. 272.

36. Weiner, ibid., p. 272

37. Sale, Kirkpatrick. *SDS,* Random House, 1970, p. 543.

38. May 5, 1969.

39. Deputy Attorney General Richard Kleindeinst, quoted by Elizabeth Drew in *The Atlantic,* May 1969.

40. Sale, Kirkpatrick. *SDS,* Random House, 1970, p. 550.

41. Sale, ibid., p. 548.

42. Sale, ibid., p. 545.

43. Oglesby, "Notes on a Decade," *Liberation,* Aug.–Sept. 1969.

44. Sale, Kirkpatrick. *SDS,* Random House, 1970, p. 636.

45. *President's Commission on Campus Unrest Report to the American People,* William Scranton, chair, 1970

46. Zinn, *A People's History of the United States,* Perennial edition, Harper Collins, 2003, p. 349.

47. Email correspondence, January 28, 2012.

48. Chomsky, Noam. "Anarchism, Intellectuals and the State," in *Chomsky on Anarchism,* AK, 2005, pp. 213–15

49. Chomsky, ibid., p. 217

50. Chomsky, ibid., pp. 194–95.

51. Linzey and Reifman, in *This Changes Everything!,* Barrett Koehler, 2011, p. 71.

52. White, Micah. "From KillCap to WikiSwarms," *Adbusters,* February 4, 2012.

53. Barry, Ellen. "Young and Connected, 'Office Plankton' Protesters Surprise Russia," *New York Times,* December 24, 2011, p. A4.

PART 2

THE WAY WE WERE AND THE WORLD NOW: REFLECTIONS BY PORT HURON VETERANS

CHAPTER 1

PORT HURON

ALIVE AND RELEVANT, BUT ADD THE EARTH

By Becky Adams

At 72, I look back with pride and compassion—as well as gratitude—to the Port Huron Conference and the years surrounding it, when I was active in Students for a Democratic Society. Pride because we were determined, organized, and active in a wide movement that accomplished sweeping changes. Compassion because we were young, intensely focused on the change we wanted and how to get there, and hurting in ways we didn't understand or didn't believe were worthy. Compassion also as a memory of how we felt for the people who were without justice or the blessings we had known as a birthright. Some of us, and I was one, were filled with fear that our world would be set ablaze in a nuclear holocaust at any moment. We were filled with guilt—or urgency—about the wrongs of segregation and poverty and couldn't spare a moment for "frivolous" personal joy. I personally was troubled (depressed, we would say now) and uncertain of my direction in the adult life I was entering after college.

I feel gratitude for the opportunity to participate in a historic movement that made grand changes in our national culture and laws governing civil rights and civil liberties, and launched a movement for equality that continues today. I wish every person could have this experience of making a difference, of their "power of conviction" and community with others who share values and commitment to act. For us, "government of the people, by the people, and for the people" was a rallying cry, not a cold historic memory of a time long gone or a cynical comment on failure of government. We were "the people"; we knew some of us were left out by injustices, and we set about to right those wrongs.

After five decades, I still find the primary message of the Port Huron Statement alive, needed, and echoed by other movements of our time both in the United States and throughout the world. It seems we slid backwards in economic rules and values rather than progressed, but in civil rights and liberties, great progress was made. However, regarding nuclear disarmament, I think the deterrence protagonists were more correct than we thought at the time, although the nuclear threat endures and triggers unjust wars in the name of avoiding nuclear proliferation. The women's movement broadened our 1960s movement and shook up our relationships and community in major ways, but for we women, it extended the movement and empowered us.

The biggest change I would make in the Port Huron Statement is to add the environment as a primary focus. The 1960s created sweeping changes in how we view and protect the environment and other species. Today those gains are all vulnerable to powerful challenges. We realize that protecting parks, wilderness, and species, and conducting environmental-impact analyses is insufficient. We must change how we live in order to live sustainably and preserve the planet's atmosphere to enable not only wildlife and native plants, but our own grandchildren to live. We understand now what our elders knew: we must work to keep the gains made long ago.

For me personally, "the movement" even created the basis for my living. I worked for many years as an equal-opportunity officer implementing the Civil Rights Act of 1964. But also, our intense focus on being "agents of change" clouded the need to balance our lives, to be supportive partners and friends and attentive parents. Buddhist practice later gave me and others the understanding that balance is important and that while we work for change, we can dance, listen to the birds, include quiet in our daily lives, and rejoice.

Becky Mills read about the first sit-in in the news while studying in Berlin in 1960, was electrified, and joined the student movement. Active in SDS from 1960–63, she led the "anti–anti-Communist" workshop at Port Huron, married a movement activist, and had two daughters. After social work and fair employment, she (lucky!) joined the National Park Service and retired as park superintendent, happy grandmother, and member of a "blended family."

Chapter 2

The Progress We Created Is Now at Stake

By Paul Booth

We were called the New Left, and justly so. The Port Huron Statement has a thrillingly youthful tone to it, still attractive after all these years.

The discontinuities between us and the Old Left were sharp. We were scornful of hackneyed, sectarian debates that seemed to characterize it. Few were the Old Leftists whose guidance we welcomed. They included Dave Dellinger, Paul Goodman, Staughton Lynd, C. Wright Mills, A. J. Muste, and William Appleman Williams.

For the most part, we had to figure things out ourselves. We got some things—a lot of things—dead right. But two things of great consequence that we got wrong, that we probably couldn't have gotten right because the evidence was not apparent, have to do with the Left that preceded us. Or, rather, what was left of the Left after the McCarthy and Eisenhower years. If there had been a still-vibrant Left, one with active connections to our generation and to the broader liberal world, we might have nailed these as well.

The more obvious of the two was mass organization, or the relationship between organization and movement. After a decade or more with nothing of the kind, we were awfully unclear about how to build and sustain mass movements when they sprung up. We were ambivalent about leadership roles. We lacked teachers, and the experiences of the '30s were way before our time, poorly accessed. We did our movements a disservice by advocating "no leaders, no structures." In a very few years one had to acknowledge that practically none of the publications, organizations, or coalitions formed in the '60s had survived.

Nevertheless, our movement changed the direction of the country, its laws, its priorities, its culture. Many of those changes, probably most of them, have persisted. Many even deepened in the '70s and later. They've lasted; the organizations that propelled them, like our own Students for a Democratic Society (SDS), did not.

Which leads to the second subject, which can now be better understood with benefit of hindsight: How is it that so much success was achieved, even after the organizational impetus has faded? The answer must be that SDS, the New Left, and the civil-rights movement were not the only forces for that change. They were actually leading a much wider social force. We typically did not do this through a coalition; nonetheless, an effective majority of America embraced much of our program and carried it forward.

That wider force was the liberal-labor coalition that was forged in the New Deal and predominated in the Democratic Party. It was the governing majority for several decades, and accomplished many great things in the '30s and '40s. (Some, like Social Security, the minimum wage, and labor-relations law seemed permanent for a long time, but now are as much at risk as the laws of the '60s.)

When we composed the Port Huron Statement, we gave scant credence to it. For good reason—the progressive energies of the New Deal coalition were more or less exhausted. Not perceiving strategic hope in the liberal-labor coalition, the Port Huron Statement satisfied itself with a rather mechanistic call for "party realignment." It was not a compelling part of the Port Huron Statement vision.

The New Left and the civil-rights movement re-energized the majority Democratic coalition—supercharged it. It not only passed the Civil Rights Act and the Voting Rights Act; it created Medicare, federal aid to education, and a host of other Great Society breakthroughs. We didn't "create" the women's movement or any of the other forces that came along to change America, but we opened many doors to change.

Even after LBJ was succeeded by Richard Nixon, this coalition was still the effective governing majority, enacting the Clean Air Act and the Occupational Safety and Health Act. The right wing has had its hands full in its recent ascendancy, attacking the social legislation of the '60s and '70s as well as the '30s and '40s. Not just the social legislation, but every form of social progress we've enjoyed is now at stake.

A rich history follows from the Port Huron Statement. There are plenty of lessons to apply to today's challenges and opportunities. Just take what it said, and combine that with what we learned in the heat of struggle and what we've figured out subsequently. With that, we can fight for the democracy we sought and seek, and we can overcome.

Paul Booth is a longtime labor-union leader, and is currently the executive assistant to the president of the American Federation of State, County and Municipal Employees (AFSCME).

Chapter 3

A Half Century Seeking to Live the Spirit and Method of Port Huron

By Robb Burlage

"Red Headed Texan Meets Red-Diaper Babies?" Old Left–bred people, along with other campus activists, including me, with little or no experience with Left politics—all were immediately challenged alike at Port Huron to articulate together nothing less than a call for a New Left in America.

The draft Statement, moving clearly beyond simple organization-launching, boldly identified realms of national and global responsibility and of action far beyond most of our experiences of campus activism or civil-rights-movement involvement. Having been editor of *The Daily Texan* at the University of Texas, I felt part of the ambitiously idealistic student-movement leaders but with an ultimately narrow band of experience.

The draft Statement declared that we were taking seriously our whole world, seeking nothing less than to transcend the old Cold War politics, domestic and international. Many of us, propelled by the civil-rights movement, felt that we must speak of the necessity and possibility of building an intelligently overarching, fluent, multi-issue, participatory democratic movement to change that whole old world.

At Port Huron, redrafting of the economy sections fell, willy-nilly, at least partly to me, then a fledgling Harvard economics graduate student who was attracted by John Kenneth Galbraith's *The Affluent Society* identifying our underlying poverty of public resources and piercing the myth of the welfare state. I became the instant economist.

In my first real engagement with explicitly Left politics, I was feeling the spirit of an instant extended family–like experience, being both deadly serious and closely jocular. In introducing to the assembly our proposed redrafting, I said it was clearly based on "Brother Hayden's" draft "with a few amendments from Brother Marx." We affirmed public infrastructure and accountable capitalism, short of socialism, but perhaps objectively/politically the essence of participatory social democracy.[1]

We, perhaps prophetically, anticipated an industrializing world; that is, beyond the globally and domestically overwhelming, bipolar Cold War, amidst "Third World" colonial resistance, including national liberation movements. We focused in particular on the wasteful and dangerous, mutually threatening, military-industrial complexes. I think many of us felt strongly then that this could inevitably lead to a global holocaust of nuclear-weapons war. We may not have anticipated, post–Cold War, the full rise of an authoritarian capitalist China nor the decline of the American political economy in the world.

Ultimately, we focused more on "political economy," participatory democratic challenge of corporate powers in the U.S.—from our universities to the commanding heights of the economy; the American corporate–planned "remote-control economy." Ours was a call for full participation in all sectors and locales of all whose lives were affected. With C. Wright Mills, exposing essentially hidden elites and calling for an oppositional political vision.

* * * *

Since Port Huron, across a mere half century, I have had the good fortune of being part of a continuity of inspiring joint ventures, which I believe have sought in some way to extend the spirit and values and to utilize the "strategic method" of Port Huron and the Statement.

The Southern Student Organizing Committee (SSOC). Within two years of Port Huron, the SSOC was standing with the yet-emerging civil-rights movement; exposing the dominant segregated economic promoters in the yet-underdeveloped "New South" region; and drafting the "We'll Take Our Stand" Statement (for an integrated and democratic New South), to help launch SSOC; and working with student activists from predominantly white campuses in the South, initially to build a civil-rights-movement partnership. It turned on its head the Southern Agrarians' statement, implicitly racist, which was written by notable Southerners, including Robert Penn Warren, three decades earlier around the same Vanderbilt University environs where we were meeting.[2]

Peoples Appalachia **journal and the multi-issue Mountain Community Union (MCU).** By the '70s, across Appalachia, organizations were taking on both the coal barons and the governor's federal-corporate Appalachian Regional Development Program; I was involved with the *Peoples Appalachia* journal and with organizing the multi-issue MCU and its community newspaper across the coal communities of northern West Virginia. MCU united race, gender, and class diversity in what I believe was an exemplary, insurgent, multi-issue local democratic-movement organization. It included the Miners for Democracy United Mine Workers of America reform movement, Black Lung Associations, and the anti–strip mining movement; welfare rights and women's-issues organizations; and healthcare insurgencies. Students organized, for example, at the University of West Virginia as a nascent anti–Vietnam War movement, forming a Vietnam Veteran Medics Group and successfully lobbying for state legislation for education and credentialing as physician-assistant medics. Later, students orchestrated a successful campaign to elect a cofounding MCU social-work professor as a decades-enduring state senator.

HealthPAC. I have been involved with HealthPAC from the mid-to-late 1960s until today. With the spirit and method of Port Huron and the Statement in mind, this organization first targeted the then–newly academic medical center–dominated empires as well as the ever-present "medical-industrial complex" while defending public health services. I have dedicated more than a quarter-century to publishing the *HealthPAC Bulletin* and books (most prominently, contributing to *The American Health Empire*, Random House, 1970); training and influencing student health professionals and health-policy analysts and planners along the way.[3] More than four decades later the message is yet alive online and in study-group sessions, holding accountable major medical complexes; advocating universal health care with unified public financing if not quite the optative model that had emerged of a working community-based U.S. national health service; and leading the development of cost-effective local and regional health systems. We see ourselves as part of a global "healthy communities" movement, just as issues of healthcare, health and well-being, and, indeed, human survival, are being joined, perhaps more than ever, across the nation and the world.

A retrospective note, as after Port Huron I believe most of us who have come to be self-identified as the "early New Left" eventually sought to sew our own seeds of approximations of participatory democracy in whatever settings, locales, and professional sectors in which we found ourselves: Self-critically, I believe we should have persevered in seeking to build a real, practical, grounded, and ongoing movement for a democratic society, despite unrelenting attacks from the Right (and much of the established Middle) on any idealism of unions, "community organizing" and decentralized collective and public control. And, without pointing historical fingers, I believe the inability to have built a "movement for a democratic society" was aggravated, if not accelerated, by an eventually disintegrating Students for a Democratic Society that, however well-intentioned, felt like an internally competitive cacophony that ultimately undermined the possibilities of building a practical American democratic political movement.

Through it all, I believe now the new global Occupy generation extends the spirit of Port Huron. And, unabashedly, I believe that in a global economic and domestic political setting very different from status quo America, we can benefit from sharing the strategic methods of challenging power and of envisioning and questing for democratic alternatives—of Port Huron and the Statement.

 *Robb Burlage pictured with his wife, Dorothy Burlage, 1962. In addition to being an ongoing editor of Health-PAC Online, Burlage is the founding director of the Joint Graduate Degree Program in Public Health and Urban Planning and emeritus professor at Columbia University; senior management consultant with the New York City Health and Hospitals Corporation (which provides public services for two million patients a year); and convener of an ongoing community and labor–health study group at SEIU.*

Dorothy Burlage grew up in Texas, lived in the same Austin intentional community as Casey Hayden, and was deeply active in the civil rights, women's, and New Left movements. She received a PhD at Harvard and is a clinical and child psychologist in Cambridge, Massachusetts.

Notes

1. The original PHS draft included this sentence: "Private enterprise is not inherently immoral or undemocratic—indeed, it may at times contribute to offset elitist tendencies—but where it decisively affects the society's functioning it should be democratically responsible to the needs and aspirations of society, not to the private interests of profit and productivity."

2. See, e.g., Michel, Gregg, *Struggle for a Better South: The Southern Student Organizing Committee, 1964–1969*, Palgrave Macmillan, 2008.

3. See, e.g., Chowkwanyun, Merlin, "The New Left and Public Health: The Health Policy Advisory Center, and the Big Business of Health, 1967–1975," *The American Journal of Public Health*, Feb. 2011.

Chapter 4

It Was a Rising Sun

By Mickey Flacks

I believe that I was asked to speak at the UCSB Port Huron Conference as an "affirmative-action appointment"—which is fine with me. Affirmative action is a useful tool to ensure women's participation, and as former chair of Santa Barbara County's Affirmative Action Commission, I am happy to accept this invitation to speak (and write) because I was indeed there (at Port Huron)! I was not a student, but was working as a research technician at the University of Michigan, and had to feign illness in order to take time off from work; as a result, I came a few days late and missed the opening events, which included addresses by various old Socialists and labor leaders—not a big loss.

When I arrived at the United Auto Workers camp, I was struck by a few things:

- The young people there were neatly dressed—not in the jeans and T-shirts of my New York left-wing student days; they weren't scruffy!
- They were incredibly articulate and smart—everyone who spoke knew how to be eloquent as well as to the point.
- They spoke a language that was not redolent of the Germanic phrases of classical Marxism, but more like the cadences of the U.S. Constitution, and had been honed by their participation in student governments at their campuses and leadership in the National Student Association, the organization of student-government leaders.

- They were masters of parliamentary procedure, using it to promote, not stifle debate—the latter is what I was used to from my Leftist student days—and ensuring a truly democratic expression of varying points of view.
- I saw a group of Southern white students, people whose existence I had imagined but had never seen. These folks—including Robb and Dorothy Burlage and Casey Hayden (Tom's new wife)—were, to my mind, sensational: I thought Robb would make a great president of the U.S. They spoke articulately, but with the soft accents of their native Texas, making their words seem softer, yet more insistent, more important. Casey in particular seemed the queen of Port Huron: she was quite beautiful, and had a regal presence, somehow, that would cause all eyes to turn to her when she entered a room, all ears to tune to whatever she had to say. I was mightily impressed, and somewhat intimidated.
- I met Michael Vester, an exchange student from Germany, leader of the German SDS, who was the first German I had ever seen who didn't call Nazism to my mind; I was prejudiced, I admit, (being a left-wing Jewish girl from NY) but Michael's presence made me confront my prejudice, and grow in understanding.
- I was stunned to see Steve Max, whom I knew from my days in the teen-age section of the Labor Youth League (LYL, the Communist Party's youth organization) and had last seen when we spent the summer of 1956 (post–Khrushchev's speech—and for us, post–high school) plotting the dismantling of the teenage section of the LYL. As I thought about it, I realized his—like mine—was a natural progression from those days to this, from the Old to the New Left.

Both Steve and I were "red-diaper babies," and had accepted a Communist Party (CP) USA perspective with our mothers' milk. The events of the mid '50s drove us from the CP orbit—but left us a bit high and dry politically. Many Socialist or liberal organizations required their members to sign a non-Communist oath—and we certainly did not feel welcomed there. We were *non*-Communists, but weren't ready to be *anti*-Communists. We believed that led to what later became known as neo-conservatism, and wanted no part of it, nor of any organization that insisted on its members' signing an oath. Although SDS, when it was essentially the Student League for Industrial Democracy, had had such an oath, part of Port Huron's task was to eliminate it and to define its *anti*–anti-Communism. Only SDS and Women's Strike for Peace (WSP) had dared to articulate such a position. (When Dagmar Wilson, founder of WSP, was called to testify before the House Un-American Activities Committee some years later, she was asked,

"You say you are open to all women. What would you do if some Russian women asked to join?" "Oh, if only they would!" she responded.) A leader of the W.E.B. Du Bois Clubs, the LYL's successor youth organization, was also at Port Huron, asking to be seated as an observer. Many SDSers rushed to get a look at him; they had never seen a Communist before! Over the objections of some of the Socialist and labor leaders, he was granted such status (and promptly left; he later quit the Du Bois Clubs and joined an SDS chapter in New York). I believe that this rejection of defining *non-Communist* as *anti-Communist* was one of the most enduring legacies of the Port Huron Statement and the organization it spawned—making it possible, for instance, to later oppose the U.S. in the Vietnam War without supporting the Viet Cong—but allowing those who liked to wave VC flags to participate in SDS-led demonstrations and marches. Port Huron was about inclusion, not exclusion.

The final work on the Statement was done at an all-night session on the last day. In the morning, a group of we bleary-eyed young people stood outside as the sun rose over the lake. I was reminded of the story of Ben Franklin at the Constitutional Convention in Philadelphia observing the sunburst design on the chairs in the hall. "I have been staring at that sun," he is said to have remarked, "trying to decide whether it is a rising or a setting sun. I now think that it is a rising one...." The sun at Port Huron was definitely rising, and while it might not have signaled the birth of the nation, it did portend a new era in American social movements, and left a legacy of a politics that seeks to maximize the participation of people in the decisions that affect their lives and promote genuine democracy. I think Ben Franklin would have been pleased.

Mickey Flacks lives in Santa Barbara, California, with her husband Richard Flacks. She is a research scientist and a local leader of Democratic Party and community coalitions.

CHAPTER 5

PORT HURON AFTER A HALF CENTURY

By Richard Flacks

If somebody had come to Port Huron when we young student activists were meeting and told us to pay attention to detailed accounts of events that had occurred in 1912 (50 years before), we would certainly have turned a cold shoulder. For 1912 was an ancient time, before two world wars, the Soviet revolution, and a massive depression. Automobiles and movies were just coming in. It was the year that the *Titanic* sank, when Woodrow Wilson was elected president, and the Republic of China was proclaimed. We may have been interested in the fact that it was a year that witnessed landmark events in the history of people's movements: it was the year of the great Lawrence Textile Strike, in which thousands of young female textile workers of many ethnicities united to prevent their wages from being cut; that year Eugene Debs ran for president as a Socialist and got nearly a million votes; that year the African National Congress was founded in South Africa. But it would have seemed unlikely that an aged veteran of those days could provide important lessons for us to draw on.

Indeed, in 1962 young politically engaged people were looking for new directions and we met precisely because we were sure that the world we inhabited could no longer be changed by relying on the categories, methods, and understandings of a Left with roots in the 19th century. That Left, constituted by a host of warring ideological tribes, was played out. On the other hand, we didn't share the conventional wisdom of the 1950s, which declared that the entire tradition of the Left had come to an end.

By "tradition of the Left" I mean the stream of action and of thought that over generations had struggled for a society freed of domination of the many by the few, that envisioned and fought for the rights and dignity of the subordinated, the propertyless, the voiceless and powerless. We identified ourselves with that tradition, even if we doubted the value of particular ideological formulations like Socialism or Marxism in their many varieties.

We were attracted to this meeting by the notion, expressed forcefully by Students for a Democratic Society (SDS) pioneer organizers like Al Haber, that these particular crises were symptoms of deeper societal crisis. The top leaders of the society as a whole were incapable of, even unwilling to, enforce the rights supposedly guaranteed in the Constitution, and certainly unwilling to end the Cold War and the threat of a hot one.

There were fewer than 60 of us there at that time, but we believed (and we were right about this) that a lot of our peers shared the mood we were in. It was time for a new politics—for new ideas and new coalitions and new modes of action. It was time for a new university—one that treated its students in adult ways, and that was a place where new ideas could be articulated and debated and acted on with student bodies that reflected the population of the country rather than a thin stratum of privilege.

The gathering was organized by the leaders of the nascent SDS. Al Haber, Tom Hayden, and a few others sensed the new mood and had the insight that the new student activists needed a national organization that would create a shared meeting ground. And, equally, the rising activism might benefit from an effort to articulate a common vision and to debate about potential strategies for political and social action. And they made the daring decision to focus the conference on the creation of a manifesto for a new political generation.

The Port Huronites were widely varied in their personal connection to the Old Left. Some, like my wife Mickey and me, were "red-diaper babies"—we were raised by parents who had been involved in political, labor, and community organizing initiated by the Communist Party in the '30s and '40s, or at least were sympathetic to the Communist left. Some others' families identified with other brands of Socialism or liberalism. Probably the majority of those in attendance did not have such leftist connections. They were instead people who had come to anger and distress when they experienced the collision between the values (religiously or secularly grounded) they'd been raised to cherish and the harsh realities of race and poverty, which the southern struggle was dramatizing. We all seemed to share a "calling" to find political roles that could make a significant difference. And we understood that none of the established parties and political identities were at all adequate to that purpose.

The Port Huron Statement provided a foundation for finding that purpose. That foundation can be found in the phrase "participatory democracy." It's an unwieldy phrase, but it provides, in capsule form, the germ of a way to imagine "another world" and, at the same time, a guide for action. Participatory democracy leads us to ask what needs to happen so that all who are affected can have some voice in deciding the rules, allocating the resources, defining the roles in each institutional setting. We're encouraged to ask such questions for society as a whole, and in the workplace, the household, the community, the school, and even the prison. The effort to find answers to such questions helps us envision possible alternatives and to investigate why more-democratic arrangements are blocked. And, as we undertake action to promote democracy, we are impelled to figure out how that action itself can be democratically organized.

"Participatory democracy" at Port Huron suggested a way to re-create the Left by culling from the Left tradition the kernels of democratic imagination that all the old warring ideologies shared. It fostered a new vocabulary for defining the Left, which would be more resonant with American culture than the terms imported from earlier centuries and other places. And it pushed us to struggle for a way to set up the new organization as a democracy that could make use of members' initiatives and experience rather than perpetuating conventional modes of hierarchical leadership.

Fifty years later, participatory democracy (whether the term itself is used or not) is defining the programs and practices of social movements everywhere. It's there in the general assemblies of the Occupiers, and in the very idea of an economy that serves the 99 Percent. It's integral to the worldwide struggle by communities to defend land, culture, identity, resources, and health in the face of corporate globalization. It's embodied in the global movement for workers' rights, for women's equality and autonomy, for student voice. When people mobilize to stop war policies, they are demanding voice in foreign policy hitherto made by politico-military elites.

Activists who got their start in the '60s have been key organizers or contributors to these new social movements. Alongside these movements, a host of experiments in participatory democratic institution-building have had historic consequences. Maybe most important has been the Internet, which provides a technological framework for participatory democracy previously unknown.

We need to know a lot more than we do about the limits, contradictions, and barriers to authentic democracy that lurk within efforts to achieve it. The pressures to succumb to authority and apathy, or to get cynical about the visionary, are very strong. But one of the beauties of struggling for democracy is that the *process* of struggle is inherently significant. A half century after Port Huron I still feel certain of that.

Dick Flacks was a graduate student in social psychology in Ann Arbor, Michigan, in 1962 and attended the Port Huron Conference with his partner Mickey Flacks. Both became active in SDS; in 1964 Dick became a sociology professor at the University of Chicago. The Flackses moved to Santa Barbara in 1969, where Dick taught for 43 years; both are longtime leaders in the Santa Barbara progressive community. Dick's book Making History: The American Left and the American Mind *(1988) has its intellectual roots in the Port Huron Statement. Mickey and Dick are working on a joint memoir about their shared lives, personal and political, called* Making History and Making Blintzes.

CHAPTER 6

THE EVOLUTION OF A RADICAL'S CONSCIOUSNESS

LIVING AN AUTHENTIC LIFE

By Sharon Jeffrey Lehrer

Even though I was a child of the Cold War and grew up in a deeply segregated country ruled by white men, I was raised by a social-activist, feminist mother, who took me to an NAACP convention when I was 13, and who worked for the United Auto Workers (UAW). I'd march with her on union picket lines and was inspired by UAW president Walter Reuther's vision and values. I met Eleanor Roosevelt when I was five in her home in Hyde Park. From then on, I wanted only to be like her.

I got my chance when I met Al Haber in 1960 at the University of Michigan. He had a vision of creating a national student political movement. Two years later, after organizing students from campuses all across the country, Students for a Democratic Society (SDS) held its famous Port Huron Conference.

Standing on the shores of Lake Huron watching the sun rise after an all-night session adopting the Port Huron Statement, I was in awe at what we had done. We knew we had accomplished something significant, that we were visionaries and map-makers who were pushing out the boundaries of the traditional Left and current American values. We were challenging authority and creating a society of empowered, authentic individuals who actively participated in the body politic.

After graduating from college, I organized college students to tutor black ghetto students, lived in Harlem organizing rent strikes, and built an integrated community in Chicago. Most significantly, I was involved in an SDS project, organizing white and black welfare mothers in Cleveland, Ohio. Living communally in a poor white neighborhood, we organized by day, and at night explored the meaning of "participatory democracy." We'd have lengthy discussions before arriving at decisions by consensus. We were committed to living our values.

In 1973 I was an organizer living in Chicago. While on a camping trip on Mt. Rainer, I had a very unusual experience that brought even more radical change to my life. It was what I now understand to have been a spiritual experience. I heard a voice speaking to me. The voice affirmed that I had a very successful professional career. Then the voice asked a question: "But how do you feel in your heart?" I had no idea how I felt in my heart. I was an organizer, serving others. I didn't know about my emotions. Who had time for that? Then it told me that I was to resign from my job. This was a shock. The next morning I awoke knowing that I was going to leave my great job of seven years. It was instantaneous: a new experience of decision-making.

I made the big leap and left my job for California. I was smitten by California's beauty, the ocean, the mountains, and by the freedom I felt. Through a series of synchronous events I ended up at Esalen Institute: a human-growth center on an old Indian burial ground on the edge of the Big Sur Coast.

For someone who was a driven political organizer, whose purpose was to change the world, finding myself sitting in a hot tub gazing into the Pacific Ocean or attending workshops exploring my emotions and inner life was truly the most radical thing I had ever done. I was out of my comfort zone, and at the same time I was intrigued by the journey.

I discovered I had a heart and it was a portal to an enormous emotional intelligence. I learned a new language and to identify and name my feelings, particularly the uncomfortable ones. I was still the adventurer, but now going outside my familiar political paradigm. Esalen gave me the opportunity to explore territories of the mind and heart that I didn't know existed.

I decided to permanently leave the comfort of the Midwest, my family, roots, and traditions, and to move to California without a job or a place to live. Through a colleague at work in San Francisco, I had the good fortune of meeting an extraordinary woman, Dr. Angeles Arrien, a cultural anthropologist who grew up in the Basque spiritual tradition in Spain. I studied Basque mysticism, archetypes, cross-cultural symbols, and the tarot with her.

Soon I was not only consulting to organizations, but also giving tarot readings. I never imagined as a child that I would become a tarot reader. This was something fortune-tellers did, not something a community organizer, social activist, intelligent person would ever do. Yet it felt so true and familiar to me. I was like a fish returning to water. The land of symbols and archetypes opened a doorway in my imagination to new worlds and connected me to my soul. I developed new ways of knowing and understanding the world. My worldview was evolving, changing and expanding beyond normal logic and reason and also the political paradigm of SDS.

I now live in California. I've come to realize there is a much larger consciousness at play in our world than I ever imagined as an activist. When I read the news and see places in the world where the old paradigm of domination and control is crumbling, I work on dismantling my own need to be dominant and control. I see how I have internalized the very things I was so actively organizing against. I realize part of changing the world is changing me. I've learned that our thoughts and feelings have energy. I continually pay attention to what is going on inside me and to process and release my negative self-critical, judgmental, self-doubting voices.

My life as a political radical as a child and with SDS was foundational for me. So strong is my commitment to live as a free spirit, I am continually compelled to explore assumptions and beliefs about reality and consciousness, as we did so courageously in 1962. I continue to learn, grow, and change, to become more authentic. Being part of the founding of SDS and living my values and vision has created a fulfilling life.

This is my life now. My values include love; beauty; joy; freedom; truth; friendship and community; exploring beyond my comfort zone; seeing complexity in life, politics, and consciousness; and having fun.

I see all the change happening in the world as being similar to the transformative process of a caterpillar giving birth to a butterfly, and something brand-new is created that is way beyond the imagination of anyone, including the caterpillar.

I believe we are in a similar transformation. We are consuming everything around us—water, air, oil, money. The old is dissolving and out of the substance of the old, the imagination in us is stirring, bringing forth new ways of being, creating, thriving, and relating with each other and the earth. My hope is in the power of our imagination to envision and birth something new, beyond what is visible now.

Sharon Jeffrey Lehrer worked for nonprofits and small businesses as a CEO and consultant for 35 years. She is an intuitive consultant for individuals, and is married to Glenn Lehrer, an internationally recognized artist. They live in San Rafael, California.

CHAPTER 7

IT'S BEEN SAID I'M STILL UNREALISTIC

By Alan Haber

In September 1959, when the old "slid"[1] adopted the name Students for a Democratic Society (SDS), I undertook to build a new organization based on action and education, affirming economic democracy and identifying in the indigenous radical tradition of "our founders" Upton Sinclair, Jack London, Clarence Darrow, and progressives like "Fighting Bob" La Follete, after whom I'm named. [*Ed. note: Al's given first name is Robert.*] From June 1960, I was SDS president and also on staff, though sometimes fired.

It was a beginning, buoyant, heady time in the movement—civil rights, peace, justice, revolution, change the world. I met a lot of beautiful people, many of whom I tried to recruit, some successfully. I made friends where I could. Our "manifesto," which we decided to compose in Ann Arbor at our December 1961 meeting, was to express who we were, what we believed, how we saw the world, and what we intended to do about it.

So, from its beginning I had a special relation to the Port Huron Convention and what became our Statement. It was my job to make it happen. When we decided to do a manifesto, we began asking ourselves and everyone on our lists, What should be in the manifesto?

Lots of suggestions came; there was a collective back-and-forth. Tom was the genius and word-crafter who put it all together, with consultants over his shoulders on different sections. The office crew was typing on typewriters, making stencils, mimeographing, collating, stapling. We didn't get the draft all pieced together until we were ready to make the drive from New York to Port Huron. Getting the place in Port Huron to gather was uncertain until hardly more than a week before we planned to meet. Stress, anxiety, excitement.

At Port Huron, this "organization in the movement" that I had devoted myself to building actually came into being. I was satisfied, tired, and ready to go back to school. It was hard work, getting us there. I looked forward to when there would be a new president of SDS and I could not have to worry about it. My last SDS job, I thought, would be getting people off the Lake Huron beach and into workshops and meetings. I was so grateful for everyone who came, giving a real-life human reality to an idea, a dream, an imagining, a commitment, a necessity. The draft manifesto gave us work to do together, to read, to think, to talk, to listen, to meet. We took the draft apart and put it back together, and debated how to make it better. We were mostly pretty respectful of each other. Sincere. As such things go, it was a good meeting, foretastes of trouble notwithstanding. We made a new something, its future unknown. We were a we. We had a taste of that beloved community that so infused the Southern movement. "Embraced by an unending love," I call it now. I was full of love. Love was what it was all about. We were brave-hearts. We believed in freedom. We would overcome. We will.

The convention then, at the very end, surprised me, passing a motion of appreciation that so touched my heart, honoring me to say I live in demonstration of my beliefs. That was true, and I have kept on doing it, or trying, and can't imagine stopping. They said I was "founder, theoretician, organizer, publicizer, and personal locus of SDS." They called me "the creator of a community of people, who, united, are the partial beginning of a visible social movement and its future power will owe much to him." They spoke of my sense of obligation, and celebrated my existence. No one had ever said anything so nice about me. I was moved. I was given a place of notice. I hope I have held it well. Of course, my part was mostly a consistent, perseverant will, and finding good people. It was everyone who made it happen, each offering something of themselves to a whole beyond any of us. I did press the importance of organization, and continue to do so.

The Port Huron Statement was linked to the organization effort and movement-building strategy of SDS. There was an impulse toward action in all the recitations of facts. Even without the organization, it still articulates a framework of activist values and a vision of "participatory democracy" that has been a reference point in many people's education and continues to serve the movements. After Port Huron, SDS made the history it did; some good, some not so. Definitely we created a heritage of controversy. Tens of thousands of young activists challenged nearly every pillar of the status quo, including among ourselves. Men discovered that women held up half the sky, and more. We all discovered war.

I wish the successors of the Port Huron early generations in SDS had kept the organization together after the '60s. I wish the Movement for a Democratic Society (an organization I attempted to create in the 1990s) had bloomed then in its many petals, as when first envisioned: intergenerational, beyond college, insurgent in its different institutional settings. Once on a panel called Remembering SDS, I said it was a good idea; we should *re-member* SDS. The political culture in America has lacked in the absence of the continuity of a multi-issue, change-the-system "education and action organization dedicated to increasing democracy in all phases of our common life."

There is now a new student SDS, to which I gave some help; and "seniors and survivors for democratic society" are all over the country, latent, remembering, active in our varied ways; and a new MDS has formed as a placeholder, at least, for that spirit of continuity, keeping the faith, and encouraging organization.

I would like to see a "manifesto for now," or, more humbly, a statement for these times, or at least the effort at collective thinking again, and more inclusively, as we attempted 50 years ago. We are now many generations active, and conscious all over the world. There are things obvious now that weren't yet on our minds at all. Thinking together is urgent.

While "mutually assured destruction" has receded, global-nuclear-war-wise, the doomsday clock is ever closer to midnight. The unimaginable, for which we attempted the unattainable, still haunts the horizon. Calamities await the whole life system. Movements around the world are needed to be more successful both in holding back the warrior beasts of global capital and in putting before the people a viable alternative. We need the option of a different government, and a winning plan of how to make it happen: shifting to a peace system from the war system, from the old order of domination, patriarchy, triumphalism, etc., to a peace economy and a culture of peace and nonviolence, partnership, caring, sharing, helping, healing, and the old virtues of generosity and hospitality. The means of communication now and the strength of the people's movements in every country make this possible.

Thinking back, I was a different person then, my eyes not so full of tears as now, seeing horrors on so many fronts. Then I was a serious student of history, an intellectual; believing in science and that there were answers to all questions, I had taken on a political task. I was doing it. At Port Huron, it was done.

When the League for Industrial Democracy attacked our document, our camaraderie was sealed, as we had to defend what we said and argue with our elders. New tasks followed: Economic Research and Action Project, The Radical Education Project, and others. I've been at it all my life.

After the '60s, I went within, as many did, boxing up my books, still on the shelves; using my "freelance-radical-intellectual" grant money to buy tools, open a "splinter group" woodshop, and begin training and working as a cabinetmaker. After my apprenticeship, I tried to organize a movement-based presidential campaign, 1975–76. (I was the only professional cabinetmaker ever to apply for the job.) We were too divided among ourselves to make a union, and perhaps still are.

Now I'm a carpenter, no longer studious or insisting on answers. Besides an activist, forever young, I think of myself as a Jew, sharing a prophetic mission, calling for a turning of hearts, lest there come the great destruction, calling the powers-that-be to the table of peace (I made the table), to end the wars, chastising Israel for its sinful ways and failures of faith (I build arks for the Torah). Jews weren't even a category when we talked politics back in those days. Now I'm near persona non grata among many fellow Jews for applying the honest human values of my Port Huron youth to current life. I advocate for union (u-n-i-o-n, the unlimited network integrating our nations). Nationalism is the scourge we didn't identify, and fascism the enemy behind the curtain. I work locally in Ann Arbor, Michigan, on the campaigns for the commons and for a community center for the homeless. It's been said I'm still unrealistic.

Al Haber lives in Ann Arbor, Michigan.

Note

1. Student League for Industrial Democracy.

CHAPTER 8

PORT HURON

A TEMPLATE FOR HOPE

By Barbara Haber

The Port Huron convention ranks high on my list of most cherished memories.

I came to Port Huron from two years of intense work in the civil-rights movement. Toward the end, I had experienced the space for whites in the movement contracting. Earlier, as a student at Brandeis University, I had come to define myself as a democratic socialist. As a Jew, the words "never again" called me to act against oppression. By 1962, I was seeking people with a broadly radical vision of change.

At Port Huron I felt I had found just what I was looking for. The people I met there were smart, humorous, politically experienced, energetic, committed, and friendly. We held a shared assumption: that through collective thinking we could understand the world and that with passionate dedication we could change it. The exuberant spirit born of shared moral purpose, a sense of historic mission, and the sweet company of kindred souls was infectious.

Our task, revising what would become the Port Huron Statement, gave us the medium in which we began to shape our collective political vision and get to know one another. We were aiming at creating a piece of literature that would actually be read, reflected upon, and remembered—as, indeed, it has been! We sought to freshly envision the radical possibilities of political culture, to provide ourselves with a rough map by which we could guide our activist lives, and to fire the social imaginations of our contemporaries. We saw ourselves not as bit players in a drama dominated by blue-collar workers, but as bona fide agents of change. We reasoned—correctly, I believe—that in a society increasingly dominated by information and high technology, students, who would serve as technicians, managers, and professionals, occupied a strategically vital position.

I came to Port Huron seeking personal transformation as well as political and social change. I believe this was true for others as well. The civil-rights movement had, for many of us, created deep personal shifts in perception and aspiration. The African American struggle, with the vibrant communities that sprang up within it, was a harsh mirror in which we saw reflected the banalities and complacencies of white, middle-class life. We saw the stereotypic and conformist social niches that were waiting for us—especially women!—and we were repelled. We had already found something better. Our political task was to translate that something better into a society in which all people could live lives of meaning, vitality, and, yes, adventure. Community, founded on political engagement, was both means and end. We had a personal as well as a political stake in this project. We needed it so that we could sustain lives beyond college that were different from those we'd been raised to expect.

This confluence of the desire for personal transformation and political agency was central to New Left politics, and the source of both strengths and weaknesses. Though the personal is political and the political is personal, sometimes the two are in conflict. Looking back, it seems to me that when we foundered, it was often because our personal ambitions, insecurities, and limited relational skills derailed us. They prevented us from being the human beings we needed to be in order to resolve our conflicts in a way that could nurture our movement, our organization, and its participants. This was true of both women and men. I know that it was true of me.

Our civil-rights experience had taught us that social change would come through a combination of tough, unyielding, grass-roots organizations and dramatic acts of protest and courage. These acts would demonstrate to the world, in irresistible images, the themes and demands on which we wanted to focus attention. I still have confidence in this model. Not too many years later, however, it shaded into intoxication with risk and disdain for the ordinary. We came to overvalue extravaganza, and sometimes confused upping the ante with being more radical and more effective. I believe that this stance also contributed to the atrophy of our abilities to sustain relationships—with people, organizations, and ideas.

Port Huron held a promise specific to women—that we could participate fully in creating a movement that would change our country, and, by implication, that we would have personal relationships of equality. I say this although on the face of it the Port Huron Statement is hopelessly sexist. The pronouns are male; the oppression of women, issues of family life, child-rearing, reproduction, sexual violence, and unequal opportunity and pay are all missing. Yet in many ways, the Port Huron Statement, and our process at the convention, held that implicit promise.

From a feminist point of view it is significant that the Port Huron Statement begins with values. This section is an evocative description of our own lives and the moral lessons we derive from them. It sees the quest for orienting human values as the first task of a social movement. Working outward from concrete, immediate experience to derive general values, then using those values as criteria for comprehending structures and evaluating events are ways of thinking that are common among women, and would later become hallmarks of feminist process.

"Participatory democracy," the defining phrase of Port Huron, though vague, also contributed to our feminist framework. As we began to confront the rigidity, remoteness, and inaccessibility of institutions of power, including those in Students for a Democratic Society (SDS), women recognized that it would take a radical transformation of decision-making if we were to gain full entry, and thereby get control over our lives. Participatory democracy legitimized our demand that we be heard and considered as equals in all matters.

The drafting process itself, at least in the values committee where I spent much of my time, exemplified the ideals that would later be articulated by the feminist movement. We met in a small group to collectively create text that would be included in our statement to the world. Much care was expended to encourage reticent members to express their views. Ideas and questions were responded to without condescension or acrimony. Good-naturedness, tolerance, and curiosity characterized our discussions. Though not perfect, Port Huron set high standards, and embodied, however briefly, how to be good people, inspiring comrades, and effective organizers.

I stayed with SDS until it was taken over by the Weathermen. By 1965, though, my frustration at intractable resistance in SDS to equality for women had pushed me to define myself primarily as a feminist, though I remained active in anti–Vietnam War organizing.

My bitterness has long melted. Looking back, I feel honored and fortunate to have been present at Port Huron and part of SDS, however painful my experience. I also feel profound sadness. We were such good and smart young people, men as well as women. We took on many of the right issues, for the right reasons, and had significant impact. Our overarching vision, though incomplete, still inspires. But sexism and personal shortcomings pulled apart those of us who might otherwise have been strong allies and partners, in it together for the long haul. As allies we might have encouraged one another to sustain our radical struggles without canned ideological certainties, to tolerate ambiguity and ambivalence, to overcome collectively our anxieties at the momentousness of our undertaking, to build an organization that could support our enormous enterprise. How might it all have turned out then?

Barbara Haber has been a psychotherapist since 1984. She has been involved in antinuclear, antiwar, and other progressive organizing. She lives in Oakland, California.

CHAPTER 9

ONLY LOVE IS RADICAL*

By Casey Hayden

I was a child of small-town Texas, and of a single-parent mom, a feminist. We were poor closet liberals. Austin was my Mecca. I excelled there, in the late '50s, and morphed into an existentialist at a residential community of learning alongside the university, the only integrated housing on campus, both by gender and by race. We met in rigorous seminars with a collegium of renegade Christian ministers, headed by a chaplain from WWII who'd seen the carnage, demythologizing the church fathers and scriptures; studying the contemporary theologians Bultmann and Bonhoeffer (based in Kierkegaard); Buber, Tillich, the Niebuhrs; and readings in cotemporary thought: Sartre, Camus, Arthur Miller, Dostoevsky, Ionesco, Beckett, and more. We lived in joy without hope, like Camus's Sisyphus pushing that rock up the hill, watching it roll down. God was dead, the word "god" empty. All words were empty of intrinsic meaning, symbols pointing to experience. The collegium attempted to create a language of experience: One struggles against the absence of final meaning, "coming up against it." Surrendering illusions through honesty, one was opened to creating meaning: an authentic life, freedom. This surrender to reality was "the Christ event." Our freedom, our commonality in receiving it, and our common task of

*Thanks to Jane Stembridge for saying my title, back in the day.

passing it on were realized in community through rituals of confession, forgiveness, surrender, and gratitude. Worship as theatre.

In but not of the world, we found a remnant of the social gospel, the campus YM-YWCA, as our outpost. I served at the Y's national conference. Men and women led workgroups as equals: Peace; Race Relations; the World of Work; The Changing Roles of Men and Women. Consciously breaking out of the silent postwar generation, we vowed to realize our values, a politics of authenticity.

The '50s unfolded into the '60s, the sit-in movement being the exalted opening of the '60s. I was discovered by SDS at a national conference of student-government leaders, where I supported the sit-ins in a speech, bringing down the house and swinging campus politics left, a white Southern girl with a drawl and a ruffled dress. I went south toward nonviolence, a methodology of nonaggression inside and outside; means and ends as one; content and process united; the beloved community ever expanding; social change as osmosis, occupation. This was my praxis: hands on, body on the line, work as love made visible. The Y paid: I organized illegal interracial meetings Southwide; rode the Freedom Train to Albany, New York; hung out with Student Nonviolent Coordinating Committee (SNCC); traveled and spoke, interpreting; and had a dangerous good time. I called myself a radical, as in going to the root. I thought the root was love.

SDS was to be the northern counterpart to SNCC, white but committed; smart. I typed its mailing list on address stencils in the office on Gramercy Park while the guys talked in the front office, ran the mimeograph machine in Mark Lane's basement for the local SDS reform Dem candidate, served on the National Executive Commission, organized a labor workshop in the South, met New York politicos, thought myself sophisticated.

I knew little about the left, ideology, or manifestos when we came to the SDS meeting in Port Huron, Tom and I, partnered since that sit-in speech. I claimed a lot of ownership in SDS—sweat equity. I'd read Tom's developing draft of a statement to be considered in Michigan, long but bright, a combo of stirring call to arms and master's thesis. I liked the phrase "participatory democracy." I thought we were that, best realized in SNCC's consensus-style self-government. In a conversation between us, Staughton Lynd recalls the time: "I shall never forget your coming back from Port Huron and telling us about the new words, 'participatory democracy,' very slowly and pronouncing each syllable separately as if you were eating a chocolate éclair."

I'd always loved Tom's writing. It was him. We were different, but side-by-side. The conference condensed and abstracted the draft to rewrite the pieces and paste up an umbrella under which we could unite. It had never occurred to me to critique Tom's work or that I should fit inside it. I tried to do so now, to belong, and felt my voice lost in his and that of the event's political culture. I couldn't find a way into the debates from my own perspective and wondered if I were dumb or these guys just talked too much. I managed an objection to a phrase about the perfectibility of man. We changed the wording, but it still wasn't right. I was surprised to learn recently that some folks remember that conversation, thought it was significant. In retrospect I can see that I was working in a different paradigm, homegrown from Christian existentialism and nonviolent theory. As compared to the Port Huron Statement, I was interested in building communities of protest and resistance rather than acting politically myself; unconvinced that independence existed essentially, much less that it was the highest societal goal; had less faith in humanity or progress; was ambivalent about control as an essential value. At the time, all this was not so clear. I left Port Huron uneasy.

SDS leadership met in New York to cope with our parent group's outrage at our non-anticommunism. I wondered if the movement could avoid implosion in the apparently inevitable drama of Left ideological schisms. It seems we couldn't. I was party to an opening act on SNCC staff a couple of years later, when our Leninist headman proposed a big centralized organizing project and similar organizational governance. Attempts at conversation from another perspective were characterized as a faction fight and vigorously combated. I took it hard. SNCC and I were both far from our beginnings.

My last action as movement activist was a letter to women of SDS and SNCC, formulating the personal as political. I wrote in the futile and somewhat ambiguous hope that women's honest and intimate interaction about our lives could, despite the cracks that were appearing, hold our movement together.

Today I live in a family, locally and simply. I study the Way, as I have for 40 years, taking the path of zen. Zen, from the Chinese word *chan,* meditation, is a method of achieving clear-sightedness without attachment to abstractions. As it is said, no hindrance in the mind, and therefore no fear. No fear of seeing things as they are, and thus with compassion.

My heart's in the 'hood, a funky, downtown, used-to-be-the-ghetto, where I'm six generations into the future, lending myself to our anarchist environmentalists, giving our yard to permaculture's water-harvesting basins and native plantings, milling our mesquite trees' beans into flour, supporting the community garden, saving up for solar. Facing into the devolution when the empire and the industrial edifice have collapsed of their own weight and we turn to each other. Loving the earth as the ship of state goes down. I see our species as short-lived, doing ourselves in with hubris, greed, and overworked left brains, blind to ourselves as one kind among many rooted in the earth our mother, herself the product of infinite time and space.

I'm happy, and my ordinary pleasures endure: movies, books, poetry, music, dance; water, earth, fire, air; perennial wisdom, tribal cultures, the Paleolithic; the intelligence of nature; the wide-open spaces of the great outdoors; clouds, flowers; women giving birth and nursing; little kids, home, and my own dear children, long since grown up.

And yet abides my passion for truth, radical truth, found, it turns out, in this very moment, gone before it can be named, unadorned and luminous.

Photo credit: Matt Heron

Casey Hayden worked in Mississippi for the Student Nonviolent Coordinating Committee from 1963 through 1964 Freedom Summer and its aftermath. She was involved in Students for a Democratic Society, the YWCA in Atlanta, and the 1960 Austin sit-ins. Hayden cowrote "Sex and Caste" with Mary King in 1965. The memo challenged activists to be aware of gender inequality in the movement and the country. She is also a coauthor of Deep in Our Hearts: Nine White Women in the Freedom Movement *(U. of Georgia Press, 2000).*

CHAPTER 10

PARTICIPATORY DEMOCRACY MEANS PUTTING YOUR BODY ON THE LINE

By Charles McDew

Tom and I go back a long way, over 50 years. I first met him and Al Haber when a Student Nonviolent Coordinating Committee (SNCC) delegation came seeking support at the 1961 National Student Association (NSA) convention in Minneapolis-St. Paul in 1961. Tom's future wife, Casey, was in our delegation. Paul Potter was there; he became the NSA officer who would be liaison to SNCC. There were right-wingers too, the Young Americans for Freedom and their intellectual founder, William F. Buckley, an old CIA person. One night there was a big encounter between Tom and Buckley, but Tom stayed on the edge of the crowd and wouldn't debate him.

Al and Tom were trying to build SDS. Tom said they were trying to recruit us and we were trying to recruit them. That's true. We were looking for support, not from intellectual revolutionaries with all their theories, but from people who wanted to put their bodies on the line. To those who were masturbating over Marxism, we said, *Fine, if you want your revolution, come down and do it yourself. We'll get you a place, a platform, and you can give a lecture in a cotton field, and get your ass killed.* You could discuss Marx, but in the meantime people had to understand what we were dealing with, and the practicality of things. We were facing white people who would kill us as quickly as a cat or a rat, with no penalty.

It would take some unusual people to join us, and we thought it most likely could be the SDS people. Tom, for example, was the first non-SNCC person who came to talk with us, meet and get to know us. We invited him down to Mississippi, and he came with Paul. Mississippi was always violent—we called it another country—and local people were getting killed for trying to start voter registration and freedom schools. Just before Tom came to McComb, for instance, a white member of the state legislature shot Herbert Lee in broad daylight in a street in Liberty. On the same day, September 25, 1961, the killer was acquitted in a courtroom filled with armed white men. Just the day before, John Doar of the justice department came to McComb and we told him every black person there wanted to vote but that the white people would kill them if they tried to register.

So when Tom and Paul came down the next week, we met with them in the basement of a house with all the curtains pulled, and they were driven around crouched down in the back seats of a car. The next day, they got whupped and arrested while they were sitting in a car observing high-school kids demonstrating and marching.

What we noticed was that the picture of Tom being beaten got national attention, because he was white, while there was no coverage when the black people were killed. We had to get whites involved, not cynically to get them killed, but as a way for our activities on behalf of voter registration to be noticed. We didn't invite Tom down to get him whupped, but he had admiration among students up north, and the SDS was growing and would get bigger. They were talkers, but some of them were doers too. They were cool. They would be around in the future, and they would become like these old radicals like A.J. Muste who would spend their entire lives working to make this place better, whose legacy would be that they made a difference.

I came to the Port Huron Conference with Tim Jenkins and Bob Zellner from SNCC because we wanted to recruit them, and also we wanted to have the discussion about participatory democracy. For us, it meant you had to align your mind and body, your ideas had to be tested; participation meant putting your body on the line. The only question was, where was your body? If your body wasn't with your passion and intellectual understanding, we didn't need to be around you.

As an aside, I don't think there's a natural energy and passion about young people. That was the problem we had with SDS. *Some of you guys can talk forever,* we said, *but you don't do shit and talk won't do it.* One of my questions about Occupy today is whether they will be fair-weather revolutionaries. It don't work that way. There is no better day for revolution than today. If you get enough people who share the same beliefs, and put their bodies behind those beliefs, you can change anything. SNCC started with 15–20 people. We knew there would be a blood price, because we lived in such a violent country. We accepted it. We were going to pay the price. Not because we wanted to, but because we didn't see any other way. We took a blood oath to give ourselves to this for five years, knowing that some of us would die, everyone would suffer, but it would end in five years. We didn't want to institutionalize SNCC like the NAACP, CORE, and so on.

We saw that the white racist power structure in Washington was built around seniority, and that was based on keeping majorities of black people disenfranchised and terrorized in these Black Belt districts. We thought that system would come down if blacks were organized and registered, and if the justice department were forced to intervene. The Voting Rights Act would pass in 1965, exactly five years after SNCC was founded.

Of the SNCC people who were left alive and made it out, we went through a thing of wondering what to do next. For example, we didn't know if we wanted to have children at all in this fucked-up country. It's funny that my friends and I were in our 40s and 50s before having toddlers.

I came from a tough steel town, Massillon, Ohio, where there was a small black community and a lot of football players who made it to the pros. That was my plan: to play football (I was a quarterback), get drafted, have a career, get married to a beautiful black woman and have some beautiful black babies, and use the money when I retired to invest in a liquor store or some other business. My father insisted, though, that I spend at least one year down south in a historically black college, and so I went to South Carolina State in Orangeburg. I had never been south before, never had black professors, never saw so many pretty black women. I was having a fine time until I left campus one night as the designated driver after a local party. The cops pulled me over and asked for my ID. They looked at it, and then the cop says, "Where you from, boy?" I said, "Ohio. Look at my driver's license; can't you read?" He says, "Don't you know how to say *Yes sir*?" I answered, "You've got to be jiving." Then he started punching me. Being from Massillon, I started stomping him, while my friends stayed back in the car, doing nothing. I didn't understand that it would cost their lives to try and help me. Then his posse arrived and the tide of battle turned. They broke my jaw, and I went to jail for the first time.

My father sent money and bailed me out the next day. So now I catch the train back to Orangeburg, my first time on a Southern train. The conductor says to get back in the baggage car, and I say, no, I like the seat I have right here. So I'm back in jail hours after getting out the first time. When I finally got out, I took the Jim Crow section of the train back to Orangeburg. I was tired and decided to cut through a public park, Edisto Park, on the way back to school. I learned that wherever there was a sign saying "Public Park" it meant no blacks. I got busted again, the third time in the weekend.

So my father said I could come home north to another school, because he couldn't afford the bail, the fines, and the medical bills. *They are going to kill you if you stay there,* he said. So we agreed I would just finish the semester and then I would never have to be in the South again.

Just then the sit-ins broke out up in North Carolina. Some students at Orangeburg came to see me about being their spokesman because they said I was a crazy nigger who would say anything to white folks. I at first said *no, thank you, because these white people here are clinically insane and you are not wrapped too tightly if you think you can change them.* This was no India, where apparently there were some cultural morals during the time of Gandhi. If people in India lay down in the road, the bus driver might consider stopping, but in South Carolina they would most likely drive over you, and back up to make sure you were dead. So I said *No thanks, and good luck to you.*

Over that weekend, though, I was reading a statement by Rabbi Hillel, a teaching from the Talmud that said, "If I am not for myself, who will be for me? If I am only for myself, what am I? And if not now, when?" I thought about that, how we were going through all this shit because my father and his generation didn't stop it, and if I don't stop it, my kids will have to deal with it, and on and on. So I called back my friends and said I would be their spokesman. It was just before I was scheduled to go home to Ohio. I was chosen as chairman of the Orangeburg Movement. The vice chairman was Jim Clyburn, who became a congressman from South Carolina. After some planning and training, we marched downtown, and on a very cold day in March. There were dogs, gas, water hoses, and 500 arrests, the largest number anywhere up to that point. They put us in a giant chicken coop when the county jail was filled.

Dr. King called a meeting on Easter Week that year to bring all the sit-in student leaders together across the South, hoping we would be organized under his Southern Christian Leadership Conference (SCLC). A big argument broke out. Ms. Ella Baker *[ed. note: a long time NAACP Southern organizer who was temporary executive director of Dr. King's organization]* told us that there were meetings going on in SCLC about how the students would be used in the movement and that we were being excluded from those meetings. There also was a debate about nonviolence. Dr. King said if we were going to be a part of his movement, we had to accept nonviolence as a way of life. I felt that nonviolence was a tactic and therefore I could not join SCLC. I said I was going down the hall to another room if anyone wanted to follow me, where the students would decide what we wanted to do. About 15 or 20 students walked over after a while, and that's where SNCC was formed, as an independent student movement, centered on our own group and not on one leader.

We started SNCC with 15 people. There are 6 of us alive today. I'm 73 now, and I just don't have the same energy. I am okay with dying, because I never expected to live this long. Anything longer than 25 years was gravy. So now we need new blood to carry on the work that we started.

This contribution is based on excerpts from two talks given by Chuck McDew in Los Angeles, California, in 2012. McDew lives in Minneapolis–St. Paul, Minnesota. He was the first chairman of the Student Nonviolent Coordinating Committee.

Just after McDew wrote this essay, a gang of white teenagers beat and drove over a 49-year-old black citizen in a parking lot in Jackson, Mississippi.[1]

Note

1. http://www.cnn.com/2011/CRIME/08/06/mississippi.hate.crime/index.html.

Chapter 11

Religion and the Spirit

By James Monsonis

Let me begin with an anecdote. I came to the Port Huron meeting with a background as a Christian activist, a seminary dropout, a former president of the National Student Christian Federation; and many others at the gathering had a religious background as well. So why is there no discussion of institutional religion in the Statement? Lots of discussion about values generally; critiques of other major institutions such as the labor movement, the educational system, political parties, etc., which shape our society. Why not the churches and the synagogues? The answer is a simple, prosaic, almost laughable one. There was a working group on religious institutions at the meeting, a critique was developed that was to be incorporated into the final draft, and I was delegated to present it to the final, all-night plenary that approved the content of the final draft. And I simply fell asleep before making the report. History is sometimes a series of accidents.

What the Port Huron Statement *would* have said, if I remember correctly, is that despite the heroic efforts of some people of faith from various religious perspectives—Martin Luther King, many of the young people in the civil-rights movement, the nameless Quakers over the decades who have "spoken truth to power"—the religious institutions generally have given their blessing to the status quo. They have simply baptized the racist-accepting, class-divided, imperialist world we all live in (remember that John Foster Dulles was a major official in the National Council of Churches). They were content with urging members to be "good men" in Hannah Arendt's lovely phrase, focusing on private morality. The segregated world was being challenged and was on the verge of coming apart (this was 1962, remember; the sit-ins and the Freedom Rides were already history), but the churches and synagogues were the most segregated institution in America. Their dominant motif was complacency. They seemed to exist to provide what Will Herberg in *Protestant, Catholic, Jew* had described as group identity, at a time when ethnic identity was becoming attenuated (except, of course, for blacks) and the suburbs suggested a family-oriented mass society.

Port Huron should have called the religious institutions back to their historical prophetic task of living out their best ideal values. It should have challenged them to "live the truth" of their confessions. That it did not is to our shame. Today a Port Huron gathering would offer a very different commentary. The complacent blessing of the status quo has been a failed strategy: all the white, established Protestant churches are smaller by a quarter to a half, the Catholic Church is holding its own mostly because of the influx of Catholic Latino immigrants, and the really big news in the white religious world is the massive expansion of fundamentalist churches. The black churches remain segregated though their numbers are holding strong. Jews and Muslims, overall a tiny percentage of the religious community, are doing well. In short the religious landscape is dramatically different. Our critique now must focus on what these groups despised by the religious and cultural establishment offer, and what this tells us about our society as a whole and about the failure of progressive forces to meet people's needs.

To begin with—and this is the most positive thing we might say about them—is that they have grown as a judgment on the established religious traditions.

People want something different, something else from their religious life than what these traditions offer. People find in these fundamentalist groupings a sense of meaning, an assertion that they, and the world of which they are a part, have purpose and value beyond simply being a cog in the great machine of capitalist expansion and profit production. Their jobs may be uninteresting and meaningless; their families are disintegrating; the educational systems are job-training systems that fail to provide them with any sense of wonder and appreciation of the achievements of science and technology, and in fact foster a profound anti-intellectualism; even sex has been reduced to a sales strategy for new goods.

Only two things have the power to seize many people and provide a sense of belonging, worth, and value: professional sports and the fundamentalist religions. Both offer the same message: You personally don't matter much, but that entity to which you give your whole heart and soul (and money, may I say; if it doesn't cost you, it can't be very valuable, right?) is a Demanding God to which you must be committed totally. If the team doesn't win this year, there's always next; this world may not be much but there is the Next One. No ambiguity, no relativity. All fans and members are assumedly equal, even though they know that the fundamentalist clergy often live *very* well, and corporations own the box seats at the stadiums.

But those two things are not only a judgment on the established churches. They also flourish as a judgment on the society in which we live, for its failure to provide people with a sense of community and worth that makes their lives worthwhile. Shopping malls and television are, ultimately, empty stimuli—interestingly, many fundamentalist churches preach against both. When I was a college teacher and taught a course on religion, I used to suggest to my students that a society in which the religious institutions are flourishing is a society in deep trouble. I see no reason to change that view. Whatever the progressive forces do towards a new institutional order, they must meet this fundamental need.

The 1962 Port Huron Statement talked a great deal about values, and a current version of the statement would demonstrate the perversion of a real concern for essential values in the absolutist claims of the dominant religious institutions of our time. They make their ostensible concern for values into a cover for a political vision, which goes far beyond any religious orientation. The new Statement would not even need to touch on the idea of God itself—whatever that term might mean to the reader. "God" and commitment to that force in their lives will continue to energize and empower individuals to act to change the world we live in. But as the priests of the Liberation Theology movement and the Fathers Berrigan discovered, the religious institutions will not allow people to live out that kind of faith if they can prevent it. They have too much at stake in the current social system, either in defending it or in reforming it in their own ways; standing in opposition to it, in their terms.

So what would a positive religious institution look like in a progressive society? I think there would be value in having an institution where people might explore some "ultimate questions" and issues of values and moral decisions, free of the necessity of taking immediate public action or of political pressures. Sometimes schools have been such a locus, but this is a hit-or-miss case, not their primary task as defined these days. Some of these explorations might be of immediate relevance to public policy, but many would not be (such as, for instance, the question of whether there is an afterlife, and what might be the consequences, if any, for daily behavior). It could be a network where people who agree on a similar course of action could connect; there will always be questions of courses of action to support or avoid in society, which involve fundamental values. It could be a place for exploring differences of value consequences. It would certainly not be a power network, empowered to act in a particular direction, but would be simply a locus of meeting. It could involve ritual—we do seem to need ritual in our lives—but also provide challenges to each other within the context of community. It could be a stimulus for thinking about questions we do not ordinarily think about. And it could be a locus for camaraderie and enjoyment (I think of both Rosa Luxembourg and Molly Ivins's insistence on having fun in the struggle).

Theologian Paul Tillich once described religion as a process of being ultimately concerned—both in the sense of being concerned with the Ultimate, and of having the utmost concern. He also meant an emphasis on being "concerned," not having a final position. We could do worse than urging this as the goal of religious life.

Jim Monsonis attended Yale Divinity School, and was involved with the Student Nonviolent Coordinating Committee in the early 1960s before he was recommended for involvement with the Southern Conference Educational Fund in 1963. He lives in New York City.

Chapter 12

A Young Christian Student
at Port Huron

By Maria Varela

My path to Port Huron was cut by others. It began early in the 20th century with Catholic "worker priests" taking jobs in factories and mines, organizing with workers to change oppressive working conditions. These experiences expressed a turn-of-the-century social-justice theology calling upon Catholics to "reconstruct society altogether, a task which would have to engage people at all levels of society."[1]

Continuing the path during World War II were Catholic religious and lay people who participated in underground resistance networks to work against the Nazis. Those caught were taken away to concentration camps. Many of these efforts involved reaching across religious lines to work ecumenically with other faith-based as well as secular people committed to opposing the horrors of the Third Reich.

After World War II, veterans of these movements developed organizations in Europe to train both Catholic clergy and lay people to change oppressive conditions in workplaces, schools, and communities. Organizations such as Young Christian Workers, Young Christian Students (YCS), and the Christian Family Movement were founded to train participants to the social inquiry method to "see, reflect, and act." The intent of this method was to move Catholics out of their religious insularity to engage in social change that would build a more just society.

I first encountered YCS in the mid 1950s in my high school on the south side of Chicago. We were a rosary-praying, mass-going traditional Mexican and Irish American family. Not being a fan of the rosary, I joined YCS because it was either that or having to join a prayer club. During this formative time in my life, by learning the social inquiry method, I became grounded in the fundamentals of community-organizing and community-based research. I went on to join YCS at Alverno College and in 1961 was invited to become a college organizer on the YCS national staff.

By the 1960s YCS was a worldwide student movement. Originating in Europe, by midcentury it had grown in strength and influence in the United States, Africa, and Latin America. While on national staff, I developed friendships with students involved in *Juventud Estudiantil Cristiana:* the YCS of Latin America. Many YCS leaders were involved in resistance and independence movements in the Americas. In Brazil especially, several were disappeared and/or killed. I believe that the praxis of this movement in Latin America resulted in the formulation of *Teología de la Liberación,* or Liberation Theology.

It was these winds of change in the 1950s and 1960s that opened a window on what we called the "Catholic ghetto." Similarly, young people on the Left were also drawn to open a window on the traditional Left. At least that is what I understood when, in late 1961, SDS founders Al Haber and Tom Hayden invited me to Port Huron. Looking for more diverse views, Hayden and Haber wanted to involve progressives and liberal religious groups to participate in writing a manifesto critiquing U.S. social and foreign policy and laying out a vision of reconstructing U.S. society through participatory democracy. No matter our origins, we all stood on the shoulders of those who went before us cutting the path of social justice and reconstruction.

Frankly, for most of the five days at Port Huron, I was at sea. The discussions and debates were intensely intellectual. I did not come from an intellectual background. The books in our home were either operations manuals for chemical plants or books my mother ordered from Reader's Digest Book Club. My father didn't initially think his five girls should go to college. As we were destined to be wives and mothers ... he thought it a waste. Then a close friend died and left a widow with few marketable skills to support four children. He changed his mind. My education was administered within the "Catholic ghetto," which eschewed critical theory. In YCS, theory grew out of experience and was expressed in everyday language. So for at least the first three days at Port Huron, Tim Jenkins, a former Howard University student-body president and later a Yale Law School student, took me aside every evening and asked if I understood the terms, discussions, and debates. I usually did not. The tutoring continued until I got my sea legs.

Where I did feel more at home was in the discussions about values, especially that "Human relationships should involve fraternity, honesty ... and human brotherhood." The discussions about participatory democracy resonated with my YCS experience. Our work reflected the Port Huron Statement's call to "establish a participatory democracy, [where] the individual shares in those social decisions determining the quality and direction of his life."

These same sentiments were reflected in the teachings of Pope John XXIII (1958–1963). We in YCS were critical Catholics, outliers to the mainstream church. John, however, gathered up the sentiments of the times and reflected back to the official church many of those principles that we and other outliers valued, trained, and worked for: democratic participation, resistance to inequity and oppression, and building communities of love. The Port Huron statement and John's encyclical *Mater et Magistra* (May 1961) could, for the most part, stand side by side in calling for the just reconstruction of society.

Speaking of that encyclical, perhaps now is the time to re-examine what is said about my role at Port Huron. Some versions describe me waving the encyclical in the air and quoting from it in order to reach a compromise between the "political realists and idealists." The end result was: "inspired by Pope John XXIII ... [Varela] suggested that we follow the doctrine that humans have 'unfulfilled' rather than 'unlimited' capacities for good, and are 'infinitely precious' rather than 'infinitely perfectible.' The theological amendment drew no objections and was incorporated without citation."[2]

Anyone who remembers me during these times knows that I generally faded into the woodwork in order to watch, a favorite coping method of mine to understand new situations. That I would insert myself as a para-theologian in this discussion and wave *anything* around does not ring true to my sense of self during those times. Furthermore, my word choices were not about doctrine, theology, or any particular encyclical. My vague remembrance is that there was a struggle over semantics, with people taking strong positions on either side. I had an insight and gathered up enough courage to speak up. (That being said, clouded memory, mine included, is a flaw in the practice of public history.) That I spoke at all during this discussion evidenced that, even though when we felt like outsiders, the discussions leading to the Port Huron Statement brought the secular and the spiritual together, helping me and others find a place in this historic event.

Another gift from Port Huron was meeting Casey Hayden, who, in late 1962, asked me to come to Atlanta to work for the Student Nonviolent Coordinating Committee (SNCC). There is not space here to relay how I got from Atlanta to Selma and eventually to Mississippi. But in my tour of duty with SNCC (1963–1967) I found more of a home than in Students for a Democratic Society (SDS). SNCC's "ideology" was very close to Liberation Theology. Liberation Theology begins with practice, working with the oppressed in their resistance, resulting in a culturally transformed theology that brings those at the margins into the center. The intellectualism I encountered at Port Huron was more theory- than experience-driven. The theories of social change encountered in SNCC grew out of practice: the nonviolent, love-infused, yet stress-filled and conflicted struggles to dismantle U.S. apartheid by nurturing indigenous leaders to develop black power: political, educational, and economic.

The thread that bound SDS to SNCC was the concept of participatory democracy. It really doesn't matter who first coined this term. What matters is that SNCC's godmother, Ella Baker, mentored us in the theory and practice of social change based on participatory democracy. She lived the practice of participatory democracy during the decades of her activist life before she helped students birth SNCC. If it weren't for her practice, SNCC workers may never have had the time or experience to plumb the deep leadership pool of indigenous leaders that Ms. Baker had worked with since the 1940s. It was this pool of veteran leaders working together with young people who changed the nation.

One significant change resulted from the Mississippi Freedom Democratic Party's (MFDP's) challenge of the seating of the all-white Mississippi Delegation at the 1964 Democratic Party Convention. While the MFDP's delegation was not seated, one of the commitments won from party leadership was that segregated delegations would, in time, no longer be accredited. By 1972 convention rules required that all state delegations be composed of "reasonable representations of women and minorities" as reflected in each state's demographics. This fruit of participatory democracy changed, over time, the body politic of the Democratic Party and the nation.

There is a lot of discussion in the literature about who influenced whom in the 1960s movements. Some credit SNCC with imprinting on SDS that praxis more than theoretical deliberations were the key to social change. Others credit SDS with coining the term "participatory democracy," which named the work SNCC did in the Black Belt South. None of this is the full truth. And the discussion is irrelevant.

Movements are more like nature than science. The tide doesn't ask from which part of the globe the sea waters originate. Movements create a synergy that crosses geographic borders, races, ethnicities, classes, and even physical matter. We were one then, with all our divisions, critiques, weaknesses, and strengths. In many ways today we remain one through our diverse activism and mentoring of succeeding generations to go beyond us to achieve a world where "We would replace power rooted in possession, privilege, or circumstance by power and uniqueness rooted in love, reflectiveness, reason, and creativity in the never ending struggle for liberation."[3]

Maria Varela worked as a community organizer and literacy campaigner for the Student Nonviolent Coordinating Committed in the Deep South, and is a longtime leader in immigrant rights, education, healthcare and Latina feminist movements in New Mexico.

Notes

1. Pope Leo XIII, *Rerum Novarum* (1891).
2. Hayden, *Reunion: A Memoir,* Random House, 1988, p. 96.
3. Port Huron Statement.

CHAPTER 13

PARTICIPATORY DEMOCRACY

A LONG REVOLUTION

By Michael Vester

On June 11, 1962, when Casey Hayden, in that huge American car, drove us from Ann Arbor to Lake Huron, through those endless Michigan forests, we could relax. Most of the labor had already been done through months of intensive work and discussions. And this work, in turn, was the reflection of a new international unrest of the young generation called the New Left.

In October 1961, I had come from Frankfurt to study sociology in the United States. I was 21 years old, just having finished my year on the national board of the German Socialist Student Federation, also called SDS. As its vice president I had been responsible for developing a new international network of Socialist student and youth organizations. These formed the New Left current inside and outside the old Socialist international organizations in the developed countries, in the decolonizing countries of the Third World, and among East European dissidents. All these young activists had a sense of a new political opening symbolized by de-colonialization and by John F. Kennedy's election as president.

Arriving in New York, I immediately resumed contact with our fraternal organizations. Most important were Al Haber and Dick Flacks of Students for a Democratic Society, but also Socialists such as Michael Harrington. Discussing with Dick and Al, I immediately found out that we shared the same enthusiasm and conviction of the new ideas. In December, they told me that they had asked Tom Hayden in Ann Arbor to formulate a public statement, which expressed those ideas for the situation of America and its young generation.

Our [German SDS] analysis to end the Cold War by diplomatic recognition of East Germany and subsequent diplomatic negotiations at that time was not very popular. The Social Democratic Party (SPD) was about to expel us on the pretext that we were Communists, which we definitely were not. From 1969 on, when Willy Brandt became head of a new German government, the Kennedy spirit spread to Germany, too, and Brandt received the Nobel Peace Prize for exactly the same policy.

The ambitious stance of the Statement—to express the political perspectives of a whole younger generation—was encouraged by the rising new movements around the world. The statement also reflected a new language, markedly differing from the stereotypes of the Old Left. The statement became a great—and, in a way, the only—synthesis of what was discussed since the international New Left had come into existence at the end of the '50s. It linked the analysis of the advanced, "affluent" Capitalist societies with that of their new social and political contradictions. It understood that these contradictions translated into a generational conflict.

The term "participatory democracy" was offered as an integrative formula of the emerging movements. It allowed us to look back to the long history of communal movements, trade unions, economic democracy, and personal emancipation in many countries. At the same time, the term became a common denominator of the manifold new movements renewing those traditions of genuine democracy. For us at that time, there was not necessarily a contradiction between unionist, Socialist, anti-racialist, feminist, and youth-cultural movements. This coincidence was symbolized by the fact that we adopted this manifesto in a holiday camp at Lake Huron, which had been built by the United Auto Workers of Detroit in the years of the Great Depression.

The formula of participatory democracy brought together the different movements for personal and political emancipation. These included gender emancipation as well as non-authoritarian pedagogy, the emancipation of ethnic and cultural minorities, the establishment of democratic publics and control in politics and economics, as well as ecological and pacifist reflection of the destructive consequences of one-dimensional modernization.

Today, after three decades of neo-conservative restoration, the spirit is still there, just recently manifested by the international chain reaction of new democratic movements. The writers of the Spanish manifesto of May 2011 rediscovered the term "genuine democracy," along with the term "democratic participation."

To me, this continuity of emancipatory movements is not just one of ideas but of the underlying changes of everyday cultures and social structures. The slow but steady spreading of participatory grass roots among the younger generations gives participatory democracy the appearance of what, in 1961, Raymond Williams called a "long revolution."

The movements of the '60s were possible only by change in three fields of action, which generally are separated:

1. On the one hand, there was a radical *change of everyday culture,* especially in the young generation. The young generation the Port Huron Statement is speaking for, whether political or not, whether intellectual or working-class, had the feeling that the old rules of social order, of discipline and of non-participation, of hierarchies, were outdated, because now there were these possibilities to be different, to not conform. This impetus of *youth culture* was largely supported by new developments of rock music, especially The Beatles.

2. This change also included *culture at work.* On the one hand, Capitalism needed a better-educated labor force, which implied higher competences and more autonomy at work. On the other hand, industrial workers and the growing faction of service employees who had experienced the rising possibilities of participation in everyday culture as well as politics wanted that same participation to be realized at work. The basic shift has continued up to now. For reasons of rising productivity, the social division of labor is accelerating, the levels of professional qualification and of educational achievements have been continuously rising—e.g., in the German work force, the percentage of academic professionals and semi-professionals rose to almost 50 percent. As their work needs more autonomy and horizontal cooperation, they increasingly get into conflict with neo-conservative politics of restoring control, discipline, and authority. This is a very long and slow process, and its translation into movements, conflicts, and politics does not occur automatically, but rather has to be organized.

3. Third, these combined with parallel movements in the *political field*: Easter marches and actions for disarmament, Freedom Rides and passive resistance against racism, sit-ins for more democratic universities, etc. Increasingly, these impulses contributed to the rise of a *participatory civil society.*

The struggle for emancipatory perspectives also went on in the field of social sciences. Dogmatic Marxists and even philosopher Herbert Marcuse could explain protest only by the assumption that increasing repression and misery alone could produce increasing protest while affluence and liberties would produce complacency, alienation, and adaptation. According to these theories, social protest movements had become impossible inside welfare Capitalism, where everybody was thought to be satisfied except small marginalized groups. Experience showed us, as it was stated at Port Huron, that the contrary was true. The "affluent students" as well as "affluent workers" of the '60s were increasingly involved in protest movements.

According to our experience, culture could not be counterposed against economics. From workers' education we knew that a certain rise in standards of consumption, welfare, and living did not suddenly convert the working class to Capitalism and make them give up their own culture for petty-bourgeois culture. There *was* a change of culture, but *within* each class culture, in the shape of an intergenerational change and conflict. The young generations already grew up in welfare Capitalism, with its slowly widening possibilities of life. For them, the restrictive morals of their parents and rigidities of the institutions were no longer necessary under conditions of relative affluence in changing Capitalism. The old, restrictive moral and institutional system had been legitimated by an economy of scarcity and want. The new conditions of relative affluence and welfare constituted an "opening of social space," as philosopher Maurice Merleau-Ponty had put it, which encouraged people to do what they always had wanted but not dared to do.

In our research projects at Hanover University, we worked to test the ever-recurring idea of the "end of classes." The finding of this research was that there was indeed a differentiation of classes in their economic as well as their cultural dimensions. But this did not change at all the vertical hierarchy. Horizontal class differentiation means rising work skills and educational achievements, and also rising needs for autonomy and participation in decisions. This is not the "end of class" but an increase of the contradictions and conflict with the neo-conservative policies of increasing exclusion, precarity, control, and disciplining.

Through this long structural revolution—rising professional competences and rising participatory capacities—the potentials for personal and social emancipation are growing. The political roll-back towards neo-liberal authoritarianism in the 1990s was not essentially translated into a mental or cultural roll-back, although authoritarian dispositions are still forcefully mobilized. Together with generational change and the new revolution of the means of communication, the values and competences of autonomy, mutual respect, reflexivity, and democratic coordination have continued to gain ground. These developments are the motive of the new democratic movements as well as the modern labor unions.

Michael Vester is professor of political science emeritus, University of Hanover, Germany. This essay is excerpted from a paper on Port Huron presented at the University of California, Santa Barbara, February 2, 2012.

PART 3

TEACHING STRATEGIES, FINAL THOUGHTS, AND THE PORT HURON STATEMENT

CHAPTER 14

TEACHING THE PORT HURON STATEMENT

By Robert Cohen, Diana Turk, and Stacie Brensilver Berman

We teach history and know the problems of getting kids today off YouTube, and their common tendency to associate past social movements only with such famous leaders as Martin Luther King, César Chávez, and Rosa Parks. It's a step forward that our students even recognize these names, and we see this top-down understanding of well-known leaders as the key entry point for getting them to see the movements that thrust those leaders into the spotlight, movements composed of young people very much like themselves.

We therefore believe that "teaching participatory democracy" is a way for us to guide young people to find themselves within the stream of history, right down to the present. What stance would they have taken when faced with choices to sit in or sit out back then, and why? And where are such choices in today's world? Among undocumented students, those fearing global warming of the planet, or those protesting against a future of high tuitions and low job opportunities? Students may find that the questions students struggled with at Port Huron 50 years ago still resonate today.

Teaching participatory democracy is not only narrating an important chapter of history, however. It also is a way of introducing a participatory pedagogical method. Political philosopher John Dewey called it learning by doing. Education theorist Paolo Freire called it liberating pedagogy. This means teaching the Port Huron Statement (PHS) in ways that foster active learning and critical thinking, so as to model democratic pedagogy as we explore this democratic document—sparking discussion and debate about both the past and the present. But to make such democratic dialogue possible, teachers of the Port Huron Statement must first identify the *enduring understandings,* those large, weighty concepts that they want their students to develop as they study this document. The PHS is so long and complex that teachers can focus on different parts of it, but no matter which section of the Statement they teach, nine enduring understandings loom large:

The PHS's central political ideal, *participatory democracy,* **was far more egalitarian and democratic than mainstream American politics.** Tom Hayden urged at a recent teacher workshop that classes on the PHS focus above all on the Statement's call for democratic renewal and individual and community empowerment via active participation in decision-making in all aspects of life. This is what Students for a Democratic Society (SDS) founder Alan Haber meant when he defined participatory democracy as looking "at democracy as not simply a political instrument of government but as a mode of relationship in all areas of our common life."[1] So teachers and students need to explore what the Port Huron Statement meant by participatory democracy, grappling with it historical meaning and implications for politics, economics, and society today. This involves inviting students to see that Port Huron's version of democracy was far deeper than that found in civics textbooks or the corridors of power in Washington. The PHS championed "a concept of democracy that's based on the quality and level of participation of a number of a people and how directly involved they are in any decisions" that impact their lives. "It goes beyond voting, although voting is crucial. It goes into birthplace democracy and neighborhood democracy and community councils and community empowerment." So Hayden concludes, as students read the PHS, the central learning goal is to promote civic engagement by "passing on" a heightened democratic sensibility. This would enable students to evaluate what a democratic life would mean, recognizing it, in Hayden's words, "as an opportunity for them to be involved because it's about creating their future through the democratic process of their own self-determining decisions and behaviors."[2]

The PHS grew out of, and reflected dissatisfaction with, the flaws, abuses, and inequities of Cold War America. The PHS cannot be understood without being nestled historically within the history of the 1950s and early 1960s. This larger historical context, and the critique of it that the PHS articulated, is summarized in the Statement's "Introduction: Agenda for a Generation." So class discussions of the PHS might well start here, with student activists describing why a college generation "bred in at least modest comfort" nonetheless looked "uncomfortably to the world we inherit."[3]

This sense of unease, which in the early 1960s moved students "from silence to activism," evolved after they awakened to the evils of Jim Crow and grew wary of the tensions bred by Cold War militarism—domestic and foreign-policy maladies "too troubling to dismiss."[4] The PHS opened, then, with an awareness that America's proclamations of its high ideals of "freedom and equality ... rang hollow before the facts of Negro life." Similarly, U.S. claims about its "peaceful intentions" on the world stage seemed hypocritical, "contradicted by its economic and military investment in the Cold War status quo."[5] The sense of urgency about ending the Cold War is linked to the baby-boomer experience as the first generation to grow up in the nuclear age, carrying a fear that the H-bomb arms race would end in total destruction. Thus the PHS's authors thought of themselves as not melodramatic but realistic in writing that "Our work is guided by the sense that we may be the last generation in the experiment with living .... If we appear to seek the unattainable, as it has been said, then let it be known that we do so to avoid the unimaginable."[6]

The New Left, represented by PHS and SDS, was more than a white, middle-class student movement; it was what historian Van Gosse terms a "movement of movements."[7] That is, it was a broad array of protest movements that surged during the long 1960s, beginning with the black-freedom movement, and continuing with the free-speech movement, the antiwar movement, second-wave feminism, gay liberation, the environmental movement, and others.

The civil-rights movement, and especially its black-led student wing, the Student Nonviolent Coordinating Committee (SNCC), gave the PHS its Gandhian tone, evident in its opening section on values: "We find violence to be abhorrent .... It is imperative that the means of violence be abolished and the institutions—local, national, and international—that encourage nonviolence as a condition of conflict be developed."[8] SNCC, which had evolved out of the integrationist lunch-counter sit-ins in the South, had shown in its courageous role in the Freedom Rides that nonviolent protest could be a powerful tool for progressive change. SNCC modeled an egalitarian organizing style, concerned with means as well as ends, so as to prefigure in its own life and work the better society it envisioned. These connections between SNCC, the black-freedom movement, and the Port Huron Statement were personal as well as political: Hayden's initial thinking about the PHS occurred when he was in an Albany, Georgia, jail as a Freedom Rider; SNCC organizers Chuck McDew and Bob Zellner were among those civil-rights-movement veterans present at the Port Huron Conference, and SNCC organizer Martha Noonan was involved both with the PHS and SDS. "SNCC," as Hayden recalls, "played a direct role in shaping my values, as it did with many SDS founders. SNCC's early organizing method was based on listening to local people and taking action on behalf of their demands .... This led to a language and a form of thinking cleansed of ideological infection, with an emphasis on trying to say what people were already thinking but hadn't put into words."[9] Through the sit-in movement and its mobilization of the black student movement, SNCC was doing in the South what SDS would intend to do in the North, and the ties between the two organizations meant that the white students not only acknowledged SNCC's goals but also joined its fight.

Although it helped set the tone for the 1960s as an era of protest and change, the Port Huron Statement was a product of a brief historical moment, amidst the 1,000 days of the Kennedy era, and that moment needs to be studied in its own right. The Statement's hopeful rhetoric, its optimism and faith in participatory democracy, reflected an America not yet polarized by the U.S. invasion of Vietnam. The PHS came before the disillusioning assassinations of Martin Luther King, Medgar Evers, Malcolm X, and the Kennedys; before the Kent, Jackson, and Orangeburg State massacres; before the ghetto rebellions; and before the national ascendance of such polarizing backlash politicians as Richard Nixon, Spiro Agnew, and Ronald Reagan. The PHS moment was one in which it still seemed possible for radically egalitarian change to be achieved without the appeals to violence and the dogmatism that came into vogue in the late '60s among the SDS's Marxifying, Weatherizing, ultramilitant factions. So students need to understand the Kennedy era, and explore why early-1960s America could seem such a time of democratic possibility, and why the *new* New Left differed from the more ideological and embittered SDS of the late 1960s.

One of the PHS's most daring characteristics was its rejection of Cold War America's obsessive anti-Communism. While the PHS criticized both the Soviet and the U.S. roles in the Cold War, the Statement stressed the damage that "McCarthyism and other forms of exaggerated and conservative anticommunism" did to American political culture. Such anti-radicalism, according to the PHS, served to "seriously weaken democratic institutions and spawn movements contrary to the interests of basic freedoms and peace. In such an atmosphere even the most intelligent of Americans fear to join political organizations, sign petitions, speak out on serious issues. Militaristic policies are easily 'sold' to a ... fearful ... public."[10]

The PHS offered a critique of political apathy, and this was an essential part of its drive to move students beyond the Silent Generation mentality inherited from the 1950s, when the Cold War and McCarthyism had rendered millions of college students socially conformist and politically quiescent. In the 1950s, as Port Huron Conference participant Steve Max recalled, "Everybody … hunkered down to the 'man in the gray flannel suit' era of conformity and then spent their weekends digging bomb shelters in their backyard …. So this was the Fifties, a period of prosperity, repression, and conformity which the New Left was reacting against at every level."[11] Early SDS believed that a challenge to this deadening political climate was not only possible, but winnable. As Hayden explained, "Our diagnosis of the prevailing apathy was that deep anxieties had fostered 'a developed indifference' about public life but also a yearning to believe in something better."[12] Connected to this was a sense that though universities had been bastions of conformity, they could, as centers of ideas, be converted into launching pads for searching social criticism and protest. Students in post-industrial society might, in this vision, play an activist role and even serve as agents of progressive social change, much as organized labor had during the industrial era.

Even though the PHS was written by student activists, it was influenced by the ideas of egalitarian elders. These include radical sociologist C. Wright Mills, the civil-rights veteran organizer Ella Baker, and political philosophers Arnold Kaufman and John Dewey. So even though the 1960s is often thought of as a decade whose protest movements were shaped by youth revolt, that revolt was, in turn, shaped by a prior generation of dissident intellectuals and activists.

Written a half century before Occupy Wall Street, the PHS anticipated Occupy's concern with economic inequity. Additionally, it was, along with Michael Harrington's classic indictment of Cold War America's blindness to poverty, *The Other America*—published the same year as the PHS—an early harbinger of the 1960s War on Poverty. In the PHS's introduction the need for greater economic equity, nationally and globally, was a major theme: "While two thirds of mankind suffers undernourishment, our own upper classes revel amidst superfluous abundance."[13] Despite the fact that most of the PHS authors grew up in fairly affluent surroundings, the PHS depicted poverty extensively, discussing the severity of the problem in one section and returning to the issue later to share ideas for alleviating it: "Poverty is shameful in that it herds people by race, region, and previous condition of infortune into 'uneconomic classes' in the so-called free society …. People in the rut of poverty are strikingly unable to overcome the collection of forces working against them .... "[14] Two years before Lyndon Johnson would launch the War on Poverty, the PHS called for "A program against poverty [that] must be just as sweeping as the nature of poverty itself. It must not be just palliative, but directed to the abolition of the structural circumstances of poverty."[15] The PHS advocated accessible housing, medical care, and welfare for the impoverished. Such concern for the poor among privileged college students reflected, as Dick Flacks explains, "that double experience of being raised in comfortable circumstances, but those circumstances were seen to be unreal in terms of the larger society, that it was morally and even emotionally important for people born in suburbia ... to connect and understand what was going on in the wider society in terms of inequality."[16]

The PHS is a distinctive document in that it is not only the longest manifesto in the history of the American Left, but one that starts off by explaining its values rather than merely offering a list of demands. This opening section explains the beliefs underlying all that follows, the common ethos that informed the politics of this activist community. As SDS veteran Todd Gitlin explains, "The genius of the Port Huron Statement, as it was structured, was placing its declaration of values up front. The movement would not be guided by interests but by values. It would not despise interests but it would insist that human life deserved to be less cruel and more lovely."[17]

Although deeply critical of U.S. racism, classism, and imperialism, the PHS was a pre-feminist document and offered no such criticism of sexism. In fact, the document was gendered male, and among its most famously eloquent passages was one that, as was common in 1962, used "men" as a synonym for humanity: "We regard *men* as infinitely precious and possessed of unfulfilled capacities for reason, freedom, and love."[18] So students need to explore the state of gender relations in early-1960s America, and to grapple with the movement's contradictory history regarding gender, that while the New Left/PHS ethos of participatory democracy later contributed (in the mid and late 1960s) to the rise of women's liberation, the early New Left and PHS were conventional with regard to gender.

Essential Questions

To help students come away from their study of the PHS with a clear sense of the importance of these enduring understandings, teachers should consider exploring the following *essential questions* to guide the teaching of the Port Huron Statement:

- How did events and attitudes of the 1950s and early 1960s create the perceived need among dissenting American college students for a manifesto like the Port Huron Statement?
- Why did the two-party system seem so ineffective in addressing concerns about racial injustice, the nuclear-arms race, and economic inequality? How might this lead to calls for deeper modes of democratic change and participation?
- How do SNCC and SDS compare? What ideas about race, youth, community organizing, and social change link these predominantly black and predominantly white activist groups?
- In what ways did SDS in 1962, with its sense of optimism as embodied in the PHS, serve as a bridge between the conformity of the 1950s and the radicalism of the later 1960s? How would you characterize SDS in 1962, in terms of its aims, efforts, and expectations? To what extent does the PHS transcend and challenge the centrist liberalism of the Kennedy administration?
- Why was the PHS so critical of Cold War anti-Communism? Anti-Communist critics, ranging from Michael Harrington on the Left to David Horowitz on the Right, complain that the PHS's anti–anti-Communism weakens the document's moral authority. Does such criticism have merit? Or was a break with America's obsessive anti-Communism a necessity for a movement seeking to free itself from the repression of the Cold War 1950s?
- Why were college students in the 1950s so politically quiescent? How effective is the Port Huron Statement in explaining and challenging that apathy? How relevant is this critique of apathy to your own student generation?
- How did C. Wright Mills's critique of elitism and inequality in Cold War America pave the way intellectually for the Port Huron Statement? How did Ella Baker's mentorship of SNCC and her collective approach to leadership impact the PHS? How did John Dewey's and Arnold Kaufman's ideas about democracy influence Tom Hayden in his drafting of the PHS? Why are progressive historian Paul Berman and others so critical of participatory democracy?
- Why was the PHS so critical of economic inequality in the U.S.? Why, a half century after the PHS, has such inequality intensified?

- How do we account for the PHS's silence on the issue of sexism? How did the ethos of participatory democracy later help to foster the emergence of the women's-liberation movement?
- Does the PHS's focus on values and the documents hefty length make it seem more or less attractive as a political manifesto? How does the PHS compare in this regard with the manifesto of conservative students in this era, the Sharon Statement of the Young Americans for Freedom? Why do you think the PHS raises the issue of racial injustice almost at the start while the Sharon Statement never even mentions it?
- Does the *Citizens United* decision and the increasing power of the super-rich and mega-corporations to shape electoral politics make the PHS's ideal of participatory democracy seem outdated or more relevant than ever?

To encourage discussion and allow all students to share their thoughts on the key PHS ideal of participatory democracy, we encourage teachers to use small groups within which students can dialogue. Obviously students first need to be able to define participatory democracy, and evaluate its meaning and relevance for the authors of the PHS. And they need to then grapple with the essential questions listed above about the New Left and the 1960s. But this discussion about the past should generate dialogue about its relationship to the present. Teachers can spark discussion by asking what 21st-century students would say if they were to write a manifesto about their own times. What problems would they stress regarding war, peace, and social justice? What would it mean to explore the democratic possibilities for righting the wrongs they see around them in their own schools, campuses, and neighborhoods? What would it take to promote democratic participation in the crucial arenas of their own lives? And beyond their own surroundings, there are obvious connections teachers can make to the Occupy movement; the Madison, Wisconsin protests of 2011; the Arab Spring; and rallies for the DREAM Act in California. Making connections such as these can enable students to formulate responses to a final essential question: "Why is the Port Huron Statement significant? In what ways can it teach us in the 21st century about the promise of participatory democracy and the challenges of making it a reality?"

Scholarly and Personal Lessons Inherent in Teaching the Port Huron Statement

There are many different formats for teaching the Port Huron Statement. The one-to-two-day lesson plan we created, available at http://steinhardt.nyu.edu/

historyintheclassroom/phs under "Teaching Resource: Lesson Plan," offers one approach, combining full class discussion and group work with an emphasis on having students wrestle with the meaning of participatory democracy, both for activists in the early 1960s and for themselves today. Classes can debate the negative portrayals of the PHS by critics such as Paul Berman, Robert Bork, and David Horowitz, whose statements are also available on our website. Teachers may also use excerpts from the oral-history transcripts of SDS members on this same website to explore the trajectory of SDS from before the Port Huron Conference to LBJ's escalation of the Vietnam War.

Social movements are ever-evolving and never complete. The changes accomplished by one generation can be reversed, necessitating a new surge of protest. The preface to the Port Huron Statement declares it to be a "living document" and, in fact, many of its goals remain unfulfilled. Hayden, Flacks, and other Port Huron coauthors look to today's students to pick up that mantle, stressing at the Port Huron Statement @50 conferences at NYU and UC Santa Barbara the importance of getting today's students politically engaged. Alan Haber urges today's teachers to "look at your students as agents of social change, as conscious people with a voice. What would they want to say if they envisioned themselves ... mak[ing] that jump from passivity, apathy and quietude and ... really wanted to say something important?"[19] Joining Haber, we call on educators to teach the Port Huron Statement in ways that enable students to see the power of democracy and collective voice so students recognize that *they too can make a difference* and build the kind of movements for democratic change that 21st-century America needs so desperately.

Professor Robert Cohen teaches social studies and history at NYU and is the author of Freedom's Orator: Mario Savio and the Radical Legacy of the 1960s.

Stacie Brensilver Berman taught U.S. history for 10 years at Edward R. Murrow High School in Brooklyn, NY. She is now in a PhD program for Teaching and Learning—Social Studies at New York University. Stacie coauthored a chapter on teaching the civil-rights movement in Teaching U.S. History: Dialogues Among Social Studies Teachers and Historians, *a volume in the Transforming Teaching series, and is currently working on a chapter on war crimes for the* Teaching Recent Global History *book in the same series.*

Diana Turk is an associate professor and director of the social studies program in the Steinhardt School at New York University. She earned her PhD in American studies from the University of Maryland at College Park. She is the author of Bound by a Mighty Vow: Sisterhood and Women's Fraternities, 1870–1920 *(New York*

University Press, 2004), coeditor of Teaching U.S. History: Dialogues Among Social Studies Teachers and Historians *(Routledge, 2010), and coauthor of the forthcoming* Teaching Recent Global History *(Routledge).*

Notes

1. Alan Haber, Speech at Port Huron @50 Conference, New York University, April 13, 2012. Video available at http://steinhardt.nyu.edu/historyintheclassroom/phs in the section "Oral History Session & Reception for Teachers."

2. Tom Hayden, Speech at Port Huron @50 conference, New York University, April 13, 2012. Video available at http://steinhardt.nyu.edu/historyintheclassroom/phs in the section "Oral History Session & Reception for Teachers."

3. Tom Hayden, *The Port Huron Statement: The Visionary Call of the 1960s Revolution.* New York: Thunder's Mouth Press, 2005, p. 45.

4. Ibid.

5. Hayden, *The Port Huron Statement,* pp. 45–6.

6. Ibid, pp. 47, 169.

7. Van Gosse, "A Movement of Movements: The Definition and Periodization of the New Left," in Roy Rosenzweig and Jean-Christophe Agnew, eds., *A Companion to Post-1945 America* (Blackwell, 2002).

8. Hayden, *The Port Huron Statement,* p. 55.

9. Tom Hayden, "Participatory Democracy from Port Huron to Occupy Wall Street." *The Nation.* April 16, 2012, p. 12.

10. Hayden, *The Port Huron Statement,* p. 103.

11. Steve Max, oral history interview with Stacie Brensilver Berman, New York City, March 9, 2012. Available at http://steinhardt.nyu.edu/historyintheclassroom/phs in the section "Teaching Resource: Oral History Transcripts."

12. Hayden, "Participatory Democracy from Port Huron to Occupy Wall Street." p. 14.

13. Hayden, *The Port Huron Statement,* p. 46.

14. Ibid, pp. 81–2.

15. Ibid, pp. 142–3.

16. Dick Flacks, telephone interview with Stacie Brensilver Berman, April 2, 2012. Available at http://steinhardt.nyu.edu/historyintheclassroom/phs in the section "Teaching Resource: Oral History Transcripts.".

17. Todd Gitlin, speech at Port Huron @50 conference, New York University, April 12, 2012. Video available at http://steinhardt.nyu.edu/historyintheclassroom/phs in the section "Port Huron Statement in Historical Perspective."

18. Hayden, *The Port Huron Statement,* p. 51.

19. Alan Haber, speech at Port Huron @50 conference, New York University in the section "Oral History Session & Reception for Teachers."

Resources for Teaching the Port Huron Statement

History in the Classroom: The Port Huron Statement @50. Retrieved from NYU Steinhardt: http://steinhardt.nyu.edu/historyintheclassroom/phs.

Berman, P. (1997). *A Tale of Two Utopias: The Political Journey of the Generation of 1968*. New York: Norton.

Flacks, R. (1988). *Making History: The American Left and the American Mind*. New York: Columbia Univ. Press.

Frost, J. (2001). *"An Interracial Movement of the Poor": Community Organizing and the New Left in the 1960s*. New York: New York University Press.

*Garvy, H. (2007). *Rebels with a Cause: A Collective Memoir of the Hopes, Rebellions, and Repression of the 1960s*. Los Gatos, CA: Shire Press.

#Gitlin, T. (1993). *The Sixties: Years of Hope, Days of Rage*. New York: Bantam Books.

Gitlin, T. (2012, April 14). Todd Gitlin on the Port Huron Statement's 50th Anniversary. Retrieved from *Daily Kos*: http://www.dailykos.com/story/2012/04/14/1083452/-Todd-Gitlin-on-the-Port-Huron-Statement-s-50th-Anniversary.

Gosse, V. (2005) *Rethinking the New Left: An Interpretative History*. New York: Palgrave.

#Harrington, M. (1997). *The Other America: Poverty in the United States*. New York: Touchstone.

Hayden, T. (1989). *Reunion: A Memoir,* New York: Collier.

Hayden, T. and Richard Flacks. (Aug 5 and 12, 2002). "The Port Huron Statement at 40." *The Nation*.

Hayden, T. (2009). *The Long Sixties: From 1960 to Barack Obama*. Boulder: Paradigm Publishers.

Hayden, T. (2012, April 16). "Participatory Democracy: From Port Huron to Occupy Wall Street." *The Nation*, pp. 11–23.

Hogan, W. (2007). *Many Minds, One Heart: SNCC's Dream for a New America*. Chapel Hill: UNC Press.

Horowitz, D. (2002, July 23). "Port Huron and the War on Terror." *FrontPage Magazine*: http://archive.frontpagemag.com/readArticle.aspx?ARTID=23534.

Kazin, M. (2011). *American Dreamers: How the Left Changed a Nation*. New York: Knopf.

Miller, J. (1987). *"Democracy Is in the Streets": From Port Huron to the Siege of Chicago*. Cambridge: Harvard University Press.

Roberts, S. (2012, March 3). "The Port Huron Statement at 50." *The New York Times*: http://www.nytimes.com/2012/03/04/sunday-review/the-port-huron-statement-at-50.html?_r=1&pagewanted=all.

Sale, K. (1973). *SDS*. New York: Vintage Books.

Reference Notes

*The documentary film *Rebels with a Cause* is also a valuable resource

#Most recent publication

CHAPTER 15

PARTICIPATORY DEMOCRACY FROM SNCC THROUGH PORT HURON TO WOMEN'S LIBERATION TO OCCUPY

STRENGTHS AND PROBLEMS OF PREFIGURATIVE POLITICS*

By Linda Gordon

The Occupy movement and the anniversary of Port Huron have sparked some reconsiderations of the New Left, particularly its call for participatory democracy, which was its core and predominant theme. We can only do that well, however, if we begin to think historically about what we mean by New Left, a category too much associated exclusively with the white student-intellectual movement that coalesced around campus and antiwar activism, then broke up into sectarian fragments from 1968 to 1970. That definition misses the continuity, the span, and the influence of the American New Left. From my perspective, that of a historian of social movements, it is important to understand the American New Left as an umbrella movement, a "cluster concept,"[1] that began in the 1950s with civil rights, traveled through the white student movement, the anti-Vietnam war movement, the women's-liberation movement, and the gay-liberation movement, taking in also the environmentalism that continued throughout.[2] These

*Thanks to Ros Baxandall, Robb Burlage, Dick Cluster, Robby Cohen, Nancy Falk, Tom Hayden, Allen Hunter, and Ann Snitow for comments.

movements shared an anti-authoritarian impulse, a recognition of the need for new analyses of injustice and exploitation, a strategic orientation toward defiance, a tactical reliance on direct action and civil disobedience, a rejection of conformist culture, and a creativity in pioneering new cultural and communitarian forms. Recognizing this "long New Left" is vital for examining the flow of participatory-democracy ideas and prefigurative politics.

Further, we need to think critically about what it means that "New Left" came to refer specifically to a predominantly white, predominantly middle-class, and male-led movement of the universities. Reducing the New Left in that way impoverishes our historical understanding of what was accomplished, and of what we can learn from its mistakes. Further, the narrative that it self-destructed after 1968 has been associated with the criticism of identity politics, as a range of movements from black power through gay liberation developed around specific constituencies. Of course the failure to develop a universal Left opposition is to be regretted. One feature of that declension story has been the mistaken view that the new feminists of the period "broke" with the New Left. It is understandable that constituencies excluded from new movements would feel rejected, but thinking politically and historically requires a broader perspective. Of course not all streams of feminism or gay-rights activism called for a radical democratization of the society and polity, any more than did all streams of antiracism or student protest. (This is why I refer to it as a cluster concept.) But within them all was an activist radicalism that is being renewed today.

We need to think of a "long New Left" that stretched from, say, the mid 1950s through, say, 1980, and one of its continuities was commitment to participatory democracy. Port Huron was part of the flow, an extraordinarily rich and eloquent moment. The statement had many intellectual parents, but the main first predecessor it acknowledged was civil rights. For the New Left, Student Nonviolent Coordinating Committee (SNCC) became not only a parent organization but an ongoing influence—through a flow of particular individuals but also through a reverence for SNCC that functioned at times like a magical amulet.

So that's where I start. The finest social-movement analysis that I know regarding civil rights is Charles Payne's *I've Got the Light of Freedom,* a study of SNCC's work in Mississippi. Payne illustrates participatory democracy in six areas: leadership, the difference between organizing and mobilizing, the intellectual content of organizing, generational relations, identity construction, and gender.

SNCC's was a participatory-democracy vision without the title. Both words were essential: active mass participation (as opposed to, say, lobbying) as the road to freedom and citizenship; democracy requiring fundamental equality before the law and in universal respect. From this followed a notion of leadership quite different from that of Saul Alinsky, who organized in Chicago around a top-down, organizer-driven model based in parishes. The duty of leadership, argued for and enacted by the experienced movement intellectual Ella Baker, was to create new leaders, to erase as much as possible the distinction between leaders and followers, even to abolish followers. Baker; her most famous protégé, Bob Moses; and many of their comrades attempted to enact these practices: listening patiently and attentively, not rushing to present an authoritative analysis, discussing decisions thoroughly. Following this utopian logic to its end, everyone becomes a leader and therefore there are no leaders because people don't need leaders. This is almost certainly impossible, because it seems that there will always be some people more confident, more charismatic, more clear-thinking, and more far-sighted than others. But as an ideal it was not only practical but extremely valuable: because it instructed those who led in a respectful way of working with nonleaders; that is, with followers. It authorized and respected a participatory-democratic approach to recruits. Trying to turn them into leaders meant, in theory, not just persuading them of a particular political analysis; it meant defining success not when the "followers" said they agreed, or even said they would try to register to vote, but when they could also reach out to others.

So SNCC tried to do two things at once: while developing analysis of the weak points of the Southern white power structure, so as to develop strategies for defeating that power structure, it had to build people's confidence in themselves. And this doubled task was again doubled, because it had to be done both among those it organized and among SNCC members themselves. Even more demanding, the confidence-building SNCC had to do was not at the level of, say, encouraging timid young women to speak in public; it was about breaking through empirically, historically justified fear and resignation that decades of terror had created in Southern blacks. It was a task different from that of subsequent New Left movements, whose activists had less to fear—with the possible exception of gays—and often already possessed considerable confidence, resources, and experience of personal efficacy. On the other hand, subsequent movements faced a task that SNCC didn't: Southern blacks, unlike later activists, did not need to be convinced that they were oppressed and exploited—they knew it from the time they were toddlers.

SNCC's conception of leadership represented also a prefigurative politics: it assumed that you cannot build a democratic and egalitarian society through undemocratic and inegalitarian means, because those means would confirm patterns of deference, resignation, and self-protection engendered by several centuries of subordination and some 75 years of violent Jim Crow. SNCC was simultaneously trying to defeat Jim Crow and to create African American citizenship. Its understanding of citizenship required active participation—a republican rather than a liberal conception of citizenship; but in its interracial universalism simultaneously liberal. Its interracial staff (and for SNCC, staff was the same as membership) tried to enact that politics. Their movement struggled to prefigure, or become a microcosm, of the society it wants to build. We see that in a small way, as organizers involved people in ongoing projects where learners in adult literacy classes and citizenship schools then became teachers.

Second, a distinction between organizing and mobilizing further clarifies what SNCC was doing. Mobilizing focused primarily on bringing together great numbers of people for large-scale and usually brief actions, notably demonstrations and petitions. Mobilizing depends heavily on public leaders who can reach people through rousing speeches and the mass media. In the long run, mobilization would not create the thoughtfulness, carefulness, and stamina that sustained social movements require. (SNCC people had an exaggerated disdain for mobilizing, deriving from their historical critique of accommodationist leaders, notably ministers; they referred to Martin Luther King, Jr., as "de Lawd.") It may well be that movements take off and spread through attractive and charismatic public figures, while permanent transformation requires organizing. Furthermore, great mobilizers are not always accountable to anyone or any group; and the more successful they are as mobilizers, the more they are publically recognized, the less they are accountable to a movement constituency—which means that they can disempower instead of empower followers.[3]

Organizing, by contrast, was a slow, usually face-to-face process. When social movements are challenging not only long-established custom, not only entrenched power capable of harsh retaliation, but also conventional wisdom—so conventional that it has come to seem common sense, like the view that "you can't win"—then the printed word or even a public lecture is unlikely to bring a new person to a meeting or a picket line populated by strangers. Some of this is owing to social anxiety: few people will come alone to a political meeting or a demonstration where they know no one, and those who will have usually had previous political experience. The organizee is more likely to respond to the physical experience of another human being, to political arguments that are part of a biography, filtered through and transformed by another subjectivity, as former SNCC volunteer (and later UFW organizer) Marshall Ganz has argued. Moreover, it helps a lot if the organizee can trust the organizer, which in turn happens through knowing her or his history, and possibly through recognizing him or her as a member of a known community, real or imagined.[4] This understanding became part of the feedback loop in which SNCC's model of leadership and organizing fed each other: the staff discovered, sought, and encouraged organizers who would be trusted by those they organized. Mobilization was also essential for the movement's most heroic and media-friendly actions, such as the freedom rides and large marches; but without organizing, few would have been able to sustain the nonviolent response to brutal beatings, or to keep on despite the terror inflicted by murders.

Third, Payne insists, in a truly remarkable claim, that courage has been over-emphasized in examining the accomplishments of the civil-rights movement. Considering the activists' extraordinary discipline in the face of power water hoses; aggressive dogs; police batons; steel bars; Southern jails; and marauding, sadistic killers, I found this an odd thing to say when I first read it. Later reflection brought me to a different interpretation. Courage is too often imagined as enduring pain and fear, and we even speak of the courage of animals—like a dog that will valiantly try to fight off a wolf. In this sense courage can be a primitivizing quality—as in the story that used to be told about Rosa Parks: that she was tired and said to herself, the hell with it, I'll sit in the white section come what may. Very frequently social movements like civil rights or the Egyptian uprising against Mubarak are seen as spontaneous expressions of people fed up with oppression. Understanding that people calculate their odds, choose their battles, and strategize their resistance reveals a different understanding of Payne's plea not to dwell too much on courage. He is arguing that social movements are complex intellectual projects. They are themselves political achievements, well before victories appear. This too is part of a prefigurative vision, one that justifies and honors building a movement with great care and thoughtfulness. It leads—in my view, not Payne's—to understanding that social-movement participation can be itself the highest form of citizenship.

Fourth, generational relations. SNCC's "youngsters" discovered that there were always some "elders" who already had a critique of their society, a sense of personal responsibility, and an analysis of the importance of collective action. They may have had no formal education or political affiliation but they usually had a history of participating in whatever small-scale efforts for social betterment and/or change had previously been possible. These older people, like the younger, typically come from families that exhibit a sense of social responsibility that might not appear as political to the new movement: they may have been active in their church or children's school, they may have been the ones who visited sick people or helped a down-and-out neighbor. SNCC learned that once the young people set up shop, these people appeared, as if they had been waiting. (This experience was the same in the early days of César Chávez's organizing among farmworkers.) As Tom Hayden put it, they arrived saying, in essence, "Where've you been? We've been waiting." SNCC worked to link young and old, and this did not always come easily, given young blacks' resentment of older generations that had not openly resisted. Overcoming that antipathy helped the youngsters draw on the material support and experience of their elders. It also helped construct an attitude of accepting with respect whatever contribution people could make, however small. This aspect of participatory democracy was a matter not of good manners but of need and strategy. And it too was prefigurative: a new society couldn't be built by a generation entirely alienated from older ones; more importantly, a movement would be strengthened through replacing a moralistic condemnation of past failure with a historical, empirical analysis of changing conditions, of the development of contradictions that weaken old regimes and allow movements for change greater chances of success. It is from understanding old failures in their context that organizers could perceive new opportunities.

Fifth, identities. Social scientists who study movements once discussed what kinds of personal identities attracted people to movements; now more of them understand that identities are reshaped through participation in movements.[5] The new identity is a sense of oneself as a person with a mission, a dedication—in this sense not entirely unlike being born again but, we can hope, more enduring. But individual identity change happens through a group process that provides a sense of belonging to a new community, in this case being part of a new civil-rights family. (This belonging among the beloved is dangerous because it creates groups that enjoy most and relax most by being with each other.) For African Americans in SNCC, identity shifted over time from an inter-racial to an intra-racial belonging, as it simultaneously transformed "black" from a race identity to a political identity. That identity transformation led to expelling whites. This was a heartbreaker for many people, black and white. But most of them never-theless understood the break as a creation not only of the racist society but also of participatory-democracy principles themselves, in the sense that it aimed to make sure that blacks were in charge of their own liberation struggle. It was, of course, a step back from immediately prefiguring a new society, but many were convinced that it was nonetheless a step toward achieving it.

Finally, gender. For better or worse, no such step was taken toward encourag-ing women to step away from their subordination to men. Inside SNCC's beloved family, male and female gender issues were not easily resolved. Just as there were powerful black leaders in interracial organizations, so there were a few powerful female leaders in mixed organizations. But as Southern black men gained self-confidence and ambition for recognition and leadership, the very principles of participatory democracy made women more sensitive to the frustration of their newly raised aspirations. It's well known by now that it is usually the collision between raised aspirations and their frustration that sparks social movements. Combine that with race, and the explosions happened all the more quickly, as black men's relations with white women infuriated black women. There were protests about sexism in SNCC, but they produced no resolution. The gender story within SNCC was a doubled loss: of female leadership and of potential cross-race female alliance. Prefiguring gender equality did not get far in SNCC.

The student/anti–Vietnam War movement did and didn't come from civil rights. Many of its members had volunteered in the Southern civil-rights movement and all of them were inspired—and their activist orientation ratcheted up—by civil rights; but most came from white privileged backgrounds and had never consciously suffered discrimination: as Port Huron said, they were *"bred in at least modest comfort, housed now in universities ... "* Their personal complaints were in part moral, a dismay at the hypocrisy and consumerism of American politics and culture; in part anxiety about nuclear war; and in part a visceral sense of alienation from both the Old Left and the U.S. mainstream. Its political strategy was not new: it called for pressuring the Democratic Party from the Left. What was new was a turn away from the working class as the exclusive agent of change (despite benefiting from funds from organized labor)—a turn that would, of course, lead to schisms a few years later.

The Port Huron statement was an existentialist manifesto, a call for taking up a moral obligation. It insisted, implicitly, that young people muster the courage to break from the conformist and fearful culture that deadened them. This aspect of the New Left's spirit was unique to the white-student-antiwar people in the movement, and remained central, perhaps, to its male members, because they were not struggling to free themselves from discrimination, unlike the black, women's, and gay movements. But with respect to the apathy that Port Huron saw on the campuses, it offered not a moralistic but a structural, historical explanation: that apathy had been constructed by the structure of higher education and by the consumerist, conformist pressures of Cold War politics. This led to perspective that was a necessary condition for the growth of the New Left: its anti–anti-Communism. Without that, its critique of the Old Left would have allowed it to be moved toward the anti-Communist liberalism of the Americans for Democratic Action.[6]

The most radical aspects of Port Huron's sensibility were the call for participatory democracy and the rejection of material incentives as a desirable basis for work and life. A call for a world where "work" was sought for self-fulfillment—*"that work should involve incentives worthier than money or survival. It should be educative, not stultifying; creative, not mechanical; self-directed, not manipulated"*—this was a dream available to prosperous people in a strong economy. It was also a youthful dream, one of people with little experience of the labor force. But precisely because of this proud assertion of a utopian aspiration, because it rejected charity and benevolence and refused to be practical, it gripped a generation of students—and the post-WWII expansion of public higher education in the U.S. had made that group far larger than previously.

That idealism foreshadowed an identifying characteristic of "the 1960s," a disdain for older people. (*"Never trust anyone over 30."*) Julius Lester, '60s civil-rights activist and writer, once remarked that the student movement began when white kids looked at their parents and didn't like what they saw. Such disparagement, despite the fact that Students for a Democratic Society (SDS) remained for a time funded by older-folks' organizations, resulting from its immersion in youth culture and campus life and its relatively prosperous class base. It would never achieve SNCC's inter-generational alliance.

The Statement called for participatory democracy only implicitly. It is in its discussion of apathy that we find its closest approach to prefigurative politics: *"The significance of these scattered movements lies not in their success or failure in gaining objectives ... [but in] breaking the crust of apathy and overcoming the inner alienation ....* "The idea is that one overcomes alienation through activism, which creates a democratic community, that must prefigure the society we would like to live in. Tom Hayden recently quoted both Thoreau's call to vote "not with a mere strip of paper but with your whole life" and John Dewey's claim that democracy should be "more than a form of government; it is primarily a mode of conjoint community experience."[7] Embryonic in Port Huron, these ideas were articulated later by Staughton Lynd, Greg Calvert, Carl Davidson, Pat Hansen, and Ken McEldowney in SDS. Calvert wrote, "While struggling to liberate the world, we would create the liberated world in our midst. While fighting to destroy the power which had created the loveless anti-community, we would ourselves create the community of love—*The Beloved Community.*"[8]

The attachment to this prefigurative vision, to creating a new world inside the old, was the more passionate because of how it was belittled. In one phrase or another, more-experienced elders (and some practical youngsters too) were constantly telling New Leftists to be realistic. Southern black elders thought SNCC and other militant groups were impatient at best and courting death at worst. Democrats and some peace-movement leaders told SDS to dress better, cut their hair, avoid over-provocation, and make alliances in the mainstream. Antifeminists told the women's-liberation activists that biology *was* destiny and earlier feminists told them to avoid shocking people. Rejecting that sort of advice was, however, close to the core spirit of the New Left. Prefigurative politics was a two-way proposition: you couldn't achieve democracy without practicing it now, and if you didn't practice it now, you would lose the vision and the commitment to a democratic world.

Besides, participatory democracy and the prefigurative mode made participation in activism attractive and pleasurable. One of the often-missed truths about social movements is that they are fun. Veterans of these movements typically describe them as the best years of their lives, and the friendships formed in them are often the most lasting. If participatory democracy works, no one can be a mere listener and no one can tune out, but everyone speaks and feels that his/

her views count. It requires energy and is therefore tiring, but it can also help prevent boredom and feeling disregarded. At the same time active participation makes it harder for a group to make irresponsible, unencumbered decisions.

But participatory democracy is exceedingly demanding and may ask more than everyone can give. To practice it while organizing—to reach out to new people—one had to begin by listening. This radical idea has had to be reinvented frequently, as it is so easily lost and so difficult to practice. (It was one of settlement-house founder Jane Addams's most democratic practices in the early years of Hull-House: her instruction that settlements should begin by learning about the neighborhood from the views and conditions of its residents, so that one could formulate a program of action directed toward its residents' needs and desires. When Sheila Rowbotham worked for the Greater London Council under Labour's Ken Livingstone, one of the first things she did was interview working-class mothers about how the city could help them.) Listening to grievances did not, of course, provide analyses, and organizers had to engage with grievances, searching for the structural roots of individual problems.

Moreover, participatory democracy was not a formula for how to get done what was needed. When it became understood primarily as a description of process within a New Left organization, as sometimes happened, it could even become an obstacle to organizing. Critics in the New as well as the Old Left charged that this requirement for internal participatory democracy and building a community of equals was self-indulgent. It signaled a move away from politics, they argued. Its purism turned the focus too much toward how meetings and the organization were run, a focus on how members of the club worked together. It created coded practices that distinguish insiders unless great care is taken to bring outsiders in. It created, critics saw, a preciousness that resulted in excluding outsiders at best, and disdaining outsiders at worst.

This was not, of course, the intention of most SDS organizers. And certainly not of those who wanted to build either campus or community organizations. They understood participatory democracy as an aspiration. They understood the tensions and problems of the ideal and tried to create an organization that combined active participation with accountable leadership. But understandings of participatory democracy seemed to change after a few years, equating it with direct democracy, allowing no structures of representation. SDSers sought to reject formal representative procedures because they had experienced how these became bureaucratized and rendered passive those at the bottom. Conflicts over the degree of centralization arose. Many "chapters" were weak and needed money and communication with a central office but others "did their own thing." None of these conflicts were insuperable. Prefigurative politics does not outlaw compromise. SDSers could live with the tension between perfect,

100-percent-equal participation, and getting things done, by compromising and improvising.

And it did. We should not underestimate what SDS accomplished. It broke through the coercive patriotism of the Cold War and educated millions to recognize domestic and international injustice. It made hundreds of thousands comfortable with dissent. Hundreds, perhaps thousands, of its veterans opted for work that promotes social justice. There might have been no Barack Obama without SDS.

But there were several problems that could not easily be compromised or improvised away, problems that may have been unsolvable. The first was the problem of fast success: the movement grew in size, in geographic spread, and in diversity beyond any possibility of making it coherent. The size of the country, the variety of campuses, the constant turnover of SDS membership due to the number of members who graduated or left the campuses, the growth of a non-student antiwar movement were quite possibly un-coordinatable. SDS and several other organizations needed staffs and offices; not everyone could volunteer and some needed wages or stipends. Their job was to try to communicate with and coordinate a mass movement. They were herding cats. (SNCC had never had to do this: it *was* its staff and only its staff, and almost all got financial support.)

Ideological divisions could not be isolated from organizational form. The very rapid spread of SDS raised the questions, Could students be agents of change? Could universities be useful sites for creating change? What came after school? "Student" was not a stable identity, nor even a temporary political identity. A combination of awareness of and guilt about the relative privilege of many SDS leaders led many to reject the idea of organizing on behalf of themselves and turn rather to organizing others who, in their varied analyses, could be agents of change: the working class, the poor, the Third World, African Americans. Different priorities, both strategic and moral, competed: the sufferings and aspirations of the Vietnamese, repression of the Black Panther Party, and the civil-rights struggles of American Indians, Asian Americans, Chicanos. These political problems, as Richard Rothstein wrote, "do not have formal solutions."[9]

How could we possibly condemn SDS for not successfully creating an organizational structure that was democratic, participatory, accountable, effective, consistent, unified, and yet decentralized? I examine its failings without a sense that another group of people could have done better. In SDS's case, an anti-leadership, participatory-democracy set of convictions became at times a religion, perfectionist in its clinging to absolutes, and failing to challenge invocations of slogans that had become scripture. Quoting Rothstein again, dissenters were "easily intimidated by their own acceptance of the moral categories in which the debate was couched."[10] Participatory democracy also gave sectarian groups freedom to recruit within the movement and, ultimately, to devastate or at least fragment the movement.

As representative leadership became disempowered by both formal and political problems, an unelected, unaccountable leadership arose. This problem was enunciated first and best within the women's movement, which I'll turn to next, but let me put it simply here. It is a version of the problem with the ultra-democratic SNCC notion of leadership; i.e., that everyone can be a leader. People are unequal in persuasive skills and reputations and confidence. Just as many musicians often come out of musical families, so many political analysts absorbed skills from their families. Others simply have a knack for strategic thinking. This inequality is magnified many times in meetings. Some people speak more persuasively, marshal arguments more powerfully, promote analyses more cogently than others. Their talk can silence others, render them more passive, or more passively resentful. Building an organization with many intellectuals magnified this inequality yet further.

National SDS decided to combat vested interests in leadership positions by requiring rotating officers. But a more continuous de facto leadership arose informally. Elected leaders, fresh every year, needed advice and consultation and for this they turned to individuals, often from the early leadership, typically the most confident, articulate, politically sophisticated (and quite possibly best-educated) men, whether they were in office or not. This behind-the-scenes leadership was literally invisible to many newer SDS members. As the paid staff at the national office became the only source of continuity, elected leadership became less influential, and their own diffidence about leading reinforced that tendency. In this way principles and structures designed to combat the accumulation of power at the top but in some ways it did the opposite, by creating an unchanging group of implicit leaders—later called "heavies." The antileadership perspective also contributed to a lack of training programs to develop skills in new people, because doing so meant recognizing that some had skills that others could learn. The antileadership aura made leaders reticent and indecisive. Lacking clear priorities set from below, they felt out on a limb, unwilling to lead. Doubts about the strategic importance of students didn't help.

The splintering of SDS into sectarian revolutionary groups was by no means caused by these internal problems. Those groups arose because of the intensity of U.S. government repression of demands for change, its continued vicious brutality in Vietnam and then throughout Indochina, and its refusal to reject a policy of supporting corrupt and repressive dictators in the rest of the world. My purpose here is not to criticize SDS. It was a great achievement in itself and its influence on the country was considerable, not to mention the campuses that were permanently revolutionized in the treatment of students and greater openness to honest intellectual dissent. I agree wholeheartedly with Hayden in his claim (made in correspondence with me) that SNCC and SDS "catalyzed more social change in their seven-year life spans than many respectable and well-funded NGOs accomplished in decades." But I am trying to articulate the challenges that face democratic activism for social justice.

The women's-liberation movement, by far the largest movement of the New Left, arose out of both SNCC and SDS. Its very name reveals its identification with the anticolonial movements of Vietnam and elsewhere, like the Third World Liberation Front. But we have to be clear about who these feminists were.

Until sometime around 1975 there were two distinct women's movements. An "industrial feminism" had arisen with considerable strength after WWII, as working-class women fought against unions' gender policies, which were at best exclusionary—refusing to put resources into organizing women's jobs—and at worst directly discriminatory. At the same time Old Left women, such as United Electrical Workers' Betty Friedan, historian Gerda Lerner, and folksinger Malvina Reynolds, were raising issues of sex discrimination in peace movements like the Women's International League for Peace and Freedom (WILPF) and Women Strike for Peace (WSP). These streams joined to form the National Organization for Women (NOW) in 1966, which was at first, oddly like SDS, dependent on the United Auto Workers. This long-standing organization was already campaigning for equal pay and equal opportunity for working women when the more radical women's-liberation movement began to emerge in 1968. But NOW did not at first challenge gender standards more broadly, or take up issues of sexual freedom, reproductive rights, or violence; it was not eager to be associated with the Left (as witness Betty Friedan's and Gerda Lerner's early efforts to expunge their Old Left history from public note). NOW was uninterested in utopian notions of democracy and process; its strength was its commitment to making legislative change through powerful lobbying.

The women's-liberation movement, by contrast, began in 1967–68, independently of NOW. Like SDS, it assumed a youthful character that rejected and even scorned the older women's efforts. No intergenerational alliance here.

Women's liberation never "broke" from the New Left. For as long as we can confidently speak of a mass New Left, the women's-liberation movement was a part of it. Its roots were in the student movements both in personnel and in ideas. Some early feminists had gone south to participate in civil-rights protests; virtually all its early members came out of or identified with anti–Vietnam War politics. They took a great deal from civil rights: the examples of solidarity, risk-taking and courage; the utopian demand that democracy live up to its name; and the energy of fighting one's own oppression. They shared with the student movement moral outrage at American brutality toward African Americans and

Vietnamese, and at the conformity, superficiality and consumerism of U.S. culture. They not only continued to appear at the demonstrations against the Vietnam war, for the Vietnamese National Liberation Front, for freeing the Black Panthers, for challenging racism, for labor unions, for disarmament—in short, for all the key causes of the New Left. But they also initiated many activities that were not exclusively focused on women's issues.

The new feminists protested sexism in SDS, of course. They were critical of male grandstanding, adventurism, machismo. The sexual objectification of women that has permeated male culture for eons was in SDS and the broader student culture too. When early SDS and women's activist Marilyn Webb spoke at an early antiwar rally in Washington, D.C., and a group of men in the front of the audience called out, "take her off the stage and fuck her; that's what she needs," this attack was not apolitical. Consciously or not, the guys who shouted that obscenity were stabbing women in their most vulnerable psychic spots—their need to be attractive and appropriately feminine and safe. (By the way, the vulnerability is not only psychic; it is also physical.) Women who had written brilliant political and historical analyses in their college courses were afraid to speak in large meetings mainly because of their awareness of being seen as a spectacle, of being evaluated on their degree of desirability.[11] No wonder they could not speak with the same authority that men exhibited in SDS meetings. It was not only men's "ways of seeing," in John Berger's sense, but also men's ways of hearing: a woman might make a point, then a man might make the same point, and the point was thereafter referred to as the man's. Men automatically regarded other men as their audience, comrades, costrategists, or adversaries. (In SNCC, the commonality of facing brutality and imprisonment may have reduced this male bonding to some extent.) Not all men participated in this appropriative culture, of course, and most did not choose it. But the culture and the male political bonding was a social structure, not an individual characteristic, and it was impossible to opt out of it entirely since men's masculinity was also vulnerable. Certainly the problem was not created by SDS or SNCC, but it resided there nevertheless.

That a newly militant women's movement emerged from disrespect for women active in mixed movements had many precedents. This was the pattern in the French revolutions of 1789, 1848, and 1870. In the U.S., attempts to shut up female abolitionists generated the women's-rights movement of the 1840s. Indeed, the opposition to women claiming public space and power contributed to a new identity that was both cause and effect of the women's-liberation movement. I am talking, of course, about a *political subjectivity,* in some ways parallel to that of black power: a realization that a gender system—although the concept was not named at first—was responsible for much of our experience; and a *political identity* as a new basis for social-justice activism.

Sexism from within the New Left pushed women toward autonomous groups, of course. But by far the more important influence toward autonomous women's groups was the need for consciousness-raising. As a feminist identity formed, however, women's organizing strategy had to differ radically from both the civil-rights and antiwar movements. Unlike African Americans, the predominantly white women who began the women's-liberation movement discovered with shock that they had long been unconscious of their own oppression because they had accepted it as a "natural" and inevitable outgrowth of their sex. Recruitment to a feminist outlook represented for many a sudden realization that they had been unaware of how discrimination had hounded and limited them all their lives. By contrast, it was a rare African American who had not understood from earliest childhood the fundamental unfairness of the oppression of her/his people. To organize, SNCC did not need to convince people that they were held down, forced into a subordination profitable to others; instead it had to convince people that they had the power to enforce change. But many women did have to unlearn what Marxists would call a false consciousness.[12]

The women's-liberation movement differed from the antiwar/student move-ment in another way: although SDS directed some of its critique toward uni-versities and cultural conformity, its greatest passion was fury at U.S. brutality toward others—the Vietnamese and African Americans. Feminists were protest-ing their own treatment. This resulted in some "guilt-tripping," both external and internal. Unlike, say, working-class women fighting for equal treatment by employers and unions, many women's-liberation-movement members had to resist feelings that their relative privilege made it unseemly to complain. They heard these criticisms not only from conservatives and liberals, but often from their New Left male comrades. As Marxism gained strength within the New Left, attacks took a classic form: come the Socialist revolution, women's second-class status would disappear, so women should join Marxist-Leninist groups and postpone their demands. Even more insidious was the claim that Marxism had already produced the best analysis of women's subjection—that it was a product of capitalism and economic exploitation—and that new analyses were pointless. Happily, most women's-liberation-movement members were part of the New, not the Old Left and understood that new circumstances necessitated new analyses.

The first women's-liberation groups were informal meetings or women's caucuses within larger New Left formations, and the key word was "autono-mous," not independent or separate. Later they took on identities of their own. Excavating and admitting to the hidden injuries of gender required women-only groups. They provided, first, freedom in which to complain and vent anger without fear of consequences, and freedom to explore the intimate. They also provided, second, the comradely comparisons that gave rise to analyses. They were learning by unlearning, so to speak, the conventions of gender and male dominance. The practice in these groups soon led to an entirely new form of prefigurative politics that came to be called consciousness-raising.[13] As is usually the case, a new practice arose from a new content, a new method of organizing from the nature of the task. The process was, ideally, one of group discovery, of shared empirical learning that led to generalization and theory.

To some extent consciousness-raising groups were reinventing an analysis of women's subordination. Women's ignorance of previous feminist analyses was not accidental or a result of our laziness but was constructed by active historical suppression. By the end of the 19th century feminists like Elizabeth Cady Stanton had elaborated a deep and sophisticated critique of male dominance and, occasionally, of gender itself. Moreover she was a sex radical, very close to the Free Lovers in her thinking. Yet no history course then taught a word she had written.[14] A generation of historians of women had published superb history in the earlier 20th century; not only were their books unread and unmentioned in other scholarship, but the universities actually became more exclusive of women in the mid 20th century than they had been earlier.

Ignorant of this earlier work, the consciousness-raising groups, unlike, say, Marxist discussion groups, did not read. Rather they started with the evidence at hand of women's lives in the 1950s and 1960s. Their process rested on existing women's gender characteristics, notably their socialization toward intimate and emotional talk with other women, and then subjected those very characteristics to critique. Having bonded with other female New Left activists, women's-liberation founders had realized that many women considered their problems to be personal and that this misconception isolated them. As in Katz and Allport's concept of pluralistic ignorance,[15] many women tended to feel that they were the only one who didn't like their job, their sexual activity, their housework, their body, etc. Enunciating their discontents, consciousness-raising-group members soon recognized that those feelings were widespread and reclassified them as social, not personal; once that was understood the search for causes began.[16] The consciousness-raising groups were not support groups, although they were supportive; they were not therapy groups, although for many they were therapeutic. What went on were conversations, usually in someone's living room, frequently accompanied by snacks.[17] People could interrupt or wander well off the topic, but there was typically careful listening. Comments were often very personal, and safety in revealing intimacies was guaranteed by a stringent (and universal, I believe) rule that nothing would be repeated outside the group. The personal comments did not, ideally, remain anecdotes but led to a rethinking of past experience from a new perspective. Encounters that had once seemed routine or idiosyncratic were reinterpreted as socially constructed patterns: why women were self-conscious in large meetings, why men didn't do housework, why women outnumbered men in peace groups. Consciousness-raising groups influenced the gay-rights movement with their critique of compulsory heterosexuality and, perhaps more important, their analysis of what counted as "normal" sex acts. Many lesbians came out in consciousness-raising groups. Consciousness-raising meetings were intense even as there might be giggles or parodies of the "boys." (Calling New Left guys "boys" was a sardonic protest by women who had for years been called "girls.") Topics ranged from menstruation to television to the latest antiwar leaflet.

Consciousness-raising was the source of most of the new feminist analyses. (Later, of course, as a generation of feminist intellectuals gained academic positions, many created feminist theory in a more traditional vein of theory: abstruse, philosophical work aimed at other academics.) The theory of the women's-liberation movement was formulated and disseminated differently, through hundreds of "underground" New Left newspapers and pamphlets—which spread surprisingly quickly in that age without digital media. These theoretical analyses invented new and redefined old concepts such as gender and exploitation, and examined with new tools problems such as war and violence, imperialism/colonialism, rape and incest, job segregation, electoral politics, organizing, education, health and medicine, mental health and psychiatry, family norms, art, and the strengths and inadequacies of Marxism and liberalism.

The groups spread virally: one week there were 10, then 100, then 500, and so on. In Boston in 1969, friends of friends asked to join the first consciousness-raising "collective," but that group knew it could not practice consciousness-raising with a constantly growing and changing group. So the first group announced in the local New Left paper (*The Old Mole*) and the weekly *Phoenix* (Boston's version of the *Village Voice*) an open meeting at which women would get help in starting their own consciousness-raising groups. At the first meeting, a hundred women showed up, and a hundred more at the second, and so on.

In Boston, these consciousness-raising groups were soon pulled together in a citywide organization, Bread and Roses. The same happened in Chicago and a few other cities, and these defined themselves as Socialist-feminist groups. In many cities, however, large organizations never formed, because the dominant mood was quite consciously anti-organizational. The sources of that antagonism came in part from the sensibility that animated Port Huron: distrust of bureaucracy, of centralism, of authority. The women's-liberation movement represented a peak of anti-authoritarianism. The new feminists directed much of their fury at the experts who had been lying to them, prescribing social conformity, holding up conventional standards of what women should be and do—doctors, psychologists, psychiatrists, lawyers, teachers, ministers, and politicians. The best-selling book series that began with *Our Bodies, Ourselves* grew out of an attempt to identify gynecologists and obstetricians who treated women with respect, an attempt that produced a very, very short list.[18]

Simultaneously the ethos of participatory democracy prevailed. The new feminists shared a constitutional understanding that every member of a consciousness-raising group was equal. There would be no leaders. There were no chairwomen, no rules of order, no agenda. Some groups enforced equality in speaking: They might choose a topic, then ask each person to speak once before anyone could add a second comment. Some groups used poker chips, allotting, say, five to each person; each time you spoke you put one in the pot, and when you were out, you couldn't speak again until everyone was out. These systems must have inhibited the development of thinking through back-and-forth responses and challenges.

This radical egalitarianism may have been the perfect form for the content being produced—consciousness-raising. It allowed all the assembled experiences to be added to the discussion, provided the group was small enough that everyone could contribute but just large enough to include a range of experience. The form was obviously prefigurative, at least in the time spent together. Consciousness-raising groups were intensely enjoyable. We ate and listened to music; we were ecstatic when Jefferson Airplane released "Volunteers." Members hated to miss a meeting. Some groups continued for decades. They constituted, of course, a respite from daily pressures, an island, a weekly free space within a far more complex and hierarchical life of jobs, bosses, coworkers, families, bureaucracies, large institutions, governments, none of which operated according to our rules. This is why consciousness-raising meetings were so much fun. They were not required to be immediately goal-oriented, so they allowed a free brainstorming that turned out to be highly productive.

In larger organizations, however, participatory, egalitarian, prefigurative practices did not function as well—though better, I think, than in SDS. (To be fair, the women's-liberation movement never tried to create a national organization.) There were, of course, women who grandstanded, who could not be terse, who craved the recognition that was accorded to politically correct rhetoric, but not as many and not so badly behaved as in SDS. Bread and Roses, with membership in the hundreds and meetings occasionally of over one hundred, experienced difficulties in sticking to the practices of its constituent consciousness-raising collectives. Let me name some of the problems: meetings were too long; those members with tighter schedules would depart, leaving decisions to be made by rumps; others quit arguing in order to go home; letting everyone have a turn to speak often meant that conversations did not remain focused but wandered onto different topics; there was no procedure for requiring comments to be succinct; people who missed previous meetings or who were new could force the group to go over old ground; no decision was permanent because all decisions could be reopened; chairing authority was easily undermined. These problems tended to drive out those who had less time, and they including working women, working-class women, mothers, older women; as in SDS, only the young and relatively unencumbered could tolerate the structurelessness. Basic organizational needs were not met: collecting dues, acculturating new members, defining members' responsibilities.

Gendered patterns exacerbated these difficulties. The experience of living with male dominance made many women even more anti-hierarchical than men, and resentment of leaders was strong. Women accustomed to being disregarded, or to being so intimidated that they feared to speak up, developed exaggerated fears of being run over by women whose confidence and articulateness seemed like that of the men they had experienced. "Collective" was a sacred liturgical word and "individualist" a damnation. Emotional expression repeatedly trumped decision-making and political argument. An interjection common in women's meetings, "I feel uncomfortable with"—whether in reference to a discussion, process, decision, etc.—could have the effect of preventing progress toward a decision.

The organizational effects of these anti-hierarchy principles—and emotions—were remarkably similar to those in SDS. In what social-movements theorist Jo Freeman called "the tyranny of structurelessness," unaccountable leaders arose. They were called the "heavies," because what they said and proposed carried disproportionate weight. Pretty much everyone knew who was and wasn't a heavy. In large meetings, statements by the heavies could carry the impression that there was a consensus, which a vote would have belied. In one sense the problem was exacerbated by too little focus on internal development of leadership and too much focus on outreach organizing. There were no formal provisions for encouraging greater participation in the large meetings, in the formulation of theory and projects; there was no training in the skills of chairing meetings, assigning responsibilities, writing press releases, and holding press conferences, managing money, maintaining organizational records. Women's-liberation schools throughout the country taught everything from Marxist theory to women's history to auto mechanics, but few taught organizing or leadership skills.

The anti-organizational, anti-hierarchical bent of women's liberation resulted, as elsewhere, in unaccountable leadership. The problem was particularly apparent as the national press began covering the women's movement, because journalists need spokespeople and the movement didn't provide them. The New York–centric media thus intersected with the nature of NYC feminism, where journalists and writers played large roles and became the face of the women's movement. Some of these spokeswomen did valuable work but they tended to present, understandably, a particular stratum of issues—those involving discrimination against professional women and disparaging media imagery.

As in SDS, organizational stability suffered from theoretical conflict as a split between Socialist feminism[19] and radical feminism developed. Within the already thin scholarship about the women's-liberation movement, its Socialist-feminist branches have been particularly neglected. In Boston, Chicago, and several other large cities, Socialist feminism predominated; and even in NYC, Socialist-feminist single-issue groups such as Committee for Abortion Rights and Against Sterilization Abuse (CARASA)[20] had lasting impact. Instead of agitating for women's equality only, Socialist feminists advocated fundamental transformation of class and race dominance as well. A reproductive-rights movement offers the best nationwide example of the Socialist feminist analysis. Rather than campaigning for abortion rights, organizations fought for public funding of abortion. Rather than focusing exclusively on birth control, they emphasized poor women's right to bear and raise children as well as not to. Having discovered a history of coercive sterilization of poor and minority women, they exposed these practices and forced the federal government to install protections that radically reduced them. Uncovering the dangers of the first contraceptive pills and IUDs, they exposed the callousness of the pharmaceutical industry and forced the FDA to install tighter oversight of big pharma. Socialist feminism rested on the premises that many forms and shapes of dominance affected women; that women's subordination was imbedded in the structures of society and economy, not primarily in the sexist attitudes of individual men; that both men and women could be both victims and beneficiaries of different patterns of dominance; that male dominance over women was not necessarily the worst or most urgent problem in various situations.

By contrast, the theoretical stream called "radical feminism"[21] moved in another direction, building on the notion that male dominance was *the* fundamental form of dominance from which all other forms grew. Its radical insights were vital early in the movement, given that the complex forms and methods of male dominance had not been well exposed previously. Yet, paradoxically, radical feminism was often the least democratic of the feminisms, its groups often deferring to individual leaders. This tendency also assumed authoritarian forms, intolerant of dissent, and people were expelled from groups. Its very theoretical principle, that maleness alone was the enemy of freedom, made democracy among women of less importance. Radical feminists did condemn class and race dominance but, in a logic similar to that of some orthodox Marxists, argued that since there was one and only one basic form of dominance, once it was abolished, all other forms of dominance would fall. As a result, by the mid 1970s radical feminism was shading into liberal and cultural feminism, focusing on women's equality and women's unique culture.

Despite these many problems, the women's-liberation movement engaged effectively in both mobilizing and organizing. There were many women's demonstrations—Take Back the Night marches protesting the threat of violence that made women fear the streets; reproductive-rights demonstrations; in Boston, a joint Bread and Roses/Combahee River Collective mobilization to protest a horrifying spate of murders of black women. Women's-liberation groups marched together with older women's groups like WSP and WILPF in antiwar demonstrations.

Moreover, the feminist version of participatory democracy gave rise to some good organizing. Activist proposals emanating from small groups then mobilized larger numbers; the reproductive rights mentioned above had that trajectory. Decentralization allowed for quick decision-making and action. I'll use Boston for examples: When an antiwar work-stoppage and classroom boycott was being planned for October 1969 (the "Moratorium"), one consciousness-raising group realized that the male organizers had not reached out to clerical workers, so the group quickly produced a leaflet inviting office staff at universities to come to a lunchtime discussion about the action.[22] There was no need for approval by the large Bread and Roses organization. A similar group began *Our Bodies, Ourselves,* another began a clerical-worker-organizing campaign that ultimately became the union 9 to 5 (now SEIU local 925). Sex/gender-education classes for teenagers were perhaps the analog to the citizenship schools in the South. One group took the early version of *Our Bodies, Ourselves* into housing projects in Somerville, where they met working-class women's rage about their lives, and their response to the book: "Why weren't we taught this in school?" Bread and Roses members picketed the for-profit abortion clinics that sprang up after states repealed their antiabortion laws (which happened well before Roe v. Wade) to protest both exploitive conditions for abortion counselors and the speed-up that resulted in inadequate time for helping pregnant women think through their decisions carefully. Members joined Mothers for Adequate Welfare, which had formed out of an SDS ERAP project, and worked with the welfare-rights movement. Other groups campaigned for daycare. All this and much more happened because of the sharp and vast burst of human energy and optimism, a fission force created by the sensation of enablement and authority.

Women's liberation was in many ways more successful than civil rights or the antiwar movement. U.S. militarism and support of right-wing dictators did not end. Structural racism did not end. Neither did sexism, but there have been truly fundamental changes in our gender system, in employment, education, religion, politics, and personal relationships.

Participatory democracy and prefigurative politics have limits, but they are not to blame for the decline of the women's movements any more than SDS or SNCC. The New Christian Right and neo-conservatism were growing apace. As the victories of the mass women's movement piled up, no one predicted the strength and virulence of the backlash. (Although, in retrospect, this failure of prediction showed that the women's-liberation movement did not understand itself well—did not understand how fundamentally its transformation of the gender system seemed to subvert the sources of security on which many people relied.)

In the fall of 2011, I'm sure, every veteran of SNCC, SDS, or the women's-liberation movement was encouraged by the emergence of Occupy (as of the Arab Spring and the Wisconsin struggle beforehand). Occupy has been especially welcome given its commitment to public activism and its focus on inequality. Its warp-speed global spread, while enabled by digital communications, was not created by technology, but rested on a global discontent—although not always conscious—with neoliberalism.

Both participants and observers have been particularly enthralled by Occupy's version of participatory democracy. In some ways Occupy has refined and developed participatory-democracy methods. Consider the "people's mic," a process that may have been brought to NY from Spain, or may have begun because NYC police would not allow microphones in Zuccotti Park—who knows? But it is a piece of tactical genius, providing practical audibility, powerful symbolism, and required participation. Having to repeat what a speaker says prevents anyone from tuning out, and asks of all those present to hear the words again, in one's own voice. One either owns the words or must consciously disavow them or, ideally, articulate one's objections. The hand gestures of support, disagreement, unsureness, or neutrality encourage active listening and signal responses even from those who may not speak. Other gestures signify attempts to manage direct democracy more efficiently: motions indicating that one has information to offer, that the speaker is going on too long, that the meeting has wandered away from the agreed-on topic. The people's mic slows down a process, but that is an extremely valuable factor when there is a need to avoid quick decisions. It combines with a distaste for voting and an emphasis rather on consensus. This is an inefficiency, to be sure, but it may have advantages. In New York in late 2011, it apparently headed off an ill-considered impulse to provoke the NYC police after a police attack on peaceful gatherers. But such events create a warning that repression is difficult for a nonviolent but radically democratic group to deal with. I find myself wondering how such a slowdown might have affected SDS.

The prefigurative nature of Occupy arose, in part, from the tactic of encampment: occupying people organized small utopian societies, providing food, toilets, showers, clothing, bedding, entertainment, art, education, policing, etc. As the occupations grew, problems multiplied. They faced disruptions by unstable and even crazy people, provocateurs, police agents, and some who were all of the above. (In NYC, reportedly, police encouraged unbalanced homeless people to head for Occupy so as to disrupt—and some did just that.) Women felt more comfortable and more respected while the movement was small, and lost substantial ground as it grew. There were some terrible failures: assaults, including rapes; thefts; fights.

Occupy has since become dispersed and decentralized into networks. Its future projects surely will require moving away from perfect democracy and from prefiguring a perfect society. But such moves do not require throwing out democratic and prefigurative goals: they are aspirations, not formulas for organizing.

Linda Gordon, university professor of the humanities at NYU, is a historian who writes and teaches about social movements, gender, and imperialism. She was active in the civil-rights, antiwar, and women's movements. Among her many books are The Moral Property of Women, *a history of birth control politics;* The Great Arizona Orphan Abduction, *a tale about Mexican Americans and vigilantes in Arizona; and* Dorothea Lange: A Life Beyond Limits, *a biography of the great depression-era photographer.*

Notes

1. Scientists define a cluster concept as one that is defined by a weighted list of criteria, such that no one of these criteria is either necessary or sufficient for membership. In plainer language it refers to a group in which each member shares many but not necessarily all characteristics.

2. This is a perspective also argued by Van Gosse in *The Movements of the New Left 1950–1975* (2004) and *Rethinking the New Left: An Interpretive History* (2005).

3. See Adolph Reed, Jr., *The Jesse Jackson Phenomenon.*

4. This particular insight of Payne's has made me less disdainful of American voters' seemingly apolitical reasoning: that Romney would be a good president because he was a good businessman; that Michele Bachmann could be a good president because she had raised so many children while holding a job.

5. Jo Reger, "Organizational Dynamics and Construction of Multiple Feminist Identities in the National Organization for Women," *Gender and Society* 16 #5, Oct. 2002.

6. "Tom Hayden's New Port Huron Statement," www.truthdig.com/report/item/20060328_hayden_port_huron/. The anti–anti-Communism may have been

rooted, paradoxically, in both its red-diaper and its non-red-diaper members: the former, because they recognized implicitly that the U.S. domestic aspects of the Communist Party included much activism that was not authoritarian or undemocratic; the latter because they had not experienced the intense anger that non-Communists in the Old Left felt toward the Communist Party.

7.   Calvert in *New Left Notes,* Dec. 25, 1966, quoted in Wini Breines, *Community and Organization in the New Left, 1962–1968: The Great Refusal* (1981, 1989).

8.   Ibid.

9.   Richard Rothstein, "Representative Democracy in SDS," *Liberation,* February 1972, pp. 11, 16.

10.   Ibid. I experienced this personally at Swarthmore College in the Quakers' insistence on consensus rather than voting.

11.   Linda Phelps, "Death in the Spectacle," 1971, in *Dear Sisters: Dispatches from the Women's Liberation Movement,* ed. Baxandall and Gordon (NY: Basic Books, 2000), pp. 175–179.

12.   This was particularly true of women who had been students recently, because colleges and universities were typically far more egalitarian than the world of employment and marriage. While the women might not speak as much in classes, their grades and papers were often just as good as men's. Many of us were shocked at our treatment in our first mainstream jobs.

13.   Some locate the origin of the term in Mao's "speak bitterness" campaigns, ironically, since the women's liberation movement version could not have been more anti-Marxist-Leninist-Maoist. But the term had also been used in the "Old Left," in speaking of raising the consciousness of workers who did not know they were oppressed.

14.   My grade school in Portland, Oregon, the Duniway school, was named after a major suffragist, but I didn't learn this until after I finished my PhD in history.

15.   Pluralistic ignorance, a term coined by Floyd H. Allport in 1931, describes "a situation where a majority of group members privately reject a norm, but assume (incorrectly) that most others accept it." Daniel Katz and Floyd H. Allport, *Students' Attitudes: A Report of the Syracuse University Reaction Study* (Syracuse, NY: Craftsman, 1931).

16.   Much of the discussion of consciousness raising that follows comes from the experiences of Bread-and-Roses groups in Boston, as well as from Chude Pamela Allen, *Free Space: A Perspective on the Small Group in Women's Liberation* (Times Change Press, 1970) and Rosalyn Baxandall and Linda Gordon, eds., *Dear Sisters: Dispatches from the Women's Liberation Movement* (2000).

17.   Serving food at meetings seems to be a characteristically female mode of operation.

18.   To cite just one example, perhaps needed for today's postfeminist generation, the 1960s was still a time when a physician would not tell a woman that she had cancer, lest she "overreact," but would give the information to her husband instead.

19. There is an important distinction between Socialist and Marxist feminism, which are frequently and mistakenly melded. The latter grew mainly in attachment to Marxist-Leninist parties, Leninist, Maoist, and Trotskyist, and was distinguished by its adherence to existing Marxist theory about women's subordination; this tendency did not see the necessity for developing analyses that broke with essential Marxist categories, while Socialist feminism did.

20. At the time there seemed to be no question about the legitimacy of contraception!

21. This is a confusing term because a radical feminist could mean a Left feminist in the UK and in some U.S. regions.

22. *Dear Sisters,* p. 273.

The Port Huron Statement of the Students for a Democratic Society*

Introduction: Agenda for a Generation

We are people of this generation, bred in at least modest comfort, housed now in universities, looking uncomfortably to the world we inherit.

When we were kids the United States was the wealthiest and strongest country in the world: the only one with the atom bomb, the least scarred by modern war, an initiator of the United Nations that we thought would distribute Western influence throughout the world. Freedom and equality for each individual, government of, by, and for the people—these American values we found good, principles by which we could live as men. Many of us began maturing in complacency.

As we grew, however, our comfort was penetrated by events too troubling to dismiss. First, the permeating and victimizing fact of human degradation, symbolized by the Southern struggle against racial bigotry, compelled most of us from silence to activism. Second, the enclosing fact of the Cold War, symbolized by the presence of the Bomb, brought awareness that we ourselves, and our friends, and millions of abstract "others" we knew more directly because of our common peril, might die at any time. We might deliberately ignore, or avoid, or fail to feel all other human problems, but not these two, for these were too immediate and crushing in their impact, too challenging in the demand that we as individuals take the responsibility for encounter and resolution.

*For this reprinting of the Port Huron Document, minor changes to syntax, punctuation, and formatting have been made for clarity.

While these and other problems either directly oppressed us or rankled our consciences and became our own subjective concerns, we began to see complicated and disturbing paradoxes in our surrounding America. The declaration "all men are created equal" rang hollow before the facts of Negro life in the South and the big cities of the North. The proclaimed peaceful intentions of the United States contradicted its economic and military investments in the Cold War status quo.

We witnessed, and continue to witness, other paradoxes. With nuclear energy whole cities can easily be powered, yet the dominant nationstates seem more likely to unleash destruction greater than that incurred in all wars of human history. Although our own technology is destroying old and creating new forms of social organization, men still tolerate meaningless work and idleness. While two-thirds of mankind suffers undernourishment, our own upper classes revel amidst superfluous abundance. Although world population is expected to double in forty years, the nations still tolerate anarchy as a major principle of international conduct and uncontrolled exploitation governs the sapping of the earth's physical resources. Although mankind desperately needs revolutionary leadership, America rests in national stalemate, its goals ambiguous and tradition-bound instead of informed and clear, its democratic system apathetic and manipulated rather than "of, by, and for the people."

Not only did tarnish appear on our image of American virtue, not only did disillusion occur when the hypocrisy of American ideals was discovered, but we began to sense that what we had originally seen as the American Golden Age was actually the decline of an era. The worldwide outbreak of revolution against colonialism and imperialism, the entrenchment of totalitarian states, the menace of war, overpopulation, international disorder, supertechnology—these trends were testing the tenacity of our own commitment to democracy and freedom and our abilities to visualize their application to a world in upheaval.

Our work is guided by the sense that we may be the last generation in the experiment with living. But we are a minority—the vast majority of our people regard the temporary equilibriums of our society and world as eternally-functional parts. In this is perhaps the outstanding paradox: we ourselves are imbued with urgency, yet the message of our society is that there is no viable alternative to the present. Beneath the reassuring tones of the politicians, beneath the common opinion that America will "muddle through," beneath the stagnation of those who have closed their minds to the future, is the pervading feeling that there simply are no alternatives, that our times have witnessed the exhaustion not only of Utopias, but of any new departures as well. Feeling the press of complexity upon the emptiness of life, people are fearful of the thought that at any moment things might thrust out of control. They fear change itself, since change might smash whatever invisible framework seems to hold back chaos for them now. For most Americans, all crusades are suspect, threatening. The fact that each individual sees apathy in his fellows perpetuates the common reluctance to organize for change. The dominant institutions are complex enough to blunt the minds of their potential critics, and entrenched enough to swiftly dissipate or entirely repel the energies of protest and reform, thus limiting human expectancies. Then, too, we are a materially improved society, and by our own improvements we seem to have weakened the case for further change.

Some would have us believe that Americans feel contentment amidst prosperity—but might it not better be called a glaze above deeply felt anxieties about their role in the new world? And if these anxieties produce a developed indifference to human affairs, do they not as well produce a yearning to believe there is an alternative to the present, that something can be done to change circumstances in the school, the workplaces, the bureaucracies, the government? It is to this latter yearning, at once the spark and engine of change, that we direct our present appeal. The search for truly democratic alternatives to the present, and a commitment to social experimentation with them, is a worthy and fulfilling human enterprise, one which moves us and, we hope, others today. On such a basis do we offer this document of our convictions and analysis: as an effort in understanding and changing the conditions of humanity in the late twentieth century, an effort rooted in the ancient, still unfulfilled conception of man attaining determining influence over his circumstances of life.

Values

Making values explicit—an initial task in establishing alternatives—is an activity that has been devalued and corrupted. The conventional moral terms of the age, the politician moralities—"free world," "people's democracies"—reflect realities poorly, if at all, and seem to function more as ruling myths than as descriptive principles. But neither has our experience in the universities brought us moral enlightenment. Our professors and administrators sacrifice controversy to public relations; their curriculums change more slowly than the living events of the world; their skills and silence are purchased by investors in the arms race; passion is called unscholastic. The questions we might want raised—What is really important? Can we live in a different and better way? If we wanted to change society, how would we do it?—are not thought to be questions of a "fruitful, empirical nature," and thus are brushed aside.

Unlike youth in other countries we are used to moral leadership being exercised and moral dimensions being clarified by our elders. But today, for us, not even the liberal and socialist preachments of the past seem adequate to the forms of the present. Consider the old slogans; Capitalism Cannot Reform Itself, United Front Against Fascism, General Strike, All Out on May Day. Or, more recently, No Cooperation with Commies and Fellow Travellers, Ideologies Are Exhausted, Bipartisanship, No Utopias. These are incomplete, and there are few new prophets. It has been said that our liberal and socialist predecessors were plagued by vision without program, while our own generation is plagued by program without vision. All around us there is astute grasp of method, technique—the committee, the ad hoc group, the lobbyist, that hard and soft sell, the make, the projected image—but, if pressed critically, such expertise is incompetent to explain its implicit ideals. It is highly fashionable to identify oneself by old categories, or by naming a respected political figure, or by explaining "how we would vote" on various issues.

Theoretic chaos has replaced the idealistic thinking of old—and, unable to reconstitute theoretic order, men have condemned idealism itself. Doubt has replaced hopefulness—and men act out a defeatism that is labeled realistic. The decline of Utopia and hope is in fact one of the defining features of social life today. The reasons are various: the dreams of the older left were perverted by Stalinism and never recreated; the congressional stalemate makes men narrow their view of the possible; the specialization of human activity leaves little room for sweeping thought; the horrors of the twentieth century, symbolized in the gas-ovens and concentration camps and atom bombs, have blasted hopefulness. To be idealistic is to be considered apocalyptic, deluded. To have no serious aspirations, on the contrary, is to be "tough-minded."

In suggesting social goals and values, therefore, we are aware of entering a sphere of some disrepute. Perhaps matured by the past, we have no sure formulas, no closed theories—but that does not mean values are beyond discussion and tentative determination. A first task of any social movement is to convenience people that the search for orienting theories and the creation of human values is complex but worthwhile. We are aware that to avoid platitudes we must analyze the concrete conditions of social order. But to direct such an analysis we must use the guideposts of basic principles. Our own social values involve conceptions of human beings, human relationships, and social systems.

We regard men as infinitely precious and possessed of unfulfilled capacities for reason, freedom, and love. In affirming these principles we are aware of countering perhaps the dominant conceptions of man in the twentieth century: that he is a thing to be manipulated, and that he is inherently incapable of directing his own affairs. We oppose the depersonalization that reduces human beings to the status of things—if anything, the brutalities of the twentieth century teach that means and ends are intimately related, that vague appeals to "posterity" cannot justify the mutilations of the present. We oppose, too, the doctrine of human incompetence because it rests essentially on the modern fact that men have been "competently" manipulated into incompetence—we see little reason why men cannot meet with increasing skill the complexities and responsibilities of their situation, if society is organized not for minority, but for majority participation in decision-making.

Men have unrealized potential for self-cultivation, self-direction, self-understanding, and creativity. It is this potential that we regard as crucial and to which we appeal, not to the human potentiality for violence, unreason, and submission to authority. The goal of man and society should be human independence: a concern not with image of popularity but with finding a meaning in life that is personally authentic: a quality of mind not compulsively driven by a sense of powerlessness, nor one which unthinkingly adopts status values, nor one which represses all threats to its habits, but one which has full, spontaneous access to present and past experiences, one which easily unites the fragmented parts of personal history, one which openly faces problems which are troubling and unresolved: one with an intuitive awareness of possibilities, an active sense of curiosity, an ability and willingness to learn.

This kind of independence does not mean egoistic individualism—the object is not to have one's way so much as it is to have a way that is one's own. Nor do we deify man—we merely have faith in his potential.

Human relationships should involve fraternity and honesty. Human interdependence is contemporary fact; human brotherhood must be willed however, as a condition of future survival and as the most appropriate form of social relations. Personal links between man and man are needed, especially to go beyond the partial and fragmentary bonds of function that bind men only as worker to worker, employer to employee, teacher to student, American to Russian.

Loneliness, estrangement, isolation describe the vast distance between man and man today. These dominant tendencies cannot be overcome by better personnel management, nor by improved gadgets, but only when a love of man overcomes the idolatrous worship of things by man.

As the individualism we affirm is not egoism, the selflessness we affirm is not self-elimination. On the contrary, we believe in generosity of a kind that imprints one's unique individual qualities in the relation to other men, and to all human activity. Further, to dislike isolation is not to favor the abolition of privacy; the latter differs from isolation in that it occurs or is abolished according to individual will. Finally, we would replace power and personal uniqueness rooted in possession, privilege, or circumstance by power and uniqueness rooted in love, reflectiveness, reason, and creativity.

As a social system we seek the establishment of a democracy of individual participation, governed by two central aims: that the individual share in those social decisions determining the quality and direction of his life; that society be organized to encourage independence in men and provide the media for their common participation.

In a participatory democracy, the political life would be based in several root principles:

- that decision-making of basic social consequence be carried on by public groupings;
- that politics be seen positively, as the art of collectively creating an acceptable pattern of social relations;
- that politics has the function of bringing people out of isolation and into community, thus being a necessary, though not sufficient, means of finding meaning in personal life;
- that the political order should serve to clarify problems in a way instrumental to their solution; it should provide outlets for the expression of personal grievance and aspiration; opposing views should be organized so as to illuminate choices and facilitate the attainment of goals; channels should be commonly available to relate men to knowledge and to power so that private problems—from bad recreation facilities to personal alienation—are formulated as general issues.

The economic sphere would have as its basis the principles:

- that work should involve incentives worthier than money or survival. It should be educative, not stultifying; creative, not mechanical; self-direct, not manipulated, encouraging independence; a respect for others, a sense of dignity and a willingness to accept social responsibility, since it is this experience that has crucial influence on habits, perceptions, and individual ethics;
- that the economic experience is so personally decisive that the individual must share in its full determination;
- that the economy itself is of such social importance that its major resources and means of production should be open to democratic participation and subject to democratic social regulation.

Like the political and economic ones, major social institutions—cultural, education, rehabilitative, and others—should be generally organized with the well-being and dignity of man as the essential measure of success.

In social change or interchange, we find violence to be abhorrent because it requires generally the transformation of the target, be it a human being or a community of people, into a depersonalized object of hate. It is imperative that the means of violence be abolished and the institutions—local, national, international—that encourage nonviolence as a condition of conflict be developed.

These are our central values, in skeletal form. It remains vital to understand their denial or attainment in the context of the modern world.

The Students

In the last few years, thousands of American students demonstrated that they at least felt the urgency of the times. They moved actively and directly against racial injustices, the threat of war, violations of individual rights of conscience and, less frequently, against economic manipulation. They succeeded in restoring a small measure of controversy to the campuses after the stillness of the McCarthy period. They succeeded, too, in gaining some concessions from the people and institutions they opposed, especially in the fight against racial bigotry.

The significance of these scattered movements lies not in their success or failure in gaining objectives—at least not yet. Nor does the significance lie in the intellectual "competence" or "maturity" of the students involved—as some pedantic elders allege. The significance is in the fact the students are breaking the crust of apathy and overcoming the inner alienation that remain the defining characteristics of American college life.

If student movements for change are rarities still on the campus scene, what is commonplace there? The real campus, the familiar campus, is a place of private people, engaged in their notorious "inner emigration." It is a place of commitment to business-as-usual, getting ahead, playing it cool. It is a place of mass affirmation of the Twist, but mass reluctance toward the controversial public stance. Rules are accepted as "inevitable," bureaucracy as "just circumstances," irrelevance as "scholarship," selflessness as "martyrdom," politics as "just another way to make people, and an unprofitable one, too."

Almost no students value activity as a citizen. Passive in public, they are hardly more idealistic in arranging their private lives: Gallup concludes they will settle for "low success, and won't risk high failure." There is not much willingness to take risks (not even in business), no setting of dangerous goals, no real conception of personal identity except one manufactured in the image of others, no real urge for personal fulfillment except to be almost as successful as the very successful people. Attention is being paid to social status (the quality of shirt collars, meeting people, getting wives or husbands, making solid contacts for later on); much too, is paid to academic status (grades, honors, the med school rat-race). But neglected generally is real intellectual status, the personal cultivation of the mind.

"Students don't even give a damn about the apathy," one has said. Apathy toward apathy begets a privately-constructed universe, a place of systematic study schedules, two nights each week for beer, a girl or two, and early marriage; a framework infused with personality, warmth, and under control, no matter how unsatisfying otherwise.

Under these conditions university life loses all relevance to some. Four hundred thousand of our classmates leave college every year.

But apathy is not simply an attitude; it is a product of social institutions, and of the structure and organization of higher education itself. The extracurricular life is ordered according to *in loco parentis* theory, which ratifies the Administration as the moral guardian of the young. The accompanying "let's pretend" theory of student extracurricular affairs validates student government as a training center for those who want to spend their lives in political pretense, and discourages initiative from more articulate, honest, and sensitive students. The bounds and style of controversy are delimited before controversy begins. The university "prepares" the student for "citizenship" through perpetual rehearsals and, usually, through emasculation of what creative spirit there is in the individual.

The academic life contains reinforcing counterparts to the way in which extracurricular life is organized. The academic world is founded in a teacher-student relation analogous to the parent-child relation which characterizes *in loco parentis*. Further, academia includes a radical separation of student from the material of study. That which is studied, the social reality, is "objectified" to sterility, dividing the student from life—just as he is restrained in active involvement by the deans controlling student government. The specialization of function and knowledge, admittedly necessary to our complex technological and social structure, has produced and exaggerated compartmentalization of study and understanding. This has contributed to: an overly parochial view, by faculty, of the role of its research and scholarship; a discontinuous and truncated understanding, by students, of the surrounding social order; a loss of personal attachment, by nearly all, to the worth of study as a humanistic enterprise.

There is, finally, the cumbersome academic bureaucracy extending throughout the academic as well as extracurricular structures, contributing to the sense of outer complexity and inner powerlessness that transforms so many students from honest searching to ratification of convention and, worse, to a numbness of present and future catastrophes. The size and financing systems of the university enhance the permanent trusteeship of the administrative bureaucracy, their power leading to a shift to the value standards of business and administrative mentality within the university. Huge foundations and other private financial interests shape under-financed colleges and universities, not only making them more commercial, but less disposed to diagnose society critically, less open to dissent. Many social and physical scientists, neglecting the liberating heritage of higher learning, develop "human relations" or morale-producing" techniques for the corporate economy, while others exercise their intellectual skills to accelerate the arms race.

Tragically, the university could serve as a significant source of social criticism and an initiator of new modes and molders of attitudes. But the actual intellectual effect of the college experience is hardly distinguishable from that of any other communications channel—say, a television set—passing on the stock truths of the day. Students leave college somewhat more "tolerant" than when they arrived, but basically unchallenged in their values and political orientations. With administrators ordering the institutions, and faculty the curriculum, the student learns by his isolation to accept elite rule within the university, which prepares him to accept later forms of minority control. The real function of the educational system—as opposed to its more rhetorical function of "searching for truth"—is to impart the key information and styles that will help the student get by, modestly but comfortably, in the big society beyond.

The Society Beyond

Look beyond the campus, to America itself. That student life is more intellectual, and perhaps more comfortable, does not obscure the fact that the fundamental qualities of life on the campus reflect the habits of society at large. The fraternity president is seen at the junior manager levels; the sorority queen has gone to Grosse Pointe: the serious poet burns for a place, any place, or work; the once-serious and never-serious poets work at the advertising agencies. The desperation of people threatened by forces about which they know little and of which they can say less; the cheerful emptiness of people "giving up" all hope of changing things; the faceless ones polled by Gallup who listed "international affairs" fourteenth on their list of "problems" but who also expected thermonuclear war in the next few years: in these and other forms, Americans are in withdrawal from public life, from any collective effort at directing their own affairs.

Some regard this national doldrums as a sign of healthy approval of the established order—but is it approval by consent or manipulated acquiescence? Others declare that the people are withdrawn because compelling issues are fast disappearing—perhaps there are fewer breadlines in America, but is Jim Crow gone, is there enough work and work more fulfilling, is world war a diminishing threat, and what of the revolutionary new peoples? Still others think the national quietude is a necessary consequence of the need for elites to resolve complex and specialized problems of modern industrial society—but, then, why should business elites help decide foreign policy, and who controls the elites anyway, and are they solving mankind's problems? Others, finally, shrug knowingly and announce that full democracy never worked anywhere in the past—but why lump qualitatively different civilizations together, and how can a social order work well if its best thinkers are skeptics, and is man really doomed forever to the domination of today?

There are no convincing apologies for the contemporary malaise. While the world tumbles toward the final war, while men in other nations are trying desperately to alter events, while the very future qua future is uncertain—America is without community, impulse, without the inner momentum necessary for an age when societies cannot successfully perpetuate themselves by their military weapons, when democracy must be viable because of its quality of life, not its quantity of rockets.

The apathy here is, first, subjective—the felt powerlessness of ordinary people, the resignation before the enormity of events. But subjective apathy is encouraged by the objective American situation—the actual structural separation of people from power, from relevant knowledge, from pinnacles of decision-making. Just as the university influences the student way of life, so do major social institutions create the circumstances in which the isolated citizen will try hopelessly to understand his world and himself.

The very isolation of the individual—from power and community and ability to aspire—means the rise of a democracy without publics. With the great mass of people structurally remote and psychologically hesitant with respect to democratic institutions, those institutions themselves attenuate and become, in the fashion of the vicious circle, progressively less accessible to those few who aspire to serious participation in social affairs. The vital democratic connection between community and leadership, between the mass and the several elites, has been so wrenched and perverted that disastrous policies go unchallenged time and again.

Politics without Publics

The American political system is not the democratic model of which its glorifiers speak. In actuality it frustrates democracy by confusing the individual citizen, paralyzing policy discussion, and consolidating the irresponsible power of military and business interests.

A crucial feature of the political apparatus in America is that greater differences are harbored within each major party than the differences existing between them. Instead of two parties presenting distinctive and significant differences of approach, what dominates the system is a natural interlocking of Democrats from Southern states with the more conservative elements of the Republican party. This arrangement of forces is blessed by the seniority system of Congress which guarantees congressional committee domination by conservatives—10 of 17 committees in the Senate and 13 of 21 in the House of Representatives are chaired currently by Dixiecrats.

The party overlap, however, is not the only structural antagonist of democracy in politics. First, the localized nature of the party system does not encourage discussion of national and international issues: thus problems are not raised by and for people, and political representatives usually are unfettered from any responsibilities to the general public except those regarding parochial matters. Second, whole constituencies are divested of the full political power they might have: many Negroes in the South are prevented from voting, migrant workers are disenfranchised by various residence requirements, some urban and suburban dwellers are victimized by gerrymandering, and poor people are too often without the power to obtain political representation. Third, the focus of political attention is significantly distorted by the enormous lobby force, composed predominantly of business interests, spending hundreds of millions each year in an attempt to conform facts about productivity, agriculture, defense, and social services to the wants of private economic groupings.

What emerges from the party contradictions and insulation of privately held power is the organized political stalemate: calcification dominates flexibility as the principle of parliamentary organization, frustration is the expectancy of legislators intending liberal reform, and Congress becomes less and less central to national decision-making, especially in the area of foreign policy. In this context, confusion and blurring is built into the formulation of issues, long-range priorities are not discussed in the rational manner needed for policymaking, the politics of personality and "image" become a more important mechanism than the construction of issues in a way that affords each voter a challenging and real option. The American voter is buffeted from all directions by pseudo-problems, by the structurally-initiated sense that nothing political is subject to human mastery. Worried by his mundane problems which never get solved, but constrained by the common belief that politics is an agonizingly slow accommodation of views, he quits all pretense of bothering.

A most alarming fact is that few, if any, politicians are calling for changes in these conditions. Only a handful even are calling on the President to "live up to" platform pledges; no one is demanding structural changes, such as the shuttling of Southern Democrats out of the Democratic Party. Rather than protesting the state of politics, most politicians are reinforcing and aggravating that state. While in practice they rig public opinion to suit their own interests, in word and ritual they enshrine "the sovereign public" and call for more and more letters. Their speeches and campaign actions are banal, based on a degrading conception of what people want to hear. They respond not to dialogue, but to pressure: and knowing this, the ordinary citizen sees even greater inclination to shun the political sphere. The politician is usually a trumpeter to "citizenship" and "service to the nation," but since he is unwilling to seriously rearrange power relationships, his trumpetings only increase apathy by creating no outlets. Much of the time the call to "service" is justified not in idealistic terms, but in the crasser terms of "defending the free world from communism"—thus making future idealistic impulses harder to justify in anything but Cold War terms.

In such a setting of status quo politics, where most if not all government activity is rationalized in Cold War anti-communist terms, it is somewhat natural that discontented, super-patriotic groups would emerge through political channels and explain their ultra-conservatism as the best means of Victory over Communism. They have become a politically influential force within the Republican Party, at a national level through Senator Goldwater, and at a local level through their important social and economic roles. Their political views are defined generally as the opposite of the supposed views of communists: complete individual freedom in the economic sphere, non-participation by the government in the machinery of production. But actually "anti-communism" becomes an umbrella by which to protest liberalism, internationalism, welfarism, the active civil rights and labor movements. It is to the disgrace of the United States that such a movement should become a prominent kind of public participation in the modern world—but, ironically, it is somewhat to the interests of the United States that such a movement should be a public constituency pointed toward realignment of the political parties, demanding a conservative Republican Party in the South and an exclusion of the "leftist" elements of the national GOP.

The Economy

American capitalism today advertises itself as the Welfare State. Many of us comfortably expect pensions, medical care, unemployment compensation, and other social services in our lifetimes. Even with one-fourth of our productive capacity unused, the majority of Americans are living in relative comfort—although their nagging incentive to "keep up" makes them continually dissatisfied with their possessions. In many places, unrestrained bosses, uncontrolled machines, and sweatshop conditions have been reformed or abolished and suffering tremendously relieved. But in spite of the benign yet obscuring effects of the New Deal reforms and the reassuring phrases of government economists and politicians, the paradoxes and myths of the economy are sufficient to irritate our complacency and reveal to us some essential causes of the American malaise.

We live amidst a national celebration of economic prosperity while poverty and deprivation remain an unbreakable way of life for millions in the "affluent society," including many of our own generation. We hear glib reference to the "welfare state," "free enterprise," and "shareholder's democracy" while military defense is the main item of "public" spending and obvious oligopoly and other forms of minority rule defy real individual initiative or popular control. Work, too, is often unfulfilling and victimizing, accepted as a channel to status or plenty, if not a way to pay the bills, rarely as a means of understanding and controlling self and events. In work and leisure the individual is regulated as part of the system, a consuming unit, bombarded by hard-sell soft-sell, lies and semi-true appeals and his basest drives. He is always told what he is supposed to enjoy while being told, too, that he is a "free" man because of "free enterprise."

The Remote Control Economy. We are subject to a remote control economy, which excludes the mass of individual "units"—the people—from basic decisions affecting the nature and organization of work, rewards, and opportunities. The modern concentration of wealth is fantastic. The wealthiest one percent of Americans own more than 80 percent of all personal shares of stock. From World War II until the mid-Fifties, the 50 biggest corporations increased their manufacturing production from 17 to 23 percent of the national total, and the share of the largest 200 companies rose from 30 to 37 percent. To regard the various decisions of these elites as purely economic is short-sighted: their decisions affect in a momentous way the entire fabric of social life in America. Foreign investments influence political policies in under-developed areas—and our efforts to build a "profitable" capitalist world blind our foreign policy to mankind's needs and destiny. The drive for sales spurs phenomenal advertising efforts; the ethical drug industry, for instance, spent more than $750 million on promotions in 1960, nearly for times the amount available to all American medical schools for their educational programs. The arts, too, are organized substantially according to their commercial appeal; aesthetic values are subordinated to exchange values, and writers swiftly learn to consider the commercial market as much as the humanistic marketplace of ideas. The tendency to over-production, to gluts of surplus commodities, encourages "market research" techniques to deliberately create pseudo-needs in consumers—we learn to buy "smart" things, regardless of their utility—and introduces wasteful "planned obsolescence" as a permanent feature of business strategy. While real social needs accumulate as rapidly as profits, it becomes evident that Money, instead of dignity of character, remains a pivotal American value and Profitability, instead of social use, a pivotal standard in determining priorities of resource allocation.

Within existing arrangements, the American business community cannot be said to encourage a democratic process nationally. Economic minorities not responsible to a public in any democratic fashion make decisions of a more profound importance than even those made by Congress. Such a claim is usually dismissed by respectful and knowing citations of the ways in which government asserts itself as keeper of the public interest at times of business irresponsibility. But the real, as opposed to the mythical, range of government "control" of the economy includes only:

1. some limited "regulatory" powers—which usually just ratify industry policies or serve as palliatives at the margins of significant business activity;
2. a fiscal policy build upon defense expenditures as pump-priming "public works"—without a significant emphasis on "peaceful public works" to meet social priorities and alleviate personal hardships;
3. limited fiscal and monetary weapons which are rigid and have only minor effects, and are greatly limited by corporate veto: tax cuts and reforms; interest rate control (used generally to tug on investment by hurting the little investor most); tariffs which protect noncompetitive industries with political power and which keep less-favored nations out of the large trade mainstream, as the removal of barriers reciprocally with the Common Market may do disastrously to emerging countries outside of Europe; wage arbitration, the use of government coercion in the name of "public interest" to hide the tensions between workers and business production controllers; price controls, which further maintains the status quo of big ownership and flushes out little investors for the sake of "stability";
4. very limited "poverty-solving" which is designed for the organized working class but not the shut-out, poverty-stricken migrants, farm workers, the indigent unaware of medical care or the lower-middle class person riddled with medical bills, the "unhireables" of minority groups or workers over 45 years of age, etc.
5. regional development programs—such as the Area Redevelopment Act—which have been only "trickle down" welfare programs without broad authority for regional planning and development and public works spending. The federal highway program has been more significant than the "depressed areas" program in meeting the needs of people, but is generally too remote and does not reach the vicious circle of poverty itself.

In short, the theory of government "countervailing" business neglects the extent to which government influence is marginal to the basic production decisions, the basic decision-making environment of society, the basic structure or distribution and allocation which is still determined by major corporations with power and wealth concentrated among the few. A conscious conspiracy—as in the case of price rigging in the electrical industry—is by no means generally or continuously operative but power undeniably does rest in comparative insulation from the public and its political representatives.

The Military-Industrial Complex. The most spectacular and important creation of the authoritarian and oligopolistic structure of economic decision-making in America is the institution called "the military-industrial complex" by former President Eisenhower, the powerful congruence of interest and structure among military and business elites which affects so much of our development and destiny. Not only is ours the first generation to live with the possibility of world-wide cataclysm—it is the first to experience the actual social preparation for cataclysm, the general militarization of American society. In 1948 Congress established Universal Military Training, the first peacetime conscription. The military became a permanent institution. Four years earlier, General Motors' Charles E. Wilson had heralded the creation of what he called the "permanent war economy," the continuous use of military spending as a solution to economic problems unsolved before the post-war boom, most notably the problem of the seventeen million jobless after eight years of the New Deal. This has left a "hidden crisis" in the allocation of resources by the American economy.

Since our childhood these two trends—the rise of the military and the installation of a defense-based economy—have grown fantastically. The Department of Defense, ironically the world's largest single organization, is worth $160 billion, owns 32 million acres of America and employs half the 7.5 million persons directly dependent on the military for subsistence, and has an $11 billion payroll, which is larger than the net annual income of all American corporations. Defense spending in the Eisenhower era totaled $350 billion and President Kennedy entered office pledging to go even beyond the present defense allocation of sixty cents from every public dollar spent. Except for a war-induced boom immediately after "our side" bombed Hiroshima, American economic prosperity has coincided with a growing dependence on military outlay—from 1941 to 1959 America's Gross National Product of $5.25 trillion included $700 billion in goods and services purchased for the defense effort, about one-seventh of the accumulated GNP. This pattern has included the steady concentration of military spending among a few corporations. In 1961, 86 percent of Defense Department contracts were awarded without competition. The ordnance industry of 100,000 people is completely engaged in military work; in the aircraft industry, 94 percent of 750,000 workers are linked to the war economy; shipbuilding, radio and communications equipment industries commit 40 percent of their work to defense; iron and steel, petroleum, metal-stamping and machine shop products, motors and generators, tools and hardware, copper, aluminum and machine tools industries all devote at least 10 percent of their work to the same cause.

The intermingling of Big Military and Big Industry is evidenced in the 1,400 former officers working for the 100 corporations who received nearly all the $21 billion spent in procurement by the Defense Department in 1961. The overlap is most poignantly clear in the case of General Dynamics, the company which received the best 1961 contracts, employed the most retired officers (187), and is directed by a former Secretary of the Army. A *Fortune* magazine profile of General Dynamics said: "The unique group of men who run Dynamics are only incidentally in rivalry with other U.S. manufacturers, with many of whom they actually act in concert. Their chief competitor is the USSR. The core of General Dynamics corporate philosophy is the conviction that national defense is a more or less permanent business." Little has changed since Wilson's proud declaration of the Permanent War Economy back in the 1944 days when the top 200 corporations possessed 80 percent of all active prime war-supply contracts.

Military-Industrial Politics

The military and its supporting business foundation have found numerous forms of political expression, and we have heard their din endlessly. There has not been a major Congressional split on the issue of continued defense spending spirals in our lifetime. The triangular relation of the business, military and political arenas cannot be better expressed than in Dixiecrat Carl Vinson's remarks as his House Armed Services Committee reported out a military construction bill of $808 million throughout the 50 states for 1960–61: "There is something in this bill for everyone," he announced. President Kennedy had earlier acknowledged the valuable anti-recession features of the bill.

Imagine, on the other hand, $808 million suggested as an anti-recession measure, but being poured into programs of social welfare: the impossibility of receiving support for such a measure identifies a crucial feature of defense spending: it is beneficial to private enterprise, while welfare spending is not. Defense spending does not "compete" with the private sector; it contains a natural obsolescence; its "confidential" nature permits easier boondoggling; the tax burdens to which it leads can be shunted from corporation to consumer as a "cost of production." Welfare spending, however, involves the government in competition with private corporations and contractors; it conflicts with imme- diate interests of private pressure groups; it leads to taxes on business. Think of the opposition of private power companies to current proposals for river and valley development, or the hostility of the real estate lobby to urban renewal; or the attitude of the American Medical Association to a paltry medical care bill; or of all business lobbyists to foreign aid; these are the pressures leading to the schizophrenic public-military, private-civilian economy of our epoch. The politicians, of course, take the line of least resistance and thickest support: warfare, instead of welfare, is easiest to stand up for: after all, the Free World is at stake (and our constituency's investments, too).

Automation, Abundance, and Challenge. But while the economy remains relatively static in its setting of priorities and allocation of resources, new conditions are emerging with enormous implications: the revolution of automation, and the replacement of scarcity by the potential of material abundance.

Automation, the process of machines replacing men in performing sensory, motoric and complex logical tasks, is transforming society in ways that are scarcely comprehensible. By 1959, industrial production regained its 1957 "pre-recession" level—but with 750,000 fewer workers required. In the Fifties as a whole, national production enlarged by 43 percent but the number of factory employees remained stationary, seven-tenths of one percent higher than in 1947. Automation is destroying whole categories of work—impersonal thinkers have efficiently labeled this "structural unemployment"—in blue-collar, service, and even middle management occupations. In addition it is eliminating employment opportunities for a youth force that numbers one million more than it did in 1950, and rendering work far more difficult both to find and do for people in the forties and up. The consequences of this economic drama, strengthened by the force of post-war recessions, are momentous: five million becomes an acceptable unemployment tabulation, and misery, uprootedness and anxiety become the lot of increasing numbers of Americans.

But while automation is creating social dislocation of a stunning kind, it paradoxically is imparting the opportunity for men the world around to rise in dignity from their knees. The dominant optimistic economic fact of this epoch is that fewer hands are needed now in actual production, although more goods and services are a real potentiality. The world could be fed, poverty abolished, the great public needs could be met, the brutish world of Darwinian scarcity could be brushed away, all men could have more time to pursue their leisure, drudgery in work could be cut to a minimum, education could become more of a continuing process for all people, both public and personal needs could be met rationally. But only in a system with selfish production motives and elitist control, a system which is less welfare- than war-based, undemocratic rather than "stockholder participative" as "sold to us," does the potentiality for abundance become a curse and a cruel irony:

1. Automation brings unemployment instead of mere leisure for all and greater achievement of needs for all people in the world—a crisis instead of economic Utopia. Instead of being introduced into a social system in a planned and equitable way, automation is initiated according to its profitability. American Telephone and Telegraph holds back modern telephone equipment, invented with public research funds, until present equipment is financially unprofitable. Colleges develop teaching machines, mass-class techniques, and TV education to replace teachers: not to proliferate knowledge or to assist the qualified professors now, but to "cut costs in education and make the academic community more efficient and less wasteful." Technology, which could be a blessing to society, becomes more and more a sinister threat to humanistic and rational enterprise.

2. Hard-core poverty exists just beyond the neon lights of affluence, and the "have-nots" may be driven still further from opportunity as the high-technology society demands better education to get into the production mainstream and more capital investment to get into "business." Poverty is shameful in that it herds people by race, region, and previous condition of infortune into "uneconomic classes" in the so-called free society—the marginal worker is made more insecure by automation and high education requirements, heavier competition for jobs, maintaining low wages or a high level of unemployment. People in the rut of poverty are strikingly unable to overcome the collection of forces working against them: poor health, bad neighborhoods, miserable schools, inadequate "welfare" services, unemployment and underemployment, weak politician and union organization.

3. Surplus and potential plenty are wasted domestically and producers suffer impoverishment because the real needs of the world and of our society are not reflected in the market. Our huge bins of decomposing grain are classic American examples, as is the steel industry which, in the summer of 1962, is producing at 53 percent of capacity.

The Stance of Labor. Amidst all this, what of organized labor, the historic institutional representative of the exploited, the presumed "countervailing power" against the excesses of Big Business? The contemporary social assault on the labor movement is of crisis proportions. To the average American, "big labor" is a growing cancer equal in impact to Big Business—nothing could be more distorted, even granting a sizable union bureaucracy. But in addition to public exaggerations, the labor crisis can be measured in several ways. First, the high expectations of the newborn AFL-CIO of 30 million members by 1965 is suffering a reverse unimaginable five years ago. The demise of the dream of "organizing the unorganized" is dramatically reflected in the AFL-CIO decision, just two years after its creation, to slash its organizing staff in half. From 15 million members when the AFL and the CIO merged, the total has slipped to 13.5 million. During the post-war generation, union membership nationally has increased by four million—but the total number of workers has jumped by 13 million. Today only 40 percent of all non-agricultural workers are protected by any form or organization. Second, organizing conditions are going to worsen. Where labor now is strongest—in industries—automation is leading to an attrition of available work. As the number of jobs dwindles, so does labor's power of bargaining, since management can handle a strike in an automated plant more easily than the older mass-operated ones.

More important perhaps, the American economy has changed radically in the last decade, as suddenly the number of workers producing goods became fewer than the number in "nonproductive" areas—government, trade, finance, services, utilities, transportation. Since World War II "white collar" and "service" jobs have grown twice as fast as have "blue collar" production jobs. Labor has almost no organization in the expanding occupational areas of the new economy, but almost all of its entrenched strength in contracting areas. As big government hires more, as business seeks more office workers and skilled technicians, and as growing commercial America demands new hotels, service stations and the like, the conditions will become graver still. Further, there is continuing hostility to labor by the Southern states and their industrial interests—meaning runaway plants, cheap labor threatening the organized trade union movement, and opposition from Dixiecrats to favorable labor legislation in Congress. Finally, there is indication that Big Business, for the sake of public relations if nothing more, has acknowledged labor's "right" to exist, but has deliberately tried to contain labor at its present strength, preventing strong unions from helping weaker ones or from spreading or unorganized sectors of the economy. Business is aided in its efforts by proliferation of "right-to-work" laws at state levels (especially in areas where labor is without organizing strength to begin with), and anti-labor legislation in Congress.

In the midst of these besetting crises, labor itself faces its own problems of vision and program. Historically, there can be no doubt as to its worth in American politics—what progress there has been in meeting human needs in this century rests greatly with the labor movement. And to a considerable extent the social democracy for which labor has fought externally is reflected in its own essentially democratic character: representing millions of people, not millions of dollars; demanding their welfare, not eternal profit. Today labor remains the most liberal "mainstream" institution—but often its liberalism represents vestigial commitments self-interestedness, unradicalism. In some measure labor has succumbed to institutionalization, its social idealism waning under the tendencies of bureaucracy, materialism, business ethics. The successes of the last generation perhaps have braked, rather than accelerated labor's zeal for change. Even the House of Labor has bay windows: not only is this true of the labor elites, but as well of some of the rank-and-file. Many of the latter are indifferent unionists, uninterested in meetings, alienated from the complexities of the labor-management negotiating apparatus, lulled to comfort by the accessibility of luxury and the opportunity of long-term contracts. "Union democracy" is not simply inhibited by labor leader elitism, but by the unrelated problem of rank-and-file apathy to the tradition of unionism. The crisis of labor is reflected in the coexistence within the unions of militant Negro discontents and discriminatory locals, sweeping critics of the obscuring "public interest" marginal tinkering of government and willing handmaidens of conservative political leadership, austere sacrificers and business-like operators, visionaries and anachronisms—tensions between extremes that keep alive the possibilities for a more militant unionism. Too, there are seeds of rebirth in the "organizational crisis" itself: the technologically unemployed, the unorganized white collar men and women, the migrants and farm workers, the unprotected Negroes, the poor, all of whom are isolated now from the power structure of the economy, but who are the potential base for a broader and more forceful unionism.

Horizon. In summary: a more reformed, more human capitalism, functioning at three-fourths capacity while one-third of America and two-thirds of the world goes needy, domination of politics and the economy by fantastically rich elites, accommodation and limited effectiveness by the labor movement, hard-core poverty and unemployment, automation confirming the dark ascension of machine over man instead of shared abundance, technological change being introduced into the economy by the criteria of profitability—this has been our inheritance. However inadequate, it has instilled quiescence in liberal hearts—partly reflecting the extent to which misery has been over-come but also the eclipse of social ideals. Though many of us are "affluent," poverty, waste, elitism, manipulation are too manifest to go unnoticed, too clearly unnecessary to go accepted. To change the Cold War status quo and other social evils, concern with the challenges to the American economic machine must expand. Now, as a truly better social state becomes visible, a new poverty impends: a poverty of vision, and a poverty of political action to make that vision reality. Without new vision, the failure to achieve our potentialities will spell the inability of our society to endure in a world of obvious, crying needs and rapid change.

The Individual in the Warfare State

Business and politics, when significantly militarized, affect the whole living condition of each American citizen. Worker and family depend on the Cold War for life. Half of all research and development is concentrated on military ends. The press mimics conventional Cold War opinion in its editorials. In less than a full generation, most Americans accept the military-industrial structure as "the way things are." War is still pictured as one more kind of diplomacy, perhaps a gloriously satisfying kind. Our saturation and atomic bombings of Germany and Japan are little more than memories of past "policy necessities" that preceded the wonderful economic boom of 1946. The facts that our once-revolutionary 20,000-ton Hiroshima Bomb is now paled by 50-megaton weapons, that our lifetime has included the creation of intercontinental ballistic missiles, that "greater" weapons are to follow, that weapons refinement is more rapid than the development of weapons of defense, that soon a dozen or more nations will have the Bomb, that one simple miscalculation could incinerate mankind: these orienting facts are but remotely felt. A shell of moral callous separates the citizen from sensitivity of the common peril: this is the result of a lifetime saturation with horror. After all, some ask, where could we begin, even if we wanted to? After all, others declare, we can only assume things are in the best of hands. A coed at the University of Kentucky says, "we regard peace and war as fairy tales." And a child has asked in helplessness, perhaps for us all, "Daddy, why is there a cold war?"

Past senselessness permits present brutality; present brutality is prelude to future deeds of still greater inhumanity; that is the moral history of the twentieth century, from the First World War to the present. A half-century of accelerating destruction has flattened out the individual's ability to make moral distinction, it has made people understandably give up, it has forced private worry and public silence.

To a decisive extent, the means of defense, the military technology itself, determines the political and social character of the state being defended—that is, defense mechanism themselves in the nuclear age alter the character of the system that creates them for protection. So it has been with America, as her democratic institutions and habits have shriveled in almost direct proportion to the growth of her armaments. Decisions about military strategy, including the monstrous decision to go to war, are more and more the property of the military and the industrial arms-race machine, with the politicians assuming a ratifying role instead of a determining one. This is increasingly a fact not just because of the installation of the permanent military, but because of constant revolutions in military technology. The new technologies allegedly require military expertise, scientific comprehension, and the mantle of secrecy. As Congress relies more and more on the Joint Chiefs of Staff, the existing chasm between people and decision-makers becomes irreconcilably wide, and more alienating in its effects.

A necessary part of the military effort is propaganda: to "sell" the need for congressional appropriations, to conceal various business scandals, and to convince the American people that the arms race is important enough to sacrifice civil liberties and social welfare. So confusion prevails about the national needs, while the three major services and the industrial allies jockey for power—the Air Force tending to support bombers and missilery; the Navy, Polaris and carriers; the Army, conventional ground forces and invulnerable nuclear arsenals; and all three feigning unity and support of the policy of weapons and agglomeration called the "mix." Strategies are advocated on the basis of power and profit, usually more so than on the basis of national military needs. In the meantime, Congressional investigating committees—most notably the House Un-American Activities Committee and the Senate Judiciary Committee—attempt to curb the little dissent that finds its way into off-beat magazines. A huge militant anti-communist brigade throws in its support, patriotically willing to do anything to achieve "total victory" in the Cold War; the government advocates peaceful confrontation with international Communism, then utterly pillories and outlaws the tiny American Communist Party. University professors withdraw prudently from public issues; the very style of social science writing becomes more qualified. Needs in housing, education, minority rights, health care, land redevelopment, hourly wages, all are subordinated—though a political tear is shed gratuitously—to the primary objective of the "military and economic strength of the Free World."

What are the governing policies which supposedly justify all this human sacrifice and waste? With few exceptions they have reflected the quandaries and confusion, stagnation and anxiety, of a stalemated nation in a turbulent world. They have shown a slowness, sometimes a sheer inability to react to a sequence of new problems.

Of these problems, two of the newest are foremost: the existence of poised nuclear weapons and the revolutions against the former colonial powers. In the both areas, the Soviet Union and the various national communist movements have aggravated international relations in inhuman and undesirable ways, but hardly so much as to blame only communism for the present menacing situation.

Deterrence Policy

The accumulation of nuclear arsenals, the threat of accidental war, the possibility of limited war becoming illimitable holocaust, the impossibility of achieving final arms superiority or invulnerability, the approaching nativity of a cluster of infant atomic powers; all of these events are tending to undermine traditional concepts of power relations among nations. War can no longer be considered as an effective instrument of foreign policy, a means of strengthening alliances, adjusting the balance of power, maintaining national sovereignty, or preserving human values. War is no longer simply a forceful extension of foreign policy; it can obtain no constructive ends in the modern world. Soviet or American "megatonnage" is sufficient to destroy all existing social structures as well as value systems. Missiles have (figuratively) thumbed their nosecones at national boundaries. But America, like other countries, still operates by means of national defense and deterrence systems. These are seen to be useful so long as they are never fully used: unless we as a national entity can convince Russia that we are willing to commit the most heinous action in human history, we will be forced to commit it.

Deterrence advocates, all of them prepared at least to threaten mass extermination, advance arguments of several kinds. At one pole are the minority of open partisans of preventive war—who falsely assume the inevitability of violent conflict and assert the lunatic efficacy of striking the first blow, assuming that it will be easier to "recover" after thermonuclear war than to recover now from the grip of the Cold War. Somewhat more reluctant to advocate initiating a war, but perhaps more disturbing for their numbers within the Kennedy Administration, are the many advocates of the "counterforce" theory of aiming strategic nuclear weapons at military installations—though this might "save" more lives than a preventive war, it would require drastic, provocative and perhaps impossible social change to separate many cities from weapons sites, it would be impossible to ensure the immunity of cities after one or two counterforce nuclear "exchanges," it would generate a perpetual arms race for less vulnerability and greater weapons power and mobility, it would make outer space a region subject to militarization, and accelerate the suspicions and arms build-ups which are incentives to precipitate nuclear action. Others would support fighting "limited wars" which use conventional (all but atomic) weapons, backed by deterrents so mighty that both sides would fear to use them—although underestimating the implications of numerous new atomic powers on the world stage, the extreme difficulty of anchoring international order with weapons of only transient invulnerability, the potential tendency for a "losing side" to push limited protracted fighting on the soil of underdeveloped countries. Still other deterrence artists propose limited, clearly defensive and retaliatory, nuclear capacity, always potent enough to deter an opponent's aggressive designs—the best of deterrence stratagems, but inadequate when it rests on the equation of an arms "stalemate" with international stability.

All the deterrence theories suffer in several common ways. They allow insufficient attention to preserving, extending, and enriching democratic values, such matters being subordinate rather than governing in the process of conducting foreign policy. Second, they inadequately realize the inherent instabilities of the continuing arms race and balance of fear. Third, they operationally tend to eclipse interest and action towards disarmament by solidifying economic, political and even moral investments in continuation of tensions. Fourth, they offer a disinterested and even patriotic rationale for the boondoggling, belligerence, and privilege of military and economic elites. Finally, deterrence stratagems invariably understate or dismiss the relatedness of various dangers; they inevitably lend tolerability to the idea of war by neglecting the dynamic interaction of problems—such as the menace of accidental war, the probable future tensions surrounding the emergence of ex-colonial nations, the imminence of several new nations joining the "Nuclear Club," the destabilizing potential of technological breakthrough by either arms race contestant, the threat of Chinese atomic might, the fact that "recovery" after World War III would involve not only human survivors but, as well, a huge and fragile social structure and culture which would be decimated perhaps irreparably by total war.

Such a harsh critique of what we are doing as a nation by no means implies that sole blame for the Cold War rests on the United States. Both sides have behaved irresponsibly—the Russians by an exaggerated lack of trust, and by much dependence on aggressive military strategists rather than on proponents of nonviolent conflict and coexistence. But we do contend, as Americans concerned with the conduct of our representative institutions, that our government has blamed the Cold War stalemate on nearly everything but its own hesitations, its own anachronistic dependence on weapons. To be sure, there is more to disarmament than wishing for it. There are inadequacies in international rule-making institutions— which could be corrected. There are faulty inspection mechanisms—which could be perfected by disinterested scientists. There is Russian intransigency and evasiveness—which do not erase the fact that the Soviet Union, because of a strained economy, an expectant population, fears of Chinese potential, and interest in the colonial revolution, is increasingly disposed to real disarmament with real controls. But there is, too, our own reluctance to face the uncertain world beyond the Cold War, our own shocking assumption that the risks of the present are fewer than the risks of a policy re-orientation to disarmament, our own unwillingness to face the implementation of our rhetorical commitments to peace and freedom.

Today the world alternatively drifts and plunges towards a terrible war.

The Colonial Revolution

While weapons have accelerated man's opportunity for self-destruction, the counter-impulse to life and creation are superbly manifest in the revolutionary feelings of many Asian, African and Latin American peoples. Against the individual initiative and aspiration, and social sense of organicism characteristic of these upsurges, the American apathy and stalemate stand in embarrassing contrast.

It is difficult today to give human meaning to the welter of facts that surrounds us. That is why it is especially hard to understand the facts of "underdevelopment": in India, man and beast together produced 65 percent of the nation's economic energy in a recent year, and of the remaining 35 percent of inanimately produced power almost three-fourths was obtained by burning dung. But in the United States, human and animal power together account for only one percent of the national economic energy—that is what stands humanly behind the vague term "industrialization." Even to maintain the misery of Asia today at a constant level will require a rate of growth tripling the national income and the aggregate production in Asian countries by the end of the century. For Asians to have the (unacceptable) 1950 standard of Europeans, less than $2,000 per year for a family, national production must increase 21-fold by the end the century, and that monstrous feat only to reach a level that Europeans find intolerable.

What has America done? During the years 1955–57 our total expenditures in economic aid were equal to one-tenth of one percent of our total Gross National Product. Prior to that time it was less; since then it has been a fraction higher. Immediate social and economic development is needed—we have helped little, seeming to prefer to create a growing gap between "have" and "have not" rather than to usher in social revolutions which would threaten our investors and our military alliances. The new nations want to avoid power entanglements that will open their countries to foreign domination—and we have often demanded loyalty oaths. They do not see the relevance of uncontrolled free enterprise in societies without accumulated capital and a significant middle class—and we have looked calumniously on those who would not try "our way." They seek empathy—and we have sided with the old colonialists, who now are trying to take credit for "giving" all the freedom that has been wrested from them, or we "empathize" when pressure absolutely demands it.

With rare variation, American foreign policy in the Fifties was guided by a concern for foreign investment and a negative anti-communist political stance linked to a series of military alliances, both undergirded by military threat. We participated unilaterally—usually through the Central Intelligence Agency—in revolutions against governments in Laos, Guatemala, Cuba, Egypt, Iran. We permitted economic investment to decisively affect our foreign policy: fruit in Cuba, oil in the Middle East, diamonds and gold in South Africa (with whom we trade more than with any African nation). More exactly: America's "foreign market" in the late Fifties, including exports of goods and services plus overseas sales by American firms, averaged about $60 billion annually. This represented twice the investment of 1950, and it is predicted that the same rates of increase will continue. The reason is obvious: Fortune said in 1958, "foreign earnings will be more than double in four years, more than twice the probable gain in domestic profits." These investments are concentrated primarily in the Middle East and Latin America, neither region being an impressive candidate for the long-run stability, political caution, and lower-class tolerance that American investors typically demand.

Our pugnacious anti-communism and protection of interests has led us to an alliance inappropriately called the "Free World." It included four major parliamentary democracies: ourselves, Canada, Great Britain, and India. It also has included through the years Batista, Franco, Verwoerd, Salazar, De Gaulle, Boun Oum, Ngo Diem, Chiang Kai-Shek, Trujillo, the Somozas, Saud, Ydigoras—all of these non-democrats separating us deeply from the colonial revolutions.

Since the Kennedy administration began, the American government seems to have initiated policy changes in the colonial and underdeveloped areas. It accepted "neutralism" as a tolerable principle; it sided more than once with the Angolans in the United Nations; it invited Souvanna Phouma to return to Laos after having overthrown his neutralist government there; it implemented the Alliance for Progress that President Eisenhower proposed when Latin America appeared on the verge of socialist revolutions; it made derogatory statements about the Trujillos; it cautiously suggested that a democratic socialist government in British Guiana might be necessary to support; in inaugural oratory, it suggested that a moral imperative was involved in sharing the world's resources with those who have been previously dominated. These were hardly sufficient to heal the scars of past activity and present associations, but nevertheless they were motions away from the Fifties. But quite unexpectedly, the President ordered the Cuban invasions, and while the American press railed about how we had been "shamed" and defied by that "monster Castro," the colonial peoples of the world wondered whether our foreign policy had really changed from its old imperialist ways (we had never supported Castro, even on the eve of his taking power, and had announced early that "the conduct of the Castro government toward foreign private enterprise in Cuba" would be a main State Department concern). Any heralded changes in our foreign policy are now further suspect in the wake of the Punta del Este foreign minister's conference where the five countries representing most of Latin America refused to cooperate in our plans to further "isolate" the Castro government.

Ever since the colonial revolution began, American policy makers have reacted to new problems with old "gunboat" remedies, often thinly disguised. The feeble but desirable efforts of the Kennedy administration to be more flexible are coming perhaps too late, and are of too little significance to really change the historical thrust of our policies. The hunger problem is increasing rapidly mostly as a result of the worldwide population explosion that cancels out the meager triumphs gained so far over starvation. The threat of population to economic growth is simply documented: in 1960–70 population in Africa south of the Sahara will increase 14 percent; in South Asia and the Far East by 22 percent; in North Africa by 26 percent; in the Middle East by 27 percent; in Latin America by 29 percent. Population explosion, no matter how devastating, is neutral. But how long will it take to create a relation of thrust between America and the newly-developing societies? How long to change our policies? And what length of time do we have?

The world is in transformation. But America is not. It can race to industrialize the world, tolerating occasional authoritarianisms, socialisms, neutralisms along the way—or it can slow the pace of the inevitable and default to the eager and self-interested Soviets and, much more importantly, to mankind itself. Only mystics would guess we have opted thoroughly for the first. Consider what our people think of this, the most urgent issue on the human agenda. Fed by a bellicose press, manipulated by economic and political opponents of change, drifting in their own history, they grumble about "the foreign-aid waste," or about "that beatnik down in Cuba," or how "things will get us by" … thinking confidently, albeit in the usual bewilderment, that Americans can go right on like always, five percent of mankind producing 40 percent of its goods.

Anti-Communism

An unreasoning anti-communism has become a major social problem for those who want to construct a more democratic America. McCarthyism and other forms of exaggerated and conservative anti-communism seriously weaken democratic institutions and spawn movements contrary to the interests of basic freedoms and peace. In such an atmosphere even the most intelligent of Americans fear to join political organizations, sign petitions, speak out on serious issues. Militaristic policies are easily "sold" to a public fearful of a democratic enemy. Political debate is restricted, thought is standardized, action is inhibited by the demands of "unity" and "oneness" in the face of the declared danger. Even many liberals and socialists share static and repetitious participation in the anti-communist crusade and often discourage tentative, inquiring discussion about "the Russian question" within their ranks—often by employing "Stalinist," "Stalinoid," "Trotskyite" and other epithets in an oversimplifying way to discredit opposition.

Thus much of the American anti-communism takes on the characteristics of paranoia. Not only does it lead to the perversion of democracy and to the political stagnation of a warfare society, but it also has the unintended consequence of preventing an honest and effective approach to the issues. Such an approach would require public analysis and debate of world politics. But almost nowhere in politics is such a rational analysis possible to make.

It would seem reasonable to expect that in America the basic issues of the Cold War should be rationally and fully debated, between persons of every opinion—on television, on platforms and through other media. It would seem, too, that there should be a way for the person or an organization to oppose communism without contributing to the common fear of associations and public actions. But these things do not happen; instead, there is finger-pointing and comical debate about the most serious of issues. This trend of events on the domestic scene, towards greater irrationality on major questions, moves us to greater concern than does the "internal threat" of domestic communism. Democracy, we are convinced, requires every effort to set in peaceful opposition the basic viewpoints of the day; only by conscious, determined, though difficult, efforts in this direction will the issue of communism be met appropriately.

Communism and Foreign Policy

As democrats we are in basic opposition to the communist system. The Soviet Union, as a system, rests on the total suppression of organized opposition, as well as on a vision of the future in the name of which much human life has been sacrificed, and numerous small and large denials of human dignity rationalized. The Communist Party has equated falsely the "triumph of true socialism" with centralized bureaucracy. The Soviet state lacks independent labor organizations and other liberties we consider basic. And despite certain reforms, the system remains almost totally divorced from the image officially promulgated by the Party. Communist parties throughout the rest of the world are generally undemocratic in internal structure and mode of action. Moreover, in most cases they subordinate radical programs to requirements of Soviet foreign policy. The communist movement has failed, in every sense, to achieve its stated intentions of leading a worldwide movement for human emancipation.

But present trends in American anti-communism are not sufficient for the creation of appropriate policies with which to relate to and counter communist movements in the world. In no instance is this better illustrated than in our basic national policy-making assumption that the Soviet Union is inherently expansionist and aggressive, prepared to dominate the rest of the world by military means. On this assumption rests the monstrous American structure of military "preparedness"; because of it we sacrifice values and social programs to the alleged needs of military power.

But the assumption itself is certainly open to question and debate. To be sure, the Soviet state has used force and the threat of force to promote or defend its perceived national interests. But the typical American response has been to equate the use of force—which in many cases might be dispassionately interpreted as a conservative, albeit brutal, action—with the initiation of a worldwide military onslaught. In addition, the Russian-Chinese conflicts and the emergency throughout the communist movement call for a re-evaluation of any monolithic interpretations. And the apparent Soviet disinterest in building a first-strike arsenal of weapons challenges the weight given to protection against surprise attack in formulations of American policy toward the Soviets.

Almost without regard to one's conception of the dynamics of Soviet society and foreign policy, it is evident that the American military response has been more effective in deterring the growth of democracy than communism. Moreover, our prevailing policies make difficult the encouragement of skepticism, anti-war or pro-democratic attitudes in the communist systems. America has done a great deal to foment the easier, opposite tendency in Russia: suspicion, suppression, and stiff military resistance. We have established a system of military alliances which are of even dubious deterrence value. It is reasonable of suggest that the Berlin and Laos crises have been earth-shaking situations partly because rival systems of deterrence make impossible the withdrawal of threats. The "status quo" is not cemented by mutual threat but by mutual fear of receding from pugnacity—since the latter course would undermine the "credibility" of our deterring system. Simultaneously, while billions in military aid were propping up right-wing Laotian, Formosan, Iranian and other regimes, American leadership never developed a purely political policy for offering concrete alternatives to either communism or the status quo for colonial revolutions. The results have been: fulfillment of the communist belief that capitalism is stagnant, its only defense being dangerous military adventurism; destabilizing incidents in numerous developing countries; an image of America allied with corrupt oligarchies counterposed to the Russian-Chinese image of rapid, though brutal, economic development. Again and again, America mistakes the static area of defense, rather than the dynamic area of development, as the master need of two-thirds of mankind.

Our paranoia about the Soviet Union has made us incapable of achieving agreements absolutely necessary for disarmament and the preservation of peace. We are hardly able to see the possibility that the Soviet Union, though not "peace loving," may be seriously interested in disarmament.

Infinite possibilities for both tragedy and progress lie before us. On the one hand, we can continue to be afraid, and out of fear commit suicide. On the other hand, we can develop a fresh and creative approach to world problems which will help to create democracy at home and establish conditions for its growth elsewhere in the world.

Discrimination

Our America is still white.

Consider the plight, statistically, of its greatest nonconformists, the "non-whites" (a Census Bureau designation).

1. Literacy: One of every four "nonwhites" is functionally illiterate; half do not complete elementary school; one in five finishes high school or better. But one in twenty whites is functionally illiterate; four of five finish elementary school; half go through high school or better.
2. Salary: In 1959 a "nonwhite" worker could expect to average $2,844 annually; a "nonwhite" family, including a college-educated father, could expect to make $5,654 collectively. But a white worker could expect to make $4,487 if he worked alone; with a college degree and a family of helpers he could expect $7,373. The approximate Negro-white wage ratio has remained nearly level for generations, with the exception of the World War II employment "boom" which opened many better jobs to exploited groups.
3. Work: More than half of all "nonwhites" work at laboring or service jobs, including one-fourth of those with college degrees; one in 20 works in a professional or managerial capacity. Fewer than one in five of all whites are laboring or service workers, including one in every 100 of the college-educated; one in four is in professional or managerial work.
4. Unemployment: Within the 1960 labor force of approximately 72 million, one of every 10 "nonwhites" was unemployed. Only one of every 20 whites suffered that condition.
5. Housing: The census classifies 57 percent of all "nonwhite" houses substandard, but only 27 percent of white-owned units so exist.
6. Education: More than 50 percent of America's "nonwhite" high school students never graduate. The vocational and professional spread of curriculum categories offered "nonwhites" is 16 as opposed to the 41 occupations offered to the white student. Furthermore, in spite of the 1954 Supreme Court decision, 80 percent of all "nonwhites" educated actually, or virtually, are educated under segregated conditions. And only one of 20 "nonwhite" students goes to college as opposed to the 1:10 ratio for white students.

7. Voting: While the white community is registered above two-thirds of its potential, the "nonwhite" population is registered below one-third of its capacity (with even greater distortion in areas of the Deep South).

Even against this background, some will say progress is being made. The facts belie it, however, unless it is assumed that America has another century to deal with its racial inequalities. Others, more pompous, will blame the situation on "those people's inability to pick themselves up," not understanding the automatic way in which such a system can frustrate reform efforts and diminish the aspirations of the oppressed. The one-party system in the South, attached to the Dixiecrat-Republican complex nationally, cuts off the Negro's independent powers as a citizen. Discrimination in employment, along with labor's accommodation to the "lily-white" hiring practices, guarantees the lowest slot in the economic order to the "nonwhite." North or South, these oppressed are conditioned by their inheritance and their surroundings to expect more of the same: in housing, schools, recreation, travel, all their potential is circumscribed, thwarted and often extinguished. Automation grinds up job opportunities, and ineffective or non-existent retraining programs make the already-handicapped "nonwhite" even less equipped to participate in "technological progress."

Horatio Alger Americans typically believe that the "nonwhites" are being "accepted" and "rising" gradually. They see more Negroes on television and so assume that Negroes are "better off." They hear the President talking about Negroes and so assume they are politically represented. They are aware of black peoples in the United Nations and so assume that the world is generally moving toward integration. They don't drive through the South, or through the slum areas of the big cities, so they assume that squalor and naked exploitation are disappearing. They express generalities about "time and gradualism" to hide the fact that they don't know what is happening.

The advancement of the Negro and other "nonwhites" in America has not been altogether by means of the crusades of liberalism, but rather through unavoidable changes in social structure. The economic pressures of World War II opened new jobs, new mobility, new insights to Southern Negroes, who then began great migrations from the South to the bigger urban areas of the North where their absolute wage was greater, though unchanged in relation to the white man of the same stratum. More important than the World War II openings was the colonial revolution. The world-wide upsurge of dark peoples against white colonial domination stirred the separation and created an urgency among American Negroes, while simultaneously it threatened the power structure of the United States enough to produce concessions to the Negro. Produced by outer pressure from the newly-moving peoples rather than by the internal conscience of the Federal government, the gains were keyed to improving the American "image" more than to reconstructing the society that prospered on top of its minorities. Thus the historic Supreme Court decision of 1954, theoretically desegregating Southern schools, was more a proclamation than a harbinger of social change—and is reflected as such in the fraction of Southern school districts which have desegregated, with Federal officials doing little to spur the process.

It has been said that the Kennedy administration did more in two years than the Eisenhower administration did in eight. Of this there can be no doubt. But it is analogous to comparing whispers to silence when positively stentorian tones are demanded. President Kennedy leapt ahead of the Eisenhower record when he made his second reference to the racial problem; Eisenhower did not utter a meaningful public statement until his last month in office when he mentioned the "blemish" of bigotry.

To avoid conflict with the Dixiecrat-Republican alliance, President Kennedy has developed a civil rights philosophy of "enforcement, not enactment," implying that existing statutory tools are sufficient to change the lot of the Negro. So far he has employed executive power usefully to appoint Negroes to various offices, and seems interested in seeing the Southern Negro registered to vote. On the other hand, he has appointed at least four segregationist judges in areas where voter registration is a desperate need. Only two civil rights bills, one to abolish the poll tax in five states and another to prevent unfair use of literacy tests in registration, have been proposed—the President giving active support to neither. But even this legislation, lethargically supported, then defeated, was intended to extend only to Federal elections. More important, the Kennedy interest in voter registration has not been supplemented with interest in giving the Southern Negro the economic protection that only trade unions can provide. It seems evident that the President is attempting to win the Negro permanently to the Democratic Party without basically disturbing the reactionary one-party oligarchy in the South. Moreover, the administration is decidedly "cool" (a phrase of Robert Kennedy's) toward mass nonviolent movements in the South, though by the support of racist Dixiecrats the Administration makes impossible gradual action through conventional channels. The Federal Bureau of Investigation in the South is composed of Southerners and their intervention in situations of racial tension is always after the incident, not before. Kennedy has refused to "enforce" the legal prerogative to keep Federal marshals active in Southern areas before, during and after any "situations" (this would invite Negroes to exercise their rights and it would infuriate the Southerners in Congress because of its "insulting" features).

While corrupt politicians, together with business interests happy with the absence of organized labor in Southern states and with the $50 billion in profits that results from paying the Negro half a "white wage," stymie and slow fundamental progress, it remains to be appreciated that the ultimate wages of discrimination are paid by individuals and not by the state. Indeed the other sides of the economic, political and sociological coins of racism represent their more profound implications in the private lives, liberties and pursuits of happiness of the citizen. While hungry nonwhites the world around assume rightful dominance, the majority of Americans fight to keep integrated housing out of the suburbs. While a fully interracial world becomes a biological probability, most Americans persist in opposing marriage between the races. While cultures generally interpenetrate, white America is ignorant still of nonwhite America—and perhaps glad of it. The white lives almost completely within his immediate, close-up world where things are tolerable, where there are no Negroes except on the bus corner going to and from work, and where it is important that daughters marry right. White, like might, makes right in America today. Not knowing the "nonwhite," however, the white knows something less than himself. Not comfortable around "different people," he reclines in whiteness instead of preparing for diversity. Refusing to yield objective social freedoms to the "nonwhite," the white loses his personal subjective freedom by turning away "from all these damn causes."

White American ethnocentrism at home and abroad reflect most sharply the self-deprivation suffered by the majority of our country which effectively makes it an isolated minority in the world community of culture and fellowship. The awe inspired by the pervasiveness of racism in American life is only matched by the marvel of its historical span in American traditions. The national heritage of racial discrimination via slavery has been a part of America since Christopher Columbus' advent on the new continent. As such, racism not only antedates the Republic and the thirteen Colonies, but even the use of the English language in this hemisphere. And it is well that we keep this as a background when trying to understand why racism stands as such a steadfast pillar in the culture and custom of the country. Racial-xenophobia is reflected in the admission of various racial stocks to the country. From the nineteenth century Oriental Exclusion Acts to the most recent updating of the McCarran-Walter Immigration Acts the nation has shown a continuous contemptuous regard for "nonwhites." More recently, the tragedies of Hiroshima and Korematsu, and our cooperation with Western Europe in the United Nations, add treatment to the thoroughness of racist overtones in national life.

But the right to refuse service to anyone is no longer reserved to the Americans. The minority groups, internationally, are changing place.

What Is Needed?

How to end the Cold War? How to increase democracy in America? These are the decisive issues confronting liberal and socialist forces today. To us, the issues are intimately related, the struggle for one invariably being a struggle for the other. What policy and structural alternatives are needed to obtain these ends?

1. Universal controlled disarmament must replace deterrence and arms control as the national defense goal. The strategy of mutual threat can only temporarily prevent thermonuclear war, and it cannot but erode democratic institutions here while consolidating oppressive institutions in the Soviet Union. Yet American leadership, while giving rhetorical due to the ideal of disarmament, persists in accepting mixed deterrence as its policy formula: under Kennedy we have seen first-strike and second-strike weapons, counter-military and counter-population inventions, tactical atomic weapons and guerilla warriors, etc. The convenient rationalization that our weapons potpourri will confuse the enemy into fear of misbehaving is absurd and threatening. Our own intentions, once clearly retaliatory, are now ambiguous since the President has indicated we might in certain circumstances be the first to use nuclear weapons. We can expect that Russia will become more anxious herself, and perhaps even prepare to "preempt" us, and we (expecting the worst from the Russians) will nervously consider "preemption" ourselves. The symmetry of threat and counter-threat leads not to stability but to the edge of hell.

It is necessary that America make disarmament, not nuclear deterrence, "credible" to the Soviets and to the world. That is, disarmament should be continually avowed as a national goal; concrete plans should be presented at conference tables; real machinery for a disarming and disarmed world—national and international—should be created while the disarming process itself goes on. The long-standing idea of unilateral initiative should be implemented as a basic feature of American disarmament strategy: initiatives that are graduated in their risk potential, accompanied by invitations to reciprocate, done regardless of reciprocation, openly planned for a significant period of future time. Their functions should not be to strip America of weapons but to induce a climate in which disarmament can be discussed with less mutual hostility and threat. They might include: a unilateral nuclear test moratorium, withdrawal of several bases near the Soviet Union, proposals to experiment in disarmament by stabilization of zone of controversy; cessation of all apparent first-strike preparations, such as the development of 41 Polaris by 1963 while naval theorists state that about 45 constitutes a provocative force; inviting a special United Nations agency to observe and inspect the launchings of all American flights into outer space; and numerous others.

There is no simple formula for the content of an actual disarmament treaty. It should be phased: perhaps on a region-by-region basis, the conventional weapons first. It should be conclusive, not open-ended, in its projection. It should be controlled: national inspection systems are adequate at first, but should be soon replaced by international devices and teams. It should be more than denuding: world or at least regional enforcement agencies, an international civil service and inspection service, and other supranational groups must come into reality under the United Nations.

2. Disarmament should be seen as a political issue, not a technical problem. Should this year's Geneva negotiations have resulted (by magic) in a disarmament agreement, the United States Senate would have refused to ratify it, a domestic depression would have begun instantly, and every fiber of American life would be wrenched drastically: these are indications not only of our unpreparedness for disarmament, but also that disarmament is not "just another policy shift." Disarmament means a deliberate shift in most of our domestic and foreign policy.

1. It will involve major changes in economic direction. Government intervention in new areas, government regulation of certain industrial price and investment practices to prevent inflation, full use of national productive capacities, and employment for every person in a dramatically expanding economy all are to be expected as the "price" of peace.
2. It will involve the simultaneous creation of international rulemaking and enforcement machinery beginning under the United Nations, and the gradual transfer of sovereignties—such as national armies and national determination of "international" law—to such machinery.
3. It will involve the initiation of an explicitly political—as opposed to military—foreign policy on the part of the two major superstates. Neither has formulated the political terms in which they would conduct their behavior in a disarming or disarmed world. Neither dares to disarm until such an understanding is reached.
4. A crucial feature of this political understanding must be the acceptance of status quo possessions. According to the universality principle all present national entities—including the Vietnams, the Koreas, the Chinas, and the Germanys—should be members of the United Nations as sovereign, no matter how desirable, states.

Russia cannot be expected to negotiate disarmament treaties for the Chinese. We should not feed Chinese fanaticism with our encirclement but Chinese stomachs with the aim of making war contrary to Chinese policy interests. Every day that we support anti-communist tyrants but refuse to even allow the Chinese communists representation in the United Nations marks a greater separation of our ideals and our actions, and it makes more likely bitter future relations with the Chinese.

Second, we should recognize that an authoritarian Germany's insistence on reunification, while knowing the impossibility of achieving it with peaceful means, could only generate increasing frustrations among the population and nationalist sentiments which frighten its Eastern neighbors who have historical reasons to suspect Germanic intentions. President Kennedy himself told the editor of *Izvestia* that he fears an independent Germany with nuclear arms, but American policies have not demonstrated cognizance of the fact that Chancellor Adenauer too, is interested in continued East-West tensions over the Germany and Berlin problems and nuclear arms precisely because this is the rationale for extending his domestic power and his influence upon the NATO-Common Market alliance.

A world war over Berlin would be absurd. Anyone concurring with such a proposition should demand that the West cease its contradictory advocacy of "reunification of Germany through free elections" and "a rearmed Germany in NATO." It is a dangerous illusion to assume that Russia will hand over East Germany to a rearmed re-united Germany which will enter the Western camp, although this Germany might have a Social Democratic majority which could prevent a reassertion of German nationalism. We have to recognize that the Cold War and the incorporation of Germany into the two power blocs was a decision of both Moscow and Washington, of both Adenauer and Ulbricht. The immediate responsibility for the Berlin wall is Ulbricht's. But it had to be expected that a regime which was bad enough to make people flee is also bad enough to prevent them from fleeing. The inhumanity of the Berlin wall is an ironic symbol of the irrationality of the Cold War, which keeps Adenauer and Ulbricht in power. A reduction of the tension over Berlin, if by internationalization or by recognition of the status quo and reducing provocations, is a necessary but equally temporary measure which could not ultimately reduce the basic Cold War tension to which Berlin owes its precarious situation. The Berlin problem cannot be solved without reducing tensions in Europe, possibly by a bilateral military disengagement and creating a neutralized buffer zone. Even if Washington and Moscow were in favor of disengagement, both Adenauer and Ulbricht would never agree to it because cold war keeps their parties in power.

Until their regimes' departure from the scene of history, the Berlin status quo will have to be maintained while minimizing the tensions necessarily arising from it. Russia cannot expect the United States to tolerate its capture by the Ulbricht regime, but neither can America expect to be in a position to indefinitely use Berlin as a fortress within the communist world. As a fair and bilateral disengagement in Central Europe seems to be impossible for the time being, a mutual recognition of the Berlin status quo, that is, of West Berlin's and East Germany's security, is needed. And it seems to be possible, although the totalitarian regime of East Germany and the authoritarian leadership of West Germany until now succeeded in frustrating all attempts to minimize the dangerous tensions of cold war.

The strategy of securing the status quo of the two power blocs until it is possible to depolarize the world by creating neutralist regions in all trouble zones seems to be the only way to guarantee peace at this time.

3. Experiments in disengagement and demilitarization must be conducted as part of the total disarming process. These "disarmament experiments" can be of several kinds, so long as they are consistent with the principles of containing the arms race and isolating specific sectors of the world from the Cold War power-play. First, it is imperative that no more nations be supplied with, or locally produce, nuclear weapons. A 1959 report of the National Academy of Arts and Sciences predicted that 19 nations would be so armed in the near future. Should this prediction be fulfilled, the prospects of war would be unimaginably expanded. For this reason the United States, Great Britain and the Soviet Union should band against France (which wants its own independent deterrent) and seek, through United Nations or other machinery, the effective prevention of the spread of atomic weapons. This would involve not only declarations of "denuclearization" in whole areas of Latin America, Africa, Asia and Europe, but would attempt to create inspection machinery to guarantee the peaceful use of atomic energy.

Second, the United States should reconsider its increasingly outmoded European defense framework, the North Atlantic Treaty Organization. Since its creation in 1949, NATO has assumed increased strength in overall determination of Western military policy, but has become less and less relevant to its original purpose, which was the defense of Central Europe. To be sure, after the Czech coup of 1948, it might have appeared that the Soviet Union was on the verge of a full-scale assault on Europe. But that onslaught has not materialized, not so much because of NATO's existence but because of the general unimportance of much of Central Europe to the Soviets. Today, when even American-based ICBMs could smash Russia minutes after an invasion of Europe, when the Soviets have no reason to embark on such an invasion, and when "thaw sectors" are desperately needed to brake the arms race, one of the least threatening but most promising courses for America would be toward the gradual diminishment of the NATO forces, coupled with the negotiated "disengagement" of parts of Central Europe.

It is especially crucial that this be done while America is entering into favorable trade relations with the European Economic Community: such a gesture, combining economic ambition with less dependence on the military, would demonstrate the kind of competitive "co-existence" America intends to conduct with the communist-bloc nations. If the disengaged states were the two Germanies, Poland and Czechoslovakia, several other benefits would accrue. First, the United States would be breaking with the lip-service commitment to "liberation" of Eastern Europe which has contributed so much to Russian fears and intransigence, while doing too little about actual liberation. But the end of "liberation" as a proposed policy would not signal the end of American concern for the oppressed in East Europe. On the contrary, disengagement would be a real, rather than a rhetorical, effort to ease military tensions, thus undermining the Russian argument for tighter controls in East Europe based on the "menace of capitalist encirclement." This policy, geared to the needs of democratic elements in the satellites, would develop a real bridge between East and West across the two most pro-Western Russian satellites. The Russians in the past have indicated some interest in such a plan, including the demilitarization of the Warsaw pact countries. Their interest should be publicly tested. If disengagement could be achieved, a major zone could be removed from the Cold War, the German problem would be materially diminished, and the need for NATO would diminish, and attitudes favorable to disarming would be generated.

Needless to say, those proposals are much different than what is currently being practiced and praised. American military strategists are slowly acceding to the NATO demand for an independent deterrent, based on the fear that America might not defend Europe from military attack. These tendencies strike just the opposite chords in Russia than those which would be struck by disengagement themes: the chords of military alertness, based on the fact that NATO (bulwarked by the German Wehrmacht) is preparing to attack Eastern Europe or the Soviet Union. Thus the alarm which underlies the NATO proposal for an independent deterrent is likely itself to bring into existence the very Russian posture that was the original cause of fear. Armaments spiral and belligerence will carry the day, not disengagement and negotiation.

The Industrialization of the World

Many Americans are prone to think of the industrialization of the newly developed countries as a modern form of American noblesse, undertaken sacrificially for the benefit of others. On the contrary, the task of world industrialization, of eliminating the disparity between have and have-not nations, is as important as any issue facing America. The colonial revolution signals the end of an era for the old Western powers and a time of new beginnings for most of the people of the earth. In the course of these upheavals, many problems will emerge: American policies must be revised or accelerated in several ways.

1. The United States' principal goal should be creating a world where hunger, poverty, disease, ignorance, violence, and exploitation are replaced as central features by abundance, reason, love, and international cooperation. To many this will seem the product of juvenile hallucination: but we insist it is a more realistic goal than is a world of nuclear stalemate. Some will say this is a hope beyond all bounds: but is far better to us to have positive vision than a "hard-headed" resignation. Some will sympathize, but claim it is impossible: if so, then we, not Fate, are the responsible ones, for we have the means at our disposal. We should not give up the attempt for fear of failure.

2. We should undertake here and now a 50-year effort to prepare for all nations the conditions of industrialization. Even with far more capital and skill than we now import to emerging areas, serious prophets expect that two generations will pass before accelerating industrialism is a worldwide act. The needs are numerous: every nation must build an adequate infrastructure (transportation, communication, land resources, waterways) for future industrial growth; there must be industries suited to the rapid development of differing raw materials and other resources; education must begin on a continuing basis for everyone in the society, especially including engineering and technical training; technical assistance from outside sources must be adequate to meet present and long-term needs; atomic power plants must spring up to make electrical energy available. With America's idle productive capacity, it is possible to begin this process immediately without changing our military allocations. This might catalyze a "peace race" since it would demand a response of such magnitude from the Soviet Union that arms spending and "coexistence" spending would become strenuous, perhaps impossible, for the Soviets to carry on simultaneously.

3. We should not depend significantly on private enterprise to do the job. Many important projects will not be profitable enough to entice the investment of private capital. The total amount required is far beyond the resources of corporate and philanthropic concerns. The new nations are suspicious, legitimately, of foreign enterprises dominating their national life. World industrialization is too huge an undertaking to be formulated

or carried out by private interests. Foreign economic assistance is a national problem, requiring long-range planning, integration with other domestic and foreign policies, and considerable public debate and analysis. Therefore the Federal government should have primary responsibility in this area.

4. We should not lock the development process into the Cold War: we should view it as a way of ending that conflict. When President Kennedy declared that we must aid those who need aid because it is right, he was unimpeachably correct—now principle must become practice. We should reverse the trend of aiding corrupt anti-communist regimes. To support dictators like Diem while trying to destroy ones like Castro will only enforce international cynicism about American "principle," and is bound to lead to even more authoritarian revolutions, especially in Latin America, where we did not even consider foreign aid until Castro had challenged the status quo. We should end the distinction between communist hunger and anti-communist hunger. To feed only anti-communists is to directly fatten men like Boun Oum, to incur the wrath of real democrats, and to distort our own sense of human values. We must cease seeing development in terms of communism and capitalism. To fight communism by capitalism in the newly-developing areas is to fundamentally misunderstand the international hatred of imperialism and colonialism and to confuse and needs of 19th century industrial America with those of contemporary nations.

Quite fortunately, we are edging away from the Dullesian "either-or" foreign policy ultimatum towards an uneasy acceptance of neutralism and nonalignment. If we really desire the end of the Cold War, we should now welcome nonalignment—that is, the creation of whole blocs of nations concerned with growth and with independently trying to break out of the Cold War apparatus.

Finally, while seeking disarmament as the genuine deterrent, we should shift from financial support of military regimes to support of national development. Real security cannot be gained by propping up military defenses, but only through the hastening of political stability, economic growth, greater social welfare, improved education. Military aid is temporary in nature, a "shoring up" measure that only postpones crisis. In addition, it tends to divert the allocations of the nation being defended to supplementary military spending (Pakistan's budget is 70 percent oriented to defense measures). Sometimes it actually creates crisis situations, as in Latin America, where we have contributed to the growth of national armies which are opposed generally to sweeping democratization. Finally, if we are really generous, it is harder for corrupt governments to exploit unfairly economic aid—especially if it is so plentiful that rulers cannot blame the absence of real reforms on anything but their own power lusts.

4. America should show its commitment to democratic institutions not by withdrawing support from undemocratic regimes, but by making domestic democracy exemplary. Worldwide amusement, cynicism and hatred toward the United States as a democracy is not simply a communist propaganda trick, but an objectively justifiable phenomenon. If respect for democracy is to be international, then the significance of democracy must emanate from America shores, not from the "soft sell" of the United States Information Agency.

5. America should agree that public utilities, railroads, mines, and plantations, and other basic economic institutions, should be in the control of national, not foreign, agencies. The destiny of any country should be determined by its nationals, not by outsiders with economic interests within. We should encourage our investors to turn over their foreign holdings (or at least 50 percent of the stock) to the national governments of the countries involved.

6. Foreign aid should be given through international agencies, primarily the United Nations. The need is to eliminate political overtones, to the extent possible, from economic development. The use of international agencies, with interests transcending those of American or Russian self-interest, is the feasible means of working on sound development. Second, internationalization will allow more long-range planning, integrate development plans adjacent countries and regions may have, and eliminate the duplication built into national systems of foreign aid. Third, it would justify more strictness of supervision than is now the case with American foreign aid efforts, but with far less chance of suspicion on the part of the developing countries. Fourth, the humiliating "hand-out" effect would be replaced by the joint participation of all nations in the general development of the earth's resources and industrial capacities. Fifth, it would eliminate national tensions, e.g., between Japan and some Southeast Asian areas, which now impair aid programs by "disguising" nationalities in the common pooling of funds. Sixth, it would make easier the task of stabilizing the world market prices of basic commodities, alleviating the enormous threat that decline in prices of commodity exports might cancel out the gains from foreign aid in the new nations. Seventh, it would improve the possibilities of non-exploitative development, especially in creating "soft-credit" rotating-fund agencies which would not require immediate progress or financial return. Finally, it would enhance the importance of the United Nations itself, as the disarming process would enhance the UN as a rule-enforcement agency.

7. Democratic theory must confront the problems inherent in social revolutions. For Americans concerned with the development of democratic societies, the anti-colonial movements and revolutions in the emerging nations pose serious problems. We need to face these problems with humility: after 180 years of constitutional government we are still striving for democracy in our own society. We must acknowledge that democracy and freedom do not magically occur, but have roots in historical experience; they cannot always be demanded for any society at any time, but must be nurtured and facilitated. We must avoid the arbitrary projection of Anglo-Saxon democratic forms onto different cultures. Instead of democratic capitalism we should anticipate more or less authoritarian variants of socialism and collectivism in many emergent societies.

But we do not abandon our critical faculties. Insofar as these regimes represent a genuine realization of national independence, and are engaged in constructing social systems which allow for personal meaning and purpose where exploitation once was, economic systems which work for the people where once they oppressed them, and political systems which allow for the organization and expression of minority opinion and dissent, we recognize their revolutionary and positive character. Americans can contribute to the growth of democracy in such societies not by moralizing, nor by indiscriminate prejudgment, but by retaining a critical identification with these nations, and by helping them to avoid external threats to their independence. Together with students and radicals in these nations we need to develop a reasonable theory of democracy which is concretely applicable to the cultures and conditions of hungry people.

Towards American Democracy

Every effort to end the Cold War and expand the process of world industrialization is an effort hostile to people and institutions whose interests lie in perpetuation of the East-West military threat and the postponement of change in the "have not" nations of the world. Every such effort, too, is bound to establish greater democracy in America. The major goals of a domestic effort would be:

1. America must abolish its political party stalemate. Two genuine parties, centered around issues and essential values, demanding allegiance to party principles shall supplant the current system of organized stalemate which is seriously inadequate to a world in flux. It has long been argued that the very overlapping of American parties guarantees that issues will be considered responsibly, that progress will be gradual instead of intemperate, and that therefore America will remain stable instead of torn by class strife. On the contrary: the enormous party overlap itself confuses issues and makes responsible presentation of choice to the electorate impossible, that guarantees Congressional listlessness and the drift of power to military and economic bureaucracies, that directs attention away from the more fundamental causes of social stability, such as a huge middle class, Keynesian economic techniques and Madison Avenue advertising. The ideals of political democracy, then, the imperative need for a flexible decision-making apparatus, makes a real two-party system an immediate social necessity. What is desirable is sufficient party disagreement to dramatize major issues, yet sufficient party overlap to guarantee stable transitions from administration to administration.

Every time the President criticizes a recalcitrant Congress, we must ask that he no longer tolerate the Southern conservatives in the Democratic Party. Every time in liberal representative complains that "we can't expect everything at once" we must ask if we received much of anything from Congress in the last generation. Every time he refers to "circumstances beyond control" we must ask why he fraternizes with racist scoundrels. Every time he speaks of the "unpleasantness of personal and party fighting" we should insist that pleasantry with Dixiecrats is inexcusable when the dark peoples of the world call for American support.

2. Mechanisms of voluntary association must be created through which political information can be imparted and political participation encouraged. Two political parties, even if realigned, would not provide adequate outlets for popular involvement. Institutions should be created that engage people with issues and express political preference, not as now with huge business lobbies which exercise undemocratic power, but which carry political influence (appropriate to private, rather than public, groupings) in national decision-making enterprise. Private in nature, these should be organized around single issues (medical care, transportation systems reform, etc.), concrete interest (labor and minority group organizations), multiple issues or general issues. These do not exist in America in quantity today. If they did exist, they would be a significant politicizing and educative force bringing people into touch with public life and affording them means of expression and action. Today, giant lobby representatives of business interests are dominant, but not educative. The Federal government itself should counter the latter forces whose intent is often public deceit for private gain, by subsidizing the preparation and decentralized distribution of objective materials on all public issues facing government.

3. Institutions and practices which stifle dissent should be abolished, and the promotion of peaceful dissent should be actively promoted. The first Amendment freedoms of speech, assembly, thought, religion and press should be seen as guarantees, not threats, to national security. While society has the right to prevent active subversion of its laws and institutions, it has the duty as well to promote open discussion of all issues—otherwise it will be in fact promoting real subversion as the only means to implementing ideas. To eliminate the fears and apathy from national life it is necessary that the institutions bred by fear and apathy be rooted out: the House Un-American Activities Committee, the Senate Internal Security Committee, the loyalty oaths on Federal loans, the Attorney General's list of subversive organizations, the Smith and McCarran Acts. The process of eliminating these blighting institutions is the process of restoring democratic participation. Their existence is a sign of the decomposition and atrophy of the participation.

4. Corporations must be made publicly responsible. It is not possible to believe that true democracy can exist where a minority utterly controls enormous wealth and power. The influence of corporate elites on foreign policy is neither reliable nor democratic; a way must be found to subordinate private American foreign investment to a democratically-constructed foreign policy. The influence of the same giants on domestic life is intolerable as well; a way must be found to direct our economic resources to genuine human needs, not the private needs of corporations nor the rigged needs of maneuvered citizenry.

We can no longer rely on competition of the many to insure that business enterprise is responsive to social needs. The many have become the few. Nor can we trust the corporate bureaucracy to be socially responsible or to develop a "corporate conscience" that is democratic. The community of interest of corporations, the anarchic actions of industrial leaders, should become structurally responsible to the people—and truly to the people rather than to an ill-defined and questionable "national interest." Labor and government as presently constituted are not sufficient to "regulate" corporations. A new re-ordering, a new calling of responsibility, is necessary: more than changing "work rules" we must consider changes in the rules of society by challenging the unchallenged politics of American corporations. Before the government can really begin to control business in a "public interest," the public must gain more substantial control of government: this demands a movement for political as well as economic realignments. We are aware that simple government "regulation," if achieved, would be inadequate without increased worker participation in management decision-making, strengthened and independent regulatory power, balances of partial and/or complete public ownership, various means of humanizing the conditions and types of work itself, sweeping welfare programs and regional public government authorities. These are examples of measures to re-balance the economy toward public—and individual—control.

5. The allocation of resources must be based on social needs. A truly "public sector" must be established, and its nature debated and planned. At present the majority of America's "public sector," the largest part of our public spending, is for the military. When great social needs are so pressing, our concept of "government spending" is wrapped up in the "permanent war economy."

In fact, if war is to be avoided, the "permanent war economy" must be seen as an "interim war economy." At some point, America must return to other mechanisms of economic growth besides public military spending. We must plan economically in peace. The most likely, and least desirable, return would be in the form of private enterprise. The undesirability lies in the fact of inherent capitalist instability, noticeable even with bolstering effects of government intervention. In the most recent post-war recessions, for example, private expenditures for plant and equipment dropped from $16 billion to $11.5 billion, while unemployment surged to nearly six million. By good fortune, investments in construction industries remained level, else an economic depression would have occurred. This will recur, and our growth in national per capita living standards will remain unsensational while the economy stagnates. The main private forces of economic expansion cannot guarantee a steady rate of growth, nor acceptable recovery from recession—especially in a demilitarizing world. Government participation in the economy is essential. Such participation will inevitably expand enormously, because the stable growth of the economy demands increasing "public" investments yearly. Our present outpour of more than $500 billion might double in a generation, irreversibly involving government solutions. And in future recessions, the compensatory fiscal action by the government will be the only means of avoiding the twin disasters of greater unemployment and a slackening rate of growth. Furthermore, a close relationship with the European Common Market will involve competition with numerous planned economies and may aggravate American unemployment unless the economy here is expanding swiftly enough to create new jobs.

All these tendencies suggest that not only solutions to our present social needs but our future expansion rests upon our willingness to enlarge the "public sector" greatly. Unless we choose war as an economic solvent, future public spending will be of a non-military nature—a major intervention into civilian production by the government. The issues posed by this development are enormous:

1. How should public vs. private domain be determined? We suggest these criteria:
    1) when a resource has been discovered or developed with public tax revenues, such as a space communications system, it should remain a public source, not be given away to private enterprise;

2) when monopolization seems inevitable, the public should maintain control of an industry;

3) when national objectives contradict seriously with business objectives as to the use of the resource, the public need should prevail.

2. How should technological advances be introduced into a society? By a public process, based on publicly-determined needs. Technological innovations should not be postponed from social use by private corporations in order to protect investment in older equipment.

3. How shall the "public sector" be made public, and not the arena of a ruling bureaucracy of "public servants"? By steadfast opposition to bureaucratic coagulation, and to definitions of human needs according to problems easiest for computers to solve. Second, the bureaucratic pileups must be at least minimized by local, regional, and national economic planning—responding to the interconnection of public problems by comprehensive programs of solution. Third, and most important, by experiments in decentralization, based on the vision of man as master of his machines and his society. The personal capacity to cope with life has been reduced everywhere by the introduction of technology that only minorities of men (barely) understand.

How the process can be reversed and we believe it can be—is one of the greatest sociological and economic tasks before human people today. Polytechnical schooling, with the individual adjusting to several work and life experiences, is one method. The transfer of certain mechanized tasks back into manual forms, allowing men to make whole, not partial, products, is not unimaginable. Our monster cities, based historically on the need for mass labor, might now be humanized, broken into smaller communities, powered by nuclear energy, arranged according to community decision. These are but a fraction of the opportunities of the new era: serious study and deliberate experimentation, rooted in a desire for human fraternity, may now result in blueprints of civic paradise.

4. America should concentrate on its genuine social priorities: abolish squalor, terminate neglect, and establish an environment for people to live in with dignity and creativeness.

5. A program against poverty must be just as sweeping as the nature of poverty itself. It must not be just palliative, but directed to the abolition of the structural circumstances of poverty. At a bare minimum it should include a housing act far larger than the one supported by the Kennedy Administration, but one that is geared more to low- and middle-income needs than to the windfall aspirations of small and large private entre-

preneurs, one that is more sympathetic to the quality of communal life than to the efficiency of city-split highways. Second, medical care must become recognized as a lifetime human right just as vital as food, shelter and clothing—the Federal government should guarantee health insurance as a basic social service, turning medical treatment into a social habit, not just an occasion of crisis, fighting sickness among the aged, not just by making medical care financially feasible but by reducing sickness among children and younger people. Third, existing institutions should be expanded so the Welfare State cares for everyone's welfare according to need. Social Security payments should be extended to everyone and should be proportionately greater for the poorest. A minimum wage of at least $1.50 should be extended to all workers (including the 16 million currently not covered at all). Equal educational opportunity is an important part of the battle against poverty.

6. A full-scale public initiative for civil rights should be undertaken despite the clamor among conservatives (and liberals) about gradualism, property rights, and law and order. The executive and legislative branches of the Federal government should work by enforcement and enactment against any form of exploitation of minority groups. No Federal cooperation with racism is tolerable—from financing of schools, to the development of Federally-supported industry, to the social gatherings of the President. Laws hastening school desegregation, voting rights, and economic protection for Negroes are needed right now. The moral force of the Executive Office should be exerted against the Dixiecrats specifically, and the national complacency about the race question generally. Especially in the North, where one-half of the country's Negro people now live, civil rights is not a problem to be solved in isolation from other problems. The fight against poverty, against slums, against the stalemated Congress, against McCarthyism, are all fights against the discrimination that is nearly endemic to all areas of American life.

7. The promise and problems of long-range Federal economic development should be studied more constructively. It is an embarrassing paradox that the Tennessee Valley Authority is a wonder to foreign visitors but a "radical" and barely influential project to most Americans. The Kennedy decision to permit private facilities to transmit power from the $1 billion Colorado River Storage Project is a disastrous one, interposing privately-owned transmitters between public-owned power generators and their publicly (and cooperatively) owned distributors. The contrary trend, to public ownership of power, should be generated in an experimental way.

The Area Redevelopment Act of 1961 is a first step in recognizing the under-developed areas of the United States, but is only a drop in the bucket financially and is not keyed to public planning and public works on a broad scale, but only to a few loan programs to lure industries and some grants to improve public facili-ties. The current public works bill in Congress is needed and a more sweeping, higher priced program of regional development with a proliferation of "TVAs" [Tennessee Valley Authorities] in such areas as the Appalachian region are needed desperately. It has been rejected by Mississippi already, however, because of the improvement it bodes for the unskilled Negro worker. This program should be enlarged, given teeth, and pursued rigorously by Federal authorities.

6. We must meet the growing complex of "city" problems; over 90 percent of Americans will live in urban areas in the next two decades. Juvenile delinquency, untended mental illness, crime increase, slums, urban tenantry and uncontrolled housing, the isolation of the individual in the city—all are problems of the city and are major symptoms of the present system of economic priorities and lack of public planning. Private property control (the real estate lobby and a few selfish landowners and businesses) is as devastating in the cities as corporations are on the national level. But there is no comprehensive way to deal with these problems now midst competing units of government, dwindling tax resources, suburban escapism (saprophytic to the sick central cities), high infrastructure costs and no one to pay them. The only solutions are national and regional. "Federalism" has thus far failed here because states are rural-dominated; the Federal government has had to operate by bootlegging and trickle-down measures dominated by private interests, and the cities themselves have not been able to catch up with their appendages through annexation or federation. A new external challenge is needed, not just a Department of Urban Affairs but a thorough national program to help the cities. The model city must be projected—more community decision-making and participation, true inte-gration of classes, races, vocations, provision for beauty, access to nature and the benefits of the central city as well, privacy without privatism, decentralized "units" spread horizontally with central, regional, democratic control, provi-sion for the basic facility-needs, for everyone, with units of planned regions and thus public, democratic control over the growth of the civic community and the allocation of resources.

7. Mental health institutions are in dire need; there were fewer mental hospital beds in relation to the numbers of mentally-ill in 1959 than there were in 1948. Public hospitals, too, are seriously wanting; existing structures alone need an estimated $1 billion for rehabilitation. Tremendous staff and faculty needs exist as well, and there are not enough medical students enrolled today to meet the anticipated needs of the future.

8. Our prisons are too often the enforcers of misery. They must be either re-oriented to rehabilitative work through public supervision or be abolished for their dehumanizing social effects. Funds are needed, too, to make possible a decent prison environment.

9. Education is too vital a public problem to be completely entrusted to the province of the various states and local units. In fact, there is no good reason why America should not progress now toward internationalizing rather than localizing, its educational system—children and young adults studying every-where in the world, through a United Nations program, would go far to create mutual understanding. In the meantime, the need for teachers and classrooms in America is fantastic. This is an area where "minimal" requirements hardly should be considered as a goal—there always are improvements to be made in the educational system, e.g., smaller classes and many more teachers for them, programs to subsidize the education of the poor but bright, etc.

10. America should eliminate agricultural policies based on scarcity and pent-up surplus. In America and foreign countries there exist tremendous needs for more food and balanced diets. The Federal government should finance small farmers' cooperatives, strengthen programs of rural electrification, and expand policies for the distribution of agricultural surpluses throughout the world (by Food-for-Peace and related UN programming). Marginal farmers must be helped to either become productive enough to survive "industrialized agriculture" or given help in making the transition out of agriculture—the current Rural Area Development program must be better coordinated with a massive national "area redevelopment" program. Science should be employed to constructively transform the conditions of life throughout the United States and the world. Yet at the present time the Department of Health, Education, and Welfare and the National Science Foundation together spend only $300 million annually for scientific purposes in contrast to the $6 billion spent by the Defense Department and the Atomic Energy Commission. One-half of all research and development in America is directly devoted to military purposes. Two imbalances must be corrected—that of military over non-military investigation, and that of biological-natural-physical science over the sciences of human behavior. Our political system must then include planning for the human use of science: by anticipating the political consequences of scientific innovation, by directing the discovery and exploration of space, by adapting science to improved production of food, to international communications systems, to technical problems of disarmament, and so on. For the newly-developing nations, American science should focus on the study of cheap sources of power, housing and building materials, mass educational techniques, etc. Further, science and scholarship should be seen less as an apparatus of conflicting power blocs, but as a bridge toward supranational community: the International Geophysical Year is a model for continuous further cooperation between the science communities of all nations.

Alternatives to Helplessness

The goals we have set are not realizable next month, or even next election—but that fact justifies neither giving up altogether nor a determination to work only on immediate, direct, tangible problems. Both responses are a sign of helplessness, fearfulness of visions, refusal to hope, and tend to bring on the very conditions to be avoided. Fearing vision, we justify rhetoric or myopia. Fearing hope, we reinforce despair.

The first effort, then, should be to state a vision: what is the perimeter of human possibility in this epoch? This we have tried to do. The second effort, if we are to be politically responsible, is to evaluate the prospects for obtaining at least a substantial part of that vision in our epoch: what are the social forces that exist, or that must exist, if we are to be at all successful? And what role have we ourselves to play as a social force?

1. In exploring the existing social forces, note must be taken of the Southern civil rights movement as the most heartening because of the justice it insists upon, exemplary because it indicates that there can be a passage out of apathy. This movement, pushed into a brilliant new phase by the Montgomery bus boycott and the subsequent nonviolent action of the sit-ins and Freedom Rides, has had three major results: first, a sense of self-determination has been instilled in millions of oppressed Negroes; second, the movement has challenged a few thousand liberals to new social idealism; third, a series of important concessions have been obtained, such as token school desegregation, increased Administration help, new laws, desegregation of some public facilities.

But fundamental social change—that would break the props from under Jim Crow—has not come. Negro employment opportunity, wage levels, housing conditions, educational privileges—these remain deplorable and relatively constant, each deprivation reinforcing the impact of the others. The Southern states, in the meantime, are strengthening the fortresses of the status quo, and are beginning to camouflage the fortresses by guile where open bigotry announced its defiance before. The white-controlled one-party system remains intact; and even where the Republicans are beginning, under the pressures of industrialization in the towns and suburbs, to show initiative in fostering a two-party system, all Southern state Republican Committees (save Georgia) have adopted militant segregationist platforms to attract Dixiecrats.

Rural dominance remains a fact in nearly all the Southern states, although the reapportionment decision of the Supreme Court portends future power shifts to the cities. Southern politicians maintain a continuing aversion to the welfare legislation that would aid their people. The reins of the Southern economy are held by conservative businessmen who view human rights as secondary to property rights. A violent anti-communism is rooting itself in the South, and threatening even moderate voices. Add the militaristic tradition of the South, and its irrational regional mystique, and one must conclude that authoritarian and reactionary tendencies are a rising obstacle to the small, voiceless, poor, and isolated democratic movements.

The civil rights struggle thus has come to an impasse. To this impasse, the movement responded this year by entering the sphere of politics, insisting on citizenship rights, specifically the right to vote. The new voter registration stage of protest represents perhaps the first major attempt to exercise the conventional instruments of political democracy in the struggle for racial justice. The vote, if used strategically by the great mass of now-unregistered Negroes theoretically eligible to vote, will be decisive factor in changing the quality of Southern leadership from low demagoguery to decent statesmanship.

More important, the new emphasis on the vote heralds the use of political means to solve the problems of equality in America, and it signals the decline of the short-sighted view that "discrimination" can be isolated from related social problems. Since the moral clarity of the civil rights movement has not always been accompanied by precise political vision, and sometimes not even by a real political consciousness, the new phase is revolutionary in its implication. The intermediate goal of the program is to secure and insure a healthy respect and realization of Constitutional liberties. This is important not only to terminate the civil and private abuses which currently characterize the region, but also to prevent the pendulum of oppression from simply swinging to an alternate extreme with a new unsophisticated electorate, after the unhappy example of the last Reconstruction. It is the ultimate objectives of the strategy which promise profound change in the politics of the nation. An increased Negro voting race in and of itself is not going to dislodge racist controls of the Southern power structure; but an accelerating movement through the courts, the ballot boxes, and especially the jails is the most likely means of shattering the crust of political intransigency and creating a semblance of democratic order on local and state levels.

Linked with pressure from Northern liberals to expunge the Dixiecrats from the ranks of the Democratic Party, massive Negro voting in the South could destroy the vice-like grip reactionary Southerners have on the Congressional legislative process.

2. The broadest movement for peace in several years emerged in 1961–62. In its political orientation and goals it is much less identifiable than the movement for civil rights: it includes socialists, pacifists, liberals, scholars, militant activists, middle-class women, some professionals, many students, a few unionists. Some have been emotionally single-issue: Ban the Bomb. Some have been academically obscurantist. Some have rejected the System (sometimes both systems). Some have attempted, too, to "work within" the System. Amidst these conflicting streams of emphasis, however, certain basic qualities appear. The most important is that the "peace movement" has operated almost exclusively through peripheral institutions—almost never through mainstream institutions. Similarly, individuals interested in peace have nonpolitical social roles that cannot be turned to the support of peace activity. Concretely, liberal religious societies, anti-war groups, voluntary associations, ad hoc committees have been the political unit of the peace movement, and its human movers have been students, teachers, housewives, secretaries, lawyers, doctors, clergy. The units have not been located in spots of major social influence, the people have not been able to turn their resources fully to the issues that concern them. The results are political ineffectiveness and personal alienation.

The organizing ability of the peace movement thus is limited to the ability to state and polarize issues. It does not have an institution or the forum in which the conflicting interests can be debated. The debate goes on in corners; it has little connection with the continuing process of determining allocations of resources. This process is not necessarily centralized, however much the peace movement is estranged from it. National policy, though dominated to a large degree by the "power elites" of the corporations and military, is still partially founded in consensus. It can be altered when there actually begins a shift in the allocation of resources and the listing of priorities by the people in the institutions which have social influence, e.g., the labor unions and the schools. As long as the debates of the peace movement form only a protest, rather than an opposition viewpoint within the centers of serious decision-making, then it is neither a movement of democratic relevance, nor is it likely to have any effectiveness except in educating more outsiders to the issue. It is vital, to be sure, that this educating go on (a heartening sign is the recent proliferation of books and journals dealing with peace and war from newly-developing countries); the possibilities for making politicians responsible to "peace constituencies" becomes greater.

But in the long interim before the national political climate is more open to deliberate, goal-directed debate about peace issues, the dedicated peace "movement" might well prepare a local base, especially by establishing civic committees on the techniques of converting from military to peacetime production. To make war and peace relevant to the problems of everyday life, by relating it to the backyard (shelters), the baby (fall-out), the job (military contracts)—and making a turn toward peace seem desirable on these same terms—is a task the peace movement is just beginning, and can profitably continue.

3. Central to any analysis of the potential for change must be an appraisal of organized labor. It would be a-historical to disregard the immense influence of labor in making modern America a decent place in which to live. It would be confused to fail to note labor's presence today as the most liberal of mainstream institutions. But it would be irresponsible not to criticize labor for losing much of the idealism that once made it a driving movement. Those who expected a labor upsurge after the 1955 AFL-CIO merger can only be dismayed that one year later, in the Stevenson-Eisenhower campaign, the AFL-CIO Committee on Political Education was able to obtain solicited $1.00 contributions from only one of every 24 unionists, and prompt only 40% of the rank and file to vote.

As a political force, labor generally has been unsuccessful in the post-war period of prosperity. It has seen the passage of the Taft-Hartley and Landrum-Griffin laws, and while beginning to receive slightly favorable National Labor Relations Board rulings, it has made little progress against right-to-work laws. Furthermore, it has seen less than adequate action on domestic problems, especially unemployment.

This labor "recession" has been only partly due to anti-labor politicians and corporations. Blame should be laid, too, to labor itself for not mounting an adequate movement. Labor has too often seen itself as elitist, rather than mass-oriented, and as a pressure group rather than as an 18-million-member body making political demands for all America. In the first instance, the labor bureaucracy tends to be cynical toward, or afraid of, rank-and-file involvement in the work of the Union. Resolutions passed at conventions are implemented only by high-level machinations, not by mass mobilization of the unionists. Without a significant base, labor's pressure function is materially reduced since it becomes difficult to hold political figures accountable to a movement that cannot muster a vote from a majority of its members.

There are some indications, however, that labor might regain its missing idealism. First, there are signs within the movement: of worker discontent with the economic progress, of collective bargaining, of occasional splits among union leaders on questions such as nuclear testing or other Cold War issues. Second, and more important, are the social forces which prompt these feelings of unrest. Foremost is the permanence of unemployment, and the threat of automation, but important, too, is the growth of unorganized ranks in white-collar fields with steady depletion in the already-organized fields. Third, there is the tremendous challenge of the Negro movement for support from organized labor: the alienation from and disgust with labor hypocrisy among Negroes ranging from the NAACP to the Black Muslims (crystallized in the formation of the Negro American Labor Council) indicates that labor must move more seriously in its attempts to organize on an interracial basis in the South and in large urban centers. When this task was broached several years ago, "jurisdictional" disputes prevented action. Today, many of these disputes have been settled—and the question of a massive organizing campaign is on the labor agenda again.

These threats and opportunities point to a profound crisis: either labor continues to decline as a social force, or it must constitute itself as a mass political force demanding not only that society recognize its rights to organize but also a program going beyond desired labor legislation and welfare improvements. Necessarily this latter role will require rank-and-file involvement. It might include greater autonomy and power for political coalitions of the various trade unions in local areas, rather than the more stultifying dominance of the international unions now. It might include reductions in leaders' salaries, or rotation from executive office to shop obligations, as a means of breaking down the hierarchical tendencies which have detached elite from base and made the highest echelons of labor more like businessmen than workers. It would certainly mean an announced independence of the center and Dixiecrat wings of the Democratic Party, and a massive organizing drive, especially in the South to complement the growing Negro political drive there.

A new politics must include a revitalized labor movement; a movement which sees itself, and is regarded by others, as a major leader of the breakthrough to a politics of hope and vision. Labor's role is no less unique or important in the needs of the future than it was in the past, its numbers and potential political strength, its natural interest in the abolition of exploitation, its reach to the grass roots of American society, combine to make it the best candidate for the synthesis of the civil rights, peace, and economic reform movements.

The creation of bridges is made more difficult by the problems left over from the generation of "silence." Middle-class students, still the main actors in the embryonic upsurge, have yet to overcome their ignorance, and even vague hostility, for what they see as "middle-class labor" bureaucrats. Students must open the campus to labor through publications, action programs, curricula, while labor opens its house to students through internships, requests for aid (on the picket-line, with handbills, in the public dialogue), and politics. And the organization of the campus can be a beginning—teachers' unions can be argued as both socially progressive, and educationally beneficial university employees can be organized—and thereby an important element in the education of the student radical.

But the new politics is still contained; it struggles below the surface of apathy, awaiting liberation. Few anticipate the breakthrough and fewer still exhort labor to begin. Labor continues to be the most liberal—and most frustrated—institution in mainstream America.

4. Since the Democratic Party sweep in 1958, there have been exaggerated but real efforts to establish a liberal force in Congress, not to balance but to at least voice criticism of the conservative mood. The most notable of these efforts was the Liberal Project begun early in 1959 by Representative Kastenmeier of Wisconsin. The Project was neither disciplined nor very influential but it was concerned at least with confronting basic domestic and foreign problems, in concert with several liberal intellectuals.

In 1960 five members of the Project were defeated at the polls (for reasons other than their membership in the Project). Then followed a "postmortem" publication of the Liberal Papers, materials discussed by the Project when it was in existence. Republican leaders called the book "further out than Communism." The New Frontier Administration repudiated any connection with the statements. Some former members of the Project even disclaimed their past roles.

A hopeful beginning came to a shameful end. But during the demise of the Project, a new spirit of Democratic Party reform was occurring: in New York City, Ithaca, Massachusetts, Connecticut, Texas, California, and even in Mississippi and Alabama where Negro candidates for Congress challenged racist political power. Some were for peace, some for the liberal side of the New Frontier, some for realignment of the parties—and in most cases they were supported by students.

Here and there were stirrings of organized discontent with the political stalemate. Americans for Democratic Action and the New Republic, pillars of the liberal community, took stands against the President on nuclear testing. A split, extremely slight thus far, developed in organized labor on the same issue. The Rev. Martin Luther King, Jr. preached against the Dixiecrat-Republican coalition across the nation.

5. From 1960 to 1962, the campuses experienced a revival of idealism among an active few. Triggered by the impact of the sit-ins, students began to struggle for integration, civil liberties, student rights, peace, and against the fast-rising right wing "revolt" as well. The liberal students, too, have felt their urgency thwarted by conventional channels: from student governments to Congressional committees. Out of this alienation from existing channels has come the creation of new ones; the most characteristic forms of liberal-radical student organizations are the dozens of campus political parties, political journals, and peace marches and demonstrations. In only a few cases have students built bridges to power: an occasional election campaign, the sit-ins, Freedom Rides, and voter registration activities; in some relatively large Northern demonstrations for peace and civil rights, and infrequently, through the United States National Student Association, whose notable work has not been focused on political change.

These contemporary social movements—for peace, civil rights, civil liberties, labor—have in common certain values and goals. The fight for peace is one for a stable and racially integrated world; for an end to the inherently volatile exploitation of most of mankind by irresponsible elites; and for freedom of economic, political and cultural organization. The fight for civil rights is also one for social welfare for all Americans; for free speech and the right to protest; for the shield of economic independence and bargaining power; for a reduction of the arms race which takes national attention and resources away from the problems of domestic injustice. Labor's fight for jobs and wages is also one labor; for the right to petition and strike; for world industrialization; for the stability of a peacetime economy instead of the insecurity of the war economy; for expansion of the Welfare State. The fight for a liberal Congress is a fight for a platform from which these concerns can issue. And the fight for students, for internal democracy in the university, is a fight to gain a forum for the issues.

But these scattered movements have more in common: a need for their concerns to be expressed by a political party responsible to their interests. That they have no political expression, no political channels, can be traced in large measure to the existence of a Democratic Party which tolerates the perverse unity of liberalism and racism, prevents the social change wanted by Negroes, peace protesters, labor unions, students, reform Democrats, and other liberals. Worse, the party stalemate prevents even the raising of controversy—a full Congressional assault on racial discrimination, disengagement in Central Europe, sweeping urban reform, disarmament and inspection, public regulation of major industries; these and other issues are never heard in the body that is supposed to represent the best thoughts and interests of all Americans.

An imperative task for these publicly disinherited groups, then, is to demand a Democratic Party responsible to their interests. They must support Southern voter registration and Negro political candidates and demand that Democratic Party liberals do the same (in the last Congress, Dixiecrats split with Northern Democrats on 119 of 300 roll-calls, mostly on civil rights, area redevelopment and foreign aid bills; and breach was much larger than in the previous several sessions). Labor should begin a major drive in the South. In the North, reform clubs (either independent or Democratic) should be formed to run against big city regimes on such issues as peace, civil rights, and urban needs. Demonstrations should be held at every Congressional or convention seating of Dixiecrats. A massive research and publicity campaign should be initiated, showing to every housewife, doctor, professor, and worker the damage done to their interests every day a racist occupies a place in the Democratic Party. Where possible, the peace movement should challenge the "peace credentials" of the otherwise-liberals by threatening or actually running candidates against them.

The University and Social Change

There is perhaps little reason to be optimistic about the above analysis. True, the Dixiecrat-GOP coalition is the weakest point in the dominating complex of corporate, military and political power. But the civil rights and peace and student movements are too poor and socially slighted, and the labor movement too quiescent, to be counted with enthusiasm. From where else can power and vision be summoned? We believe that the universities are an overlooked seat of influence.

First, the university is located in a permanent position of social influence. Its educational function makes it indispensable and automatically makes it a crucial institution in the formation of social attitudes. Second, in an unbelievably complicated world, it is the central institution for organizing, evaluating, and transmitting knowledge. Third, the extent to which academic resources presently are used to buttress immoral social practice is revealed first by the extent to which defense contracts make the universities engineers of the arms race. Too, the use of modern social science as a manipulative tool reveals itself in the "human relations" consultants to the modern corporation, who introduce trivial sops to give laborers feelings of "participation" or "belonging," while actually deluding them in order to further exploit their labor. And, of course, the use of motivational research is already infamous as a manipulative aspect of American politics. But these social uses of the universities' resources also demonstrate the unchangeable reliance by men of power on the men and storehouses of knowledge: this makes the university functionally tied to society in new ways, revealing new potentialities, new levers for change. Fourth, the university is the only mainstream institution that is open to participation by individuals of nearly any viewpoint.

These, at least, are facts, no matter how dull the teaching, how paternalistic the rules, how irrelevant the research that goes on. Social relevance, the accessibility to knowledge, and internal openness together make the university a potential base and agency in a movement of social change.

1. Any new left in America must be, in large measure, a left with real intellectual skills, committed to deliberativeness, honesty, reflection as working tools. The university permits the political life to be an adjunct to the academic one, and action to be informed by reason.
2. A new left must be distributed in significant social roles throughout the country. The universities are distributed in such a manner.
3. A new left must consist of younger people who matured in the post-war world, and partially be directed to the recruitment of younger people. The university is an obvious beginning point.
4. A new left must include liberals and socialists, the former for their relevance, the latter for their sense of thoroughgoing reforms in the system. The university is a more sensible place than a political party for these two traditions to begin to discuss their differences and look for political synthesis.
5. A new left must start controversy across the land, if national policies and national apathy are to be reversed. The ideal university is a community of controversy, within itself and in its effects on communities beyond.
6. A new left must transform modern complexity into issues that can be understood and felt close-up by every human being. It must give form to the feelings of helplessness and indifference, so that people may see the political, social and economic sources of their private troubles and organize to change society. In a time of supposed prosperity, moral complacency and political manipulation, a new left cannot rely on only aching stomachs to be the engine force of social reform. The case for change, for alternatives that will involve uncomfortable personal efforts, must be argued as never before. The university is a relevant place for all of these activities.

But we need not indulge in illusions: the university system cannot complete a movement of ordinary people making demands for a better life. From its schools and colleges across the nation, a militant left might awaken its allies, and by beginning the process towards peace, civil rights, and labor struggles, reinsert theory and idealism where too often reign confusion and political barter. The power of students and faculty united is not only potential; it has shown its actuality in the South, and in the reform movements of the North.

The bridge to political power, though, will be built through genuine cooperation, locally, nationally, and internationally, between a new left of young people, and an awakening community of allies. In each community we must look within the university and act with confidence that we can be powerful, but we must look outwards to the less exotic but more lasting struggles for justice.

To turn these possibilities into realities will involve national efforts at university reform by an alliance of students and faculty. They must wrest control of the educational process from the administrative bureaucracy. They must make fraternal and functional contact with allies in labor, civil rights, and other liberal forces outside the campus. They must import major public issues into the curriculum—research and teaching on problems of war and peace is an outstanding example. They must make debate and controversy, not dull pedantic cant, the common style for educational life. They must consciously build a base for their assault upon the loci of power.

As students, for a democratic society, we are committed to stimulating this kind of social movement, this kind of vision and program on campuses and in communities across the country. If we appear to seek the unattainable, it has been said, then let it be known that we do so to avoid the unimaginable.

Index

United Auto Workers (UAW), 17, 51
United Farm Workers (UFW), 9
United Nations, 161–162, 167
universal controlled disarmament,
160–161
universities: criticism of in PHS, 133–
135; as knowledge factories, 18; and
progressive social change, 95; revival
of idealism among students, 181–182;
and social change, 183–185
urban areas, problems related to, 174
urgency, sense of in Port Huron
Statement, 93
Utopia, decline of, 130

"Values" section, PHS: as distinctive
feature, 96; essential questions
regarding, 98; and feminism, 61;
overview, 5; and religion, 75, 79; text
of, 129–133
Varela, Maria, 77–81
Vester, Michael, 44, 83–87
Vietnam War: effect of Kennedy's
assassination on, 12; impact on Port
Huron vision, 12–13; lessons learned
from, 16; movement against, 21–22,
109
violence: surrounding civil-rights
movement, 67–70; view of in Port
Huron Statement, 93, 132–133
voluntary association, mechanisms of,
169
Voter Education Fund, 8
voting: discrimination in, 157; politics
of emphasis on, 177–178; strategy of
realignment in fight for rights, 7–9.
See also civil-rights movement
Voting Rights Act, 8

wages, of nonwhites, 156
Walker, Scott, 23
war economy, permanent, 141–142, 171
warfare state. *See* "The Individual in the
Warfare State" section, PHS
War on Poverty, effect of Vietnam War
on, 13
wars: antiwar defendants, exoneration

of, 21–22; antiwar movement, 109,
114–115, 116, 178–179; Cold War,
15–17, 92–93; deterrence policy,
148–150; Vietnam, 12–13, 16,
21–22, 109; World War II, Catholic
underground resistance networks
during, 77
waste, 144
wealth, concentration of, 139
weapons, 147–150, 163. *See also*
disarmament
Weatherman (Weather Underground),
19–20
Webb, Marilyn, 115
W.E.B. Du Bois Clubs, 45
welfare Capitalism, and protests, 86
welfare spending, 142–143, 173
West Germany, 162–163
"What Is Needed?" section, PHS:
The Industrialization of the World,
164–168; overview, 160–164
White, Micah, 26
white Americans, and discrimination,
156–159
White House, connections of SDS in, 16
white students: effect of civil-rights
movement on, 60; importance of in
civil-rights movement, 68; in New
Left, 109; Southern, at Port Huron
Conference, 44
Wikipedia, 2
Wilson, Dagmar, 44–45
Wisconsin, revolt against Tea Party
governor Scott Walker in, 23
Wobblies, 24
Wofford, Harris, 8
women's-liberation movement: overview,
34; participatory democracy and,
98, 114–123; and Port Huron
Conference, 61–62; in Port Huron
Statement, 96
Women Strike for Peace (WSP), 15,
44–45
work: comments on in PHS, 139; culture
at, and emancipatory movements,
85; discrimination in, 156; effect of
automation on, 143; labor movement,